FIREFLY
Wildlife Atlas

A comprehensive guide to animal habitats

John Farndon

FIREFLY BOOKS

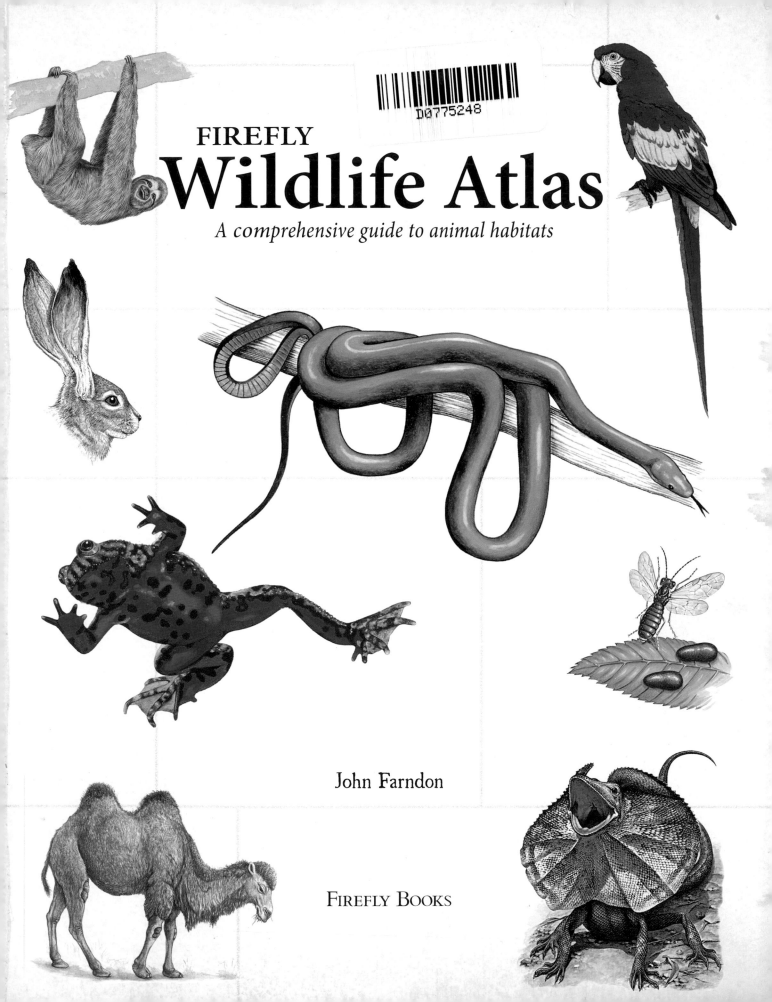

A FIREFLY BOOK

Published by Firefly Books Ltd. 2017

Copyright © 2017 Marshall Editions

Designed and edited by Tall Tree Ltd.
Consultant: Camilla de la Bédoyère

First printing

Publisher Cataloging-in-Publication Data (U.S.)

Library of Congress Cataloging-in-Publication Data is available

Library and Archives Canada Cataloguing in Publication

Farndon, John, author
Firefly wildlife atlas : a comprehensive guide to animal habitats/
John Farndon.

Ages 9-12.

ISBN 978-1-77085-932-6 (softcover)

1. Habitat (Ecology)—Juvenile literature.
2. Animal ecology—Juvenile literature. I. Title.
QH541.14.F37 2017   j591.7   C2017-902898-7

Published in the United States by
Firefly Books (U.S.) Inc.
P.O. Box 1338, Ellicott Station
Buffalo, New York 14205

Published in Canada by
Firefly Books Ltd.
50 Staples Avenue, Unit 1
Richmond Hill, Ontario L4B 0A7

Printed in China

CONTENTS

TEMPERATE WOODLANDS

TEMPERATE GRASSLANDS

TAIGA AND TUNDRA

WETLANDS

MOUNTAINS AND POLAR REGIONS

ANIMAL CLASSIFICATION

INTRODUCTION

PERHAPS uniquely in the universe, our planet teems with life. As human exploration penetrates to the darkest corners of the Earth, we are finding life in every nook and cranny, in every environment no matter how extreme. Strange fish lurk in the pitch black of the very deepest oceans. Birds are found nesting atop some of the world's highest mountains.

But what is most astounding, perhaps, is the sheer variety of life — swimming in the vast oceans, flying through the air, and slithering, crawling or running over the world's land surfaces. More than 1.7 million species of animals have been named so far, and most zoologists believe there may be many, many more as yet undiscovered. There are over 5,500 known species of mammals, 10,000 species of reptiles, 7,300 amphibians, 10,400 species of birds, 32,900 fish, 1 million insects, and perhaps 400,000 other tiny creatures that go by the general name "invertebrates," including 103,000 kinds of spider.

We owe this rich diversity of life to hundreds of millions of years of evolution, hundreds of millions of years of subtle changes, generation by generation, as some creatures survived to pass on their quirks to their offspring and as others with their own quirks died out. Of course, those creatures best equipped for the prevailing conditions survived; those poorly equipped passed into the oblivion of extinction.

Conditions change, and, over time, many creatures have found themselves in the same position as the dinosaurs — initially well adapted to their environment, but then ill-equipped to survive the changes occurring in the world around them. But conditions do not only vary over time; they vary across the face of the planet, too.

Every region on Earth has its own unique conditions, and, during the long roll of evolution, a unique range of creatures has developed to suit each particular place. An endless sequence of chance changes has created the host of different animal species that inhabit the Earth today, each particularly adapted to survive in its own special place, each occupying its own niche in the environment.

Every species has its home and every home has its species. Just as the gentle deciduous woodlands of Northeast America provide a habitat for sawflies, raccoons and black bears, so the wide open savanna of Africa is home to elephants, baboons and lions. Climate, plant life, terrain, the availability of food and shelter, and many other factors have given every region its own distinctive range of creatures.

This book provides an overview of where the world's animals live and why they live there. The book travels the world, habitat by habitat, from the scorched grasslands of the tropics to the frozen wastes of the

Arctic and Antarctic. Each chapter focuses on a particular habitat and introduces, continent by continent, the range of creatures that make this habitat their home — the predators, the grazing mammals, the birds of the air, the insects, the reptiles and all the rest. Within each chapter, special feature pages explore the nature of the habitat and the complex web of inter-relationships between all the animals that live there. Yet it is a sad fact that by the time you read this book, some of the animals in it may have vanished forever. Today, we are witnessing what may be one of the greatest waves of animal extinctions ever, as more and more species fall victim to rampaging human activity. There are now over 11,800 species in the high-risk category and many more, as yet undiscovered, may also be under threat.

Many factors are to blame for this impending tragedy. Climate change, the loss of habitats, the relentless spread of cities, the poisoning of the land by pollutants, the deadly gun of the hunter. The more we know and understand the reasons for this massacre, the better equipped we will be to prevent it.

Despite this, the world is still blessed with an astonishing wealth of wildlife, and it is this that the *Children's Wildlife Atlas* celebrates in presenting a unique view of the animal and plant life of our planet.

JOHN FARNDON

ANIMAL HOMES

There are many ways of dividing the world into natural regions. Zoologists divide it into five regions. Climatologists divide it by climate. Botanists divide it by plant type. There is a close relationship between climate and vegetation type, and both play a key role in determining where each kind of animal lives. In this book, the world is divided into broad "habitats" — regions where a particular environment for animals is created by the climate and plant life — such as tropical rain forests and deserts.

Grassland food web (*see page 11*)

ANIMAL GROUPS

The animal world is divided into animals that have backbones, called vertebrates, and those that have none, called invertebrates. Invertebrates are mostly small creatures, such as insects and mollusks — although giant squids grow up to 55 feet (17 m) long. The main groups of vertebrates are: fish, birds, amphibians, reptiles and mammals. In this book, birds and mammals are further grouped according to where they spend most of their time (birds of the air and ground birds) or how they find their food (birds of prey, predatory mammals, browsers, foragers and grazing mammals).

TROPICAL GRASSLANDS

MORE than one-third of the world's land surface is covered in grass. Much of the grassland was created by farmers who cleared forests for their livestock to graze on, but there is still a great deal of grassland that is entirely natural, especially in the tropics.

Tropical grasslands occur where there is rain for only half the year, and the rest of the time it is too dry for trees to grow. Apart from a few isolated thorn and palm trees, grass here stretches as far as the eye can see, under wide-open skies. In the wet season, the grass is green and lush. In the dry season, the land is parched and the grass turns yellow.

Even so, grasslands are incredibly productive habitats. Every square yard (0.8 sq m) of African grassland grows more than 4 pounds (1.8 kg) of plant matter a year — half as much as pine forest produces — from just a thin covering of grass. So tropical grasslands can support a huge amount of wildlife and are home to some of the world's most spectacular creatures.

WHERE ARE TROPICAL GRASSLANDS?

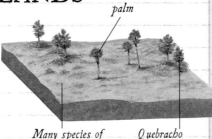

Tropic of Cancer

Equator

Tropic of Capricorn

Asian grassland

African grassland

South American grassland

Australian grassland

COMPARING GRASSLANDS

SOUTH AMERICA

South American grasslands are often parklike landscapes of clustered trees and shrubs dotted with tall palm trees. Here and there is espinal, a dry forest of spiny, thorny shrubs and low trees. The thorny quebracho tree sometimes forms dense thickets that rise like islands amid the sea of grasses.

Herbaceous palm

Many species of grass and sedge

Quebracho thorn tree

AFRICA

The savanna is the tropical grassland covering much of central Africa, especially in the east. The savanna varies with the length of the dry season. Stretching along the dry southern edge of the Sahara Desert is the Sahel — a vast area of thorn savanna that is dry, sparse grassland scattered with thin trees.

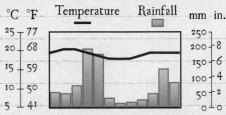

Acacia thorn   Euphorbia tree

Elephant grass up to 10 feet (3 m) tall

Baobab tree with thick trunk for water storage

AUSTRALIA

In Australia, the tropical grass of the bush covers a huge arc around the north of the continent from east to west. In Queensland, the dry Mitchell grassland is distinctive. In the moister areas, tall spear grass and shorter kangaroo grass grow. Most grassland trees have waxy leaves to reduce water loss, which helps them to survive the dry season.

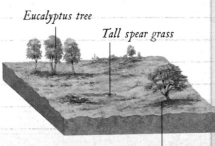

Eucalyptus tree

Tall spear grass

Short kangaroo grass

TROPICAL GRASSLAND ENVIRONMENTS

Tropical grasslands are warm, with temperatures usually in the range of 65–80°F (19–27°C). In the dry season, temperatures can be higher. Most of the rain falls in a five- to eight-month wet season, with less than 2½ inches (60 mm) of rain in the driest month.

SUN AND RAIN

This graph shows rainfall month by month, and the average monthly temperature for part of the African savanna.

°C °F   Temperature   Rainfall   mm in.

25 — 77   250 —
20 — 68   200 — 8
15 — 59   150 — 6
10 — 50   100 — 4
 5 — 41   50 — 2
                                         0 — 0
J F M A M J J A S O N D

THUNDERSTORMS

When it does rain on tropical grasslands, it rains in torrents. Huge thunderclouds build up in the heat of the morning, then the storm begins in midafternoon. Isolated trees are often struck by lightning, starting fires in the dry grass.

NEW GRASS

In the hot dry season, the grass can turn to straw and may even be burned away by bush fires. It looks dead, but even though the grass is burned, its roots are safe under the soil. The grass soon sprouts new shoots when the rains finally come.

7

SOUTH AMERICAN TROPICAL GRASSLANDS

THE tropical grasslands of South America are very different from those of Africa. African savannas are huge expanses of grass, where vast herds of large grazing animals can thrive. But South America's grasslands are much more varied, with bogs and dense scrub in many places. So, instead of grazers, the dominant animals are large rodents, such as capybaras and agoutis, and foragers, such as tapirs and peccaries, as well as many birds.

Andes Mountains

Pacific Ocean

GROUND BIRDS

The scarcity of trees means that many birds in these grasslands are ground-dwellers. Besides the rhea, others including tinamous and helmeted guineafowl strut through the grass, and various finches forage for seeds.

Greater rhea
(see p. 142)

Boa constrictor
(see p. 124)

BIRDS OF PREY

The birds and small creatures of the South American grasslands make rich pickings for predatory birds, such as hawk eagles, Swainson's hawk, caracaras, falcons and kites. Black vultures and king vultures swoop down on carrion.

King vulture
(see p. 144)

RODENTS

The grassland swamps are a good habitat for large rodents. Besides the capybara (the world's largest rodent), agoutis, pacs, plains viscacha, coatis and various cavies scrabble through the reeds. Many small rodents live here, too, such as water rats and various mice.

Capybara
(see p. 110)

REPTILES AND AMPHIBIANS

Swamps and rivers provide ample habitats for many reptiles and amphibians. Besides snakes, such as boas and pit vipers, there are other reptiles, including crocodilelike caimans, river turtles, iguanas, and lizards like the teyu. Poisonous tree frogs and toads, such as cane toads, are often seen here.

LLANOS

The Llanos is a vast area of low-lying grass and swampland covering 220,000 sq miles (570,000 sq km) of Venezuela and northeast Colombia.

GRAN SABANA

The Gran Sabana is a high tableland of grass and scrub, bounded by steep cliffs. Its inaccessibility makes it a valuable refuge for many rare species.

Amazon River

Paraguay River

Parana River

Atlantic Ocean

Nine-banded armadillo
(see p. 108)

FORAGING MAMMALS

Among the foragers are the piglike peccary and tapir, which are related to horses. Ants and termites are food for quite large animals, such as the giant anteater and the giant armadillos.

Army ant *(see p. 145)*

INSECTS

The grasslands are home to a huge range of insects, including many beetles and butterflies. However, the dominant species are termites and ants, especially fire ants and army ants.

CERRADO

The Cerrado is a land of grasses and shrubs south of the Amazon rain forest. Covering one-quarter of Brazil, it is home to 5 percent of all the world's animal species.

GRAN CHACO

The Gran Chaco is a vast, dry lowland plain covering 280,000 square miles (725,000 sq km) of central South America between the Andes and the Paraguay and Parana rivers.

Red piranha

FISH

The rivers and swamps hold many species of fish. There are characins such as the golden dorado, meat-eating red piranhas and their harmless cousins, the pacus.

Rufous-tailed jacamar *(see p. 137)*

BIRDS OF THE AIR

Many of the birds seen in the air above the South American grasslands are seasonal migrants such as swifts and wrens. Resident species include anhingas, New World orioles, woodpeckers, parakeets, hyacinth and other macaws, doves and tyrant flycatchers. Insect eaters include ovenbirds and tanagers.

GRAZING MAMMALS

The grasslands support few large grazing animals due to the spread of cattle ranches, except for llamalike guanaco and deer such as brockets and pampas deer.

Guanaco
(see p. 113)

Puma
(see p. 115)

PREDATORY MAMMALS

Four big cats prowl the grasslands — jaguars, jaguarundis, ocelots and pumas — plus smaller cats like the pampas cat and Geoffroy's cat. Two large dogs also hunt here: the rare maned wolf and the bush dog.

SURVIVAL IN GRASSLANDS

FOR the animals of the South American grasslands, life is a constant battle for survival. The long months of the dry season mean that every creature has to struggle to find food and water, while the lack of hiding places among trees makes life dangerous all year round. For plant-eating animals, survival means eating grass or the roots and tiny fruit of scrubby trees. But these herbivores provide food for a range of large predators, such as jaguars, pumas and maned wolves.

WHO EATS WHAT?

As in every environment, animals in the South American grasslands depend on each other for survival. Plant eaters get the food they need from surrounding vegetation, but all other animals need to eat other animals to survive. Jaguars eat animals like rhea and deer, while wolves eat armadillos, and armadillos eat termites. Indeed, all grassland animals are linked together in chains of food dependence, and these food chains are interwoven in a complex, finely balanced web of dependence. A change to even one tiny part of this web — perhaps due to human intervention — can upset the whole balance.

Flies play a vital part in the grassland ecology, spreading pollen as they feed on plants, and clearing waste as they feed on dung and dead creatures.

Caracaras often feed on carrion early in the morning. They also swoop down on small birds like ovenbirds and puffbirds.

Agoutis are too small to cope with the tall grass, so live in the shorter grass where they scrabble for fallen fruit. Their hearing is so acute that they can find the fruit by listening for the quiet thud as it falls.

Giant armadillos are tough, armored creatures with incredibly powerful front claws. They use these to dig out termites' nests to get at the termites, which they eat.

Termites eat the wood of rotting trees and roots. Their activity helps in the breakdown of vegetation to soil.

Earthworms play a vital role in processing the soil and making it fertile. The soil goes in one end, passes through their gut and emerges from the other end.

The South American caecilian is a blind, burrowing amphibian related to frogs. It lives in the soil and feeds on earthworms.

ADAPTATION: LONG LEGS

With nowhere to hide, many creatures rely on speed to escape predators. Indeed, grassland animals are among the world's fastest runners. Thomson's gazelles in Africa reach 50 miles per hour (80 kmph). The rhea's African cousin, the ostrich, can tear along at 40 miles per hour (65 kmph). To achieve these speeds, grazing animals such as gray brockets and rheas have developed long, slender legs. Some predators, such as pumas, can run just as fast to catch them.

Gray brocket

Most of the hind limb is packed with powerful muscle and protected within the body wall.

The ankle rotates a long way for maximum thrust.

Unlike most other mammals, deer have two toes and run on the tips for maximum speed.

The leg bones are very long.

Puffbirds sally out from perches on branches to catch large insects in flight. Sometimes, they drop to the ground to forage for ants.

Maned wolves prey on armadillos and agoutis, as well as cavy (wild guinea pigs), rabbits and viscachas (burrowing rodents). They also eat insects and birds as well as fruit and sugarcane.

The ovenbirds are a large group of drab insect eaters that are common in the savanna and scrub, where they forage for bugs and seeds.

Gray brockets are small deer that live only in tall grass where they can hide. They feed on the tops of grass stalks and fruit from caesalpina and zizyphus trees.

Greater rheas live in the tall grass and feed on the grass tops – often feeding with deer herds. They also eat fruit and insects.

Jaguars prey on the larger grassland animals – brockets, rheas, and capybaras. They also attack peccaries, but the peccaries can often fight them off.

Capybaras feed on the short grasses by the waterside, and so avoid competing with deer (and farmers' cattle).

Rhea

The rhea's toes have grown enormously long to propel it at high speed.

Some ankle bones are long and fused to become part of the leg, not the foot.

JAGUAR

The jaguar has a bulky build, but, like many predators, in grass it is very quick and graceful. It can reach high speeds over short distances, climb trees and swim well. It relies on getting in close to its prey unnoticed, or lying silently in wait to make a kill. When it catches prey, its strong jaws can pulverize skulls.

AFRICAN GRASSLANDS

THE vast savanna grasslands of Africa are among the most spectacular of all wildlife habitats, home to some of the world's largest mammals. The vast grassy plains also host herds of large grazing animals, such as antelopes and zebras. There are browsers, too, such as elephants and rhinos. Then there are large predators — most famously the big cats, such as lions and cheetahs.

Congo

Lake Victoria

Lake Tanganyka

Zambesi River

Limpopo River

Lake Nyasa

N

BROWSERS AND FORAGERS

Savanna trees provide food for browsers, such as elephants, giraffes, black and white rhinos, warthogs and various antelopes — eland, kudu, gerenuk, steenbok and Kirk's dik-dik. As more savanna is used for farming, however, trees are becoming less abundant as a food source.

African elephant *(see p. 112)*

BUSHVELD
In the south, the dry savanna fringes are called bushveld. Large herds of tsessebe, kudu, springbok and hartebeest live here, as well as small groups of dik-dik.

PRIMATES

Olive baboon *(see p. 108)*

Baboons and vervet monkeys sleep in trees to avoid predators, and vervet monkeys often forage in the trees, too. Many primates spend their lives entirely in the trees and leap agilely from branch to branch.

GRAZING MAMMALS

Savanna grasses provide food for huge herds of grazers, including zebras, buffalo and many species of antelope, among them wildebeest, hartebeest, sable antelope, Thomson's gazelle and Grant's gazelle.

Impala *(see p. 114)*

BIRDS OF PREY

Secretary bird *(see p. 142)*

Many birds of prey find rich pickings here, including bataleur snake eagles, gabar goshawks, augur buzzards and vultures, such as Ruppell's vulture. These feed on the carcasses of large animals killed by lions and African wild dogs.

SAHEL

The Sahel is where the dry northern bushlands or "Sudan" savanna merge into the Sahara. Rare oryx, dama gazelles, and red-fronted gazelles live here.

Nile River

SERENGETI

East Africa is the heartland of the savanna. The Serengeti in Tanzania is home to over half a million buffaloes, wildebeests, zebras and gazelles, as well as elephants, giraffes, rhinos, lions and cheetahs, plus 450 species of birds.

REPTILES AND AMPHIBIANS

The lack of moisture means few amphibians live in the savanna, but there are many reptiles, including numerous chameleons such as Meller's chameleon, barking geckos, lizards, leopard tortoises and snakes.

Red-crested turaco
(see p. 144)

BIRDS OF THE AIR

The savanna air has plenty of birds, such as "go-away" birds (turacos), shrikes, flycatchers, starlings, hoopoes, rollers, bee-eaters and many weaver birds, including vast flocks of quelea.

Boomslang snake
(see p. 124)

INSECTS

Under the savanna are vast nests of termites that send out workers to forage for grass to feed the young. Flesh flies and carrion beetles feed on rotting carcasses left by vultures. Occasionally, vast swarms of locusts appear and may devastate crops.

Praying mantis
(see p. 151)

Rock hyrax
(see p. 113)

SMALL MAMMALS

The savanna is famed for its large animals, but many small mammals scurry among the grasses, including elephant shrews, striped mice and spring hares. Zorillas are skunklike mammals that hunt at night and rest in burrows by day. Like skunks, they spray an odor when alarmed.

GROUND BIRDS

With scant cover in the open savanna, there are fewer ground birds here than in some habitats. The flightless ostrich relies on running fast on its long legs to escape from predators. Other ground birds include yellow-billed and ground hornbills, kori bustards and helmeted guinea fowls.

Ostrich
(see p. 139)

PREDATORY MAMMALS

The herds of hoofed grazers provide prey for big cats, such as lions, cheetahs and leopards, and for dogs, such as jackals, wolves, foxes and African wild dogs. Cheetahs use speed to catch prey such as gazelles, while hyenas and lions rely on teamwork.

Lion
(see p. 115)

GRAZERS AND BROWSERS

THE alternating wet and dry seasons in East Africa's Serengeti create the world's most amazing animal migrations. Every May, the rains stop, the land dries up and vast herds of wildebeests begin to move in search of grass and water. They are joined in their trek by a multitude of zebras and antelopes — and are tailed by hungry lions and African wild dogs. When the rains come again and fresh grass springs up, the herds return to complete a yearly migration cycle, during which they cover more than 1,500 miles (2,400 km).

The giraffe uses its tongue to twist off leaves and twigs from branches 16 feet (4.9 m) up in the air.

With its trunk, an elephant can pull down branches almost as high.

Gerenuk stand on their hind legs to reach high branches.

Eland use their horns to twist off shoulder-high branches.

1) In the wet season, when the grass is plentiful, herds of zebras, wildebeests, and Thomson's gazelles intermingle on the high southeastern plains. Calves and foals are born in February.

2) Toward the end of the wet season, the herds begin to gather for their migration and males start their ritual mating fights, or ruts.

WET SEASON

SOUTH EAST

7) Toward the end of October, the skies darken, the rains begin to fall, and the herds begin their journey back to the grassy plains of the southeast.

6) As the drought takes its toll, Ruppell's vultures that have been trailing the herds swoop down on animals that have died.

BROWSING LEVELS

Just as each grazer has adapted to make the most of certain grass conditions, so each browsing animal in the savanna has adapted to reach branches at different heights. Many browsers, such as rhinos and dik-diks, can reach lower branches, so competition here is severe, but big animals such as elephants and giraffe, can reach much higher.

THE GREAT MIGRATION

The great animal migration in the Serengeti has developed over tens of thousands of years, and is minutely attuned to variations in the environment. The herds rarely move at exactly the same time, or along the same route, and the migration changes in response to local variations in grass growth. In some years, a dry spell may set the herds moving from the open plains earlier; fire damage may block the path in others — then attract the animals the following year as fresh growth springs up. The timing of the rut, too, seems to vary to coincide with a full moon.

Thomson's gazelles trail behind the wildebeest feeding on the high-protein seeds and young shoots left behind after the wildebeests have eaten down the leafy grass stalks.

3) By the time the trek begins, zebra herds are 200,000 strong, Thomson's gazelle herds are half a million strong, and wildebeests are a million and a half strong.

Wildebeests follow the zebras and feed on the lower leafy part of the grass left behind after the zebras have eaten.

Zebras lead the way, eating the coarse top layer of red oat grass. As they push on through the tall grass, they make a path for the small animals to follow.

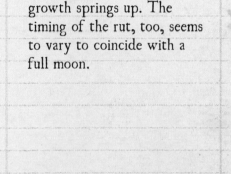

DRY SEASON

NORTH WEST

4) As the dry season progresses, the herds move on farther to the northwest into more wooded areas. Many die as they cross crocodile-infested rivers.

5) Toward the end of the dry season, rivers dry up and water holes shrink. The herds, led by zebras, reach the woodlands of the northwest.

HUNTING CHEETAH

The cheetah is the world's greatest sprinter. Because cover is sparse on the savanna, a cheetah relies on an explosive burst of speed to catch prey, such as a gazelle, and can reach 60 miles per hour (100 kmph) in just five seconds. It leaves the ground twice in its running cycle — first with front and hind legs bunched up (pictured), then with them fully extended. During one of these leaps, the cheetah can travel almost 23 feet (7 m) through the air.

AUSTRALIAN GRASSLANDS

THE vast, scrubby, rolling plains and plateaus of Australia's empty interior, or outback, are home to many of the continent's unique range of creatures, from kangaroos and wallabies to bandicoots and marsupial moles. Much of the outback is very arid, and creatures that live here must cope with little water. In lusher areas, wild animals have to compete with sheep and other livestock.

THE GREAT WESTERN PLATEAU

Covering most of western Australia, the Great Western Plateau is vast. It is 1,000–1,500 foot (300–460 m) high and is mostly covered in mulga and mallee scrub.

Gulf of Carpentaria

Great Sandy Desert

Gibson Desert

Great Victoria Desert

Great Australian Bight

GRAZING MAMMALS

Australia has no native hoofed grazers. Instead, it has the kangaroo family with their strong back legs and long feet for hopping. There are 76 species, divided into two families — macropods (kangaroos, walleroos and wallabies) and the smaller potoroids (potoroos and bettongs).

Red kangaroo
(see p. 114)

INSECTS AND SPIDERS

Australia's grasslands are home to many ants and termites, including the magnetic termite which aligns its nest north-south. There are many cicadas, beetles, flies, and spiders, too.

Cicada
(see p. 147)

Brahminy kite
(see p. 138)

BIRDS OF PREY

Since big birds of prey are able to reach Australia, many species here are also found elsewhere, such as Brahminy kites. There are local varieties, too, such as the Australian kestrel and the gray goshawk.

GROUND BIRDS

With few large predators, ground birds have flourished. Besides the emu, there are ground parrots, bowerbirds and "megapodes" — large birds such as malleefowl and brush-turkey that lay their eggs in mounds.

Emu (see p. 135)

REPTILES AND AMPHIBIANS

In the Australian grasslands lurk many venomous snakes of the elapid family, including the brown snake and the taipan. Australia also has about 500 species of lizard, including geckos and skinks. In the north, there are smaller cousins of the giant saltwater crocodiles.

Frilled lizard *(see p. 126)*

Golden perch

FISH

The interior is dry, but its rivers and billabongs are teeming with fish, including the huge Murray cod, golden perch, rainbowfish and gudgeons. Murray cod and golden perch feed on yabbies (crayfish) that are found in hot, muddy pools.

Flinders Ranges

Darling River

Murray River

N

SMALL MAMMALS

The grasslands are home to many small mammals, including marsupials unique to Australia such as the hairy-nosed wombat. Many estivate (stay dormant) in summer to cope with the heat.

Common wombat *(see p. 123)*

PREDATORY MAMMALS

Before dingoes arrived more than 3,000 years ago, Australia's only large predator was the thylacine, a wolflike marsupial. Since the thylacine was driven to extinction, dingoes have been the only large mammal predators.

Dingo *(see p. 111)*

Budgerigar *(see p. 133)*

BIRDS OF THE AIR

The Australian grasslands' rich bird life includes many parakeets and cockatoos, best known of which is the colorful galah, known for its raucous call. There are also many nectar-sipping honey-eaters and one species of bee-eater.

EGG-LAYING MAMMALS

Australia's long isolation has allowed two unique primitive egg-laying mammals, or "monotremes," to survive — the platypus and the echidna.

Long-nosed echidna *(see p. 112)*

POUCHED MAMMALS

ONE hundred million years ago, Australia began to drift away from the rest of the world's continents, and a unique range of wildlife developed there in isolation. In particular, there are two kinds of mammal found almost nowhere else — marsupials, which raise their young in pouches, and monotremes, which lay eggs. Remarkably, these creatures have evolved to fill niches similar to those of their counterparts elsewhere.

MARSUPIAL NICHES

Marsupials first evolved 100 million years ago and once lived all over the world. Placental mammals, whose young are born more fully developed, were thought to have evolved later, and to have driven marsupials into extinction almost everywhere but Australia, where they survived in isolation. Recent finds of 115-million-year-old placental mammal fossils in Australia, and analysis of DNA from both kinds of mammal, suggest that they may have lived alongside each other for millions of years. Whatever the truth, it is clear that the Australian marsupials have evolved to fill roles similar to those occupied elsewhere. This is known as convergent evolution.

The small Tasmanian devil is now almost the only marsupial hunter, although there was once a marsupial lion.

Bandicoots and numbats (banded anteaters) are insect eaters, with long snouts and strong digging claws.

The marsupial mole is a blind burrowing animal with strong front paws for tunneling through the ground.

CARNIVORES
LEOPARD
Big cats and wild dogs are the large predators of the placental world. They now have no marsupial counterparts.

ADAPTATION: HOPPING

Placental grazing animals run on four legs to escape predators, whereas many marsupials hop on strong hind legs and feet (and tails). The hind legs of a red kangaroo are roughly 10 times the size of its front legs. When moving slowly, kangaroos use all four legs, but when they need to move fast, they rise up on their hind legs and hop. It takes a lot of energy to start hopping, but very little energy is needed to hop faster. In contrast, four-legged mammals need more and more energy as they run faster.

Rock wallaby

The inner toes of the kangaroo family have grown especially large and strong.

Wombats fill a similar niche to marmots and badgers but grow larger because there is no competition. Oddly, there are no large marsupial foragers.

Koalas, possums and cuscuses are tree-dwelling marsupials that feed on vegetation.

The red kangaroo is a big grazing animal like antelope, deer and buffalo, but is strikingly different. It has few predators to avoid and relies on hopping on its two big feet, rather than running, to escape.

HERBIVORES
ELEPHANT
Elsewhere in the world, there are not only small foragers like badgers, but also giants such as elephants.

TREE DWELLERS
VERVET MONKEY
Squirrels, marmosets, and monkeys, such as the vervet, are the placental equivalent of marsupial tree dwellers.

GRAZERS
AFRICAN BUFFALO
In the rest of the world, big grazers like the buffalo have developed long legs and hooves — and safety in numbers — to escape from predators.

INSECTIVORES
GIANT PANGOLIN
Placental anteaters like giant pangolins and anteaters also have long snouts and strong digging claws.

BURROWERS
GIANT GOLDEN MOLE
Placental moles are remarkably similar to their marsupial counterparts.

Besides marsupials, many rodents hop, including the northern hopping mouse and the United States' kangaroo rat. They also have long inner toes.

Northern hopping mouse

MALLEE FOWL
The mallee fowl is a large ground bird that builds a compost heap to keep its eggs warm. In fall, the male digs a hole and fills it with vegetation. When it rains in spring, the vegetation rots and heats up. The female then lays her egg in the warm rotting vegetation. The male tests the temperature, and adds sand to save heat if it is too cold, or opens up the mound if it is too hot. This way the mound stays at exactly 91°F (33°C), which is why the mallee is known as the "thermometer bird."

TROPICAL RAIN FORESTS

WHERE there is enough rain in the tropics, forests grow — and the combination of year-round warmth and moisture makes tropical rain forests the lushest, greenest, densest and most richly varied natural habitats on Earth.

Tropical rain forests cover barely 6 percent of the world's land surface. Yet they contain 50 percent of its plant and animal species. Some scientists think it may be as much as 90 percent. Indeed, more species of amphibian, bird, insect, mammal, and reptile live here than in all the other habitats put together.

Yet rain forests are incredibly fragile environments — partly because the plants and animals depend on each other to an exceptional degree. Here, almost all trees rely on animals to disperse their seeds; elsewhere, dispersal by the wind is the most common method. As more and more rain forest is affected by human activity, the very existence of thousands of animal species is endangered.

WHERE ARE TROPICAL RAIN FORESTS?

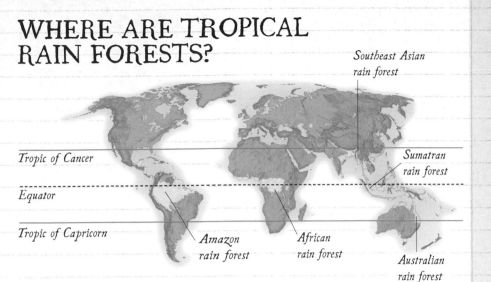

Southeast Asian
rain forest

Tropic of Cancer

Sumatran
rain forest

Equator

Tropic of Capricorn

Amazon
rain forest

African
rain forest

Australian
rain forest

COMPARING TROPICAL RAIN FORESTS

SOUTH AMERICA

The Amazon rain forest has a rich variety of trees both large (e.g., rubber, Brazil nut, silk-cotton, sapucaia and sucupir), and small. They are all covered with lianas and epiphytes (plants that grow on other plants), such as orchids and bromeliads.

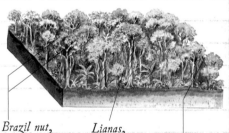

Brazil nut,
sacupaia trees

Lianas,
vines

Bromeliads,
orchids

AFRICA

African rain forests are less varied than those of the Amazon. The trees are large hardwoods, such as mahogany, iroko and sapele, and smaller trees. Beneath them grow fibrous plants as well as numerous fungi.

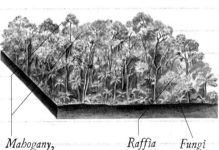

Mahogany,
iroko trees

Raffia

Fungi

AUSTRALASIA AND ASIA

Southeast Asian rain forests are dominated by huge dipterocarps (tea trees) along with teak, under which grow small trees, including fruit trees such as lychee and mango. Trees are covered with mosses and climbers. Exotic flowers such as rafflesia and titan arum grow on the ground.

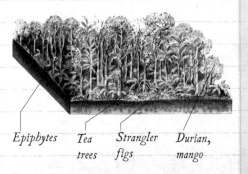

Epiphytes

Tea
trees

Strangler
figs

Durian,
mango

TROPICAL RAIN FOREST ENVIRONMENTS

Rain forests are typically hot and steamy. Temperatures rarely rise above 93°F (34°C) nor fall below 68°F (20°C). The rainfall totals over 4 inches (100 mm) each month.

SUN AND RAIN

Rainfall month by month and average daily temperature is shown for the Uaupés River, in the Amazon. The hottest month is often little more than 3–9°F (2–5°C) warmer than the coldest month.

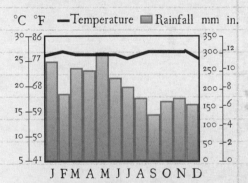

°C °F — Temperature ▪ Rainfall mm in.

J F M A M J J A S O N D

TREETOP POOLS

The dense canopy of leaves catches much of the rain. The trees are so damp that some frogs even live in pools that collect on these plants.

THUNDERCLOUDS

Most rain comes in thundershowers, which occur at least 200 days a year. Heat and humidity combine to build up thunderclouds each morning, which release rain in the afternoon.

AUSTRALASIAN AND ASIAN RAIN FORESTS

U NLIKE the immense Amazon rain forest, the tropical rain forests of southern Asia, Indonesia, and Australia occupy quite small areas, and many of the larger animals, such as elephants, rhino and tigers, are under threat from human activity. Even so, these forests remain home to an incredibly rich diversity of wildlife, including some of the world's most colorful birds and butterflies.

GANGES FOREST
Ganges forest is much depleted but is still home to tigers, rhinos, elephants and gaurs.

BIRDS

In Asia, the forest canopy is full of colorful hornbills, lorikeets, sunbirds, leafbirds and fairy-bluebirds, along with wood swallows and tree swifts.
On the ground run bleeding heart doves, pheasants, pittas, crowned pigeons and flowerpeckers.

King of Saxony's bird of paradise (see p. 137)

MALAYSIA
The rain forest here is home to at least 200 species of mammal, including tigers, rhinos, elephants, clouded leopards and sun bears.

BORNEO
Borneo has a rich rain forest fauna, including at least 600 bird species, such as white-rumped shamas, and at least 10 primate species, such as orangutans.

Pileated gibbon (see p. 113)

PRIMATES

There are no primates in Australia, but many in southeast Asia. Best known are apes, such as gibbons and orangutans. There are also many monkeys, including langurs and leaf monkeys, the rhesus macaque and the proboscis monkey.

SMALL MAMMALS

Among the many small mammals that live in the rain forests are marsupials such as echidnas, bandicoots and cuscuses.
There are also numerous rodents, brush-tailed porcupines and tree shrews.

Tree shrew (see p. 120)

Greater fruit bat (see p. 108)

FLYING CREATURES

As well as numerous kinds of bat, the forests of Australasia have a unique range of gliding animals, such as flying squirrels, snakes, frogs and geckos.
The most skillful are the gliding lemurs or colugos, which can glide huge distances.

Komodo dragon
(see p. 126)

Water
chevrotain
(see p. 110)

REPTILES AND AMPHIBIANS

Australasian rain forests are home to many snakes, including venomous taipans, and constrictors such as the reticulated pythons. There are also hundreds of species of lizard, including many agamids and monitors.

BROWSERS AND FORAGERS

The biggest browsers and foragers are Asian elephants, but they are now very rare in the wild. So, too, are the various species of rhinoceros found on different islands, such as the Javan and Sumatran rhinos.

WALLACE'S LINE

West of a line called "Wallace's Line," which runs through Southeast Asia, there are deer, monkeys, pigs, cats, elephants and rhinos. To the east, in New Guinea and Australia, are marsupials like possums, cuscuses, tree kangaroos and bandicoots.

Queen Alexandra's
birdwing butterfly
(see p. 147)

INSECTS

Besides countless tiny insects, such as termites, there are many huge ones, including giant stick insects, leaf insects, giant atlas beetles, beautiful Indian luna moths and birdwing butterflies.

NEW GUINEA

There are many species of mammals here that are found nowhere else on the planet.

QUEENSLAND FORESTS

Here live many marsupials, including tree kangaroos and possums, and birds, such as cassowaries.

Leopard
(see p. 115)

PREDATORY MAMMALS

There are still tigers and leopards in the forests of southern Asia, Sumatra and Java, but they are rare. The clouded leopard is also rare, with only about 20,000 left. Small civets such as the masked palm civet are still quite common.

GRAZING MAMMALS

There are many small deer, including the tiny mouse deer (chevrotain), tufted deer, sambar deer and barking deer. The larger grazers are wild cattle, including the water buffalo, the anoa and banteng.

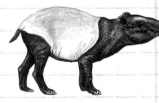

Malayan tapir
(see p. 121)

JUNGLE SURVIVAL

TROPICAL rain forests contain an incredible range of animals. In an area of just 40 square miles (100 sq km), there may be more than 400 different species, 150 kinds of reptile and amphibian, 125 types of mammal, and tens of thousands of different insects. With this range of wildlife, there is a remarkable degree of interdependence. Rain forests are among the most stable and ancient of environments, and, over millions of years, a complex web of food relationships has developed between different animals and also between plants and animals.

RAIN FOREST FOOD CHAINS

At the top of the food chains are the large predators. Big cats such as leopards, and wild dogs like the dhole stalk the jungle floor. In the lower branches, there are smaller cats like the clouded leopard, and snakes, such as the green tree python. In the canopy, there are snakes like the flying snake, and predatory birds such as the bat hawk, crested serpent eagle and variable goshawk. Below each of these top predators is a food chain of species feeding upon species.

Flies and beetles

Sheath-tailed bat

Masked palm civet

Water monitor lizard

Ants

Moon rat

Banteng

Dhole

FOREST FLOOR ANIMALS
Dholes hunt in packs to bring down animals as big as banteng as well as small deer like mouse deer. Small predators, like the water monitor lizard feed mainly on insects, such as termites, that crawl on the forest floor.

ADAPTATION: GLIDING

In the rain forests of Southeast Asia, a number of canopy animals have developed the ability to take to the air, both to move within the canopy and to escape predators. They are not true fliers, but have grown winglike extensions to help them glide from tree to tree, or to the ground. They include Wallace's flying frogs, which can glide 50 feet (15 m), flying squirrels, such as Thomas's and the black flying squirrel, and Ptychozoon flying geckos.

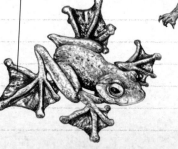

Flying frog
The flying frog planes on huge webs between its toes.

Flying squirrel
Flying squirrels have gliding membranes stretched between their front and rear limbs.

Bat hawk

Bar-winged flycatcher

Crested serpent eagle

BIRDS OF PREY
High up in the treetops, birds of prey hunt. Bat hawks swoop on birds, such as flycatchers, swallows and swiftlets. They also prey on bats, gliding at dusk, snapping them up as they emerge from their bat caves. Crested serpent eagles feed on reptile, such as tree snakes. They usually watch their prey from branches in the canopy, then dive through the branches to strike.

BATS AND FLYCATCHERS
Bats such as the sheath-tailed bat, and birds like the bar-winged flycatcher, catch flies in midair high above the forest floor in the canopy. Bats hunt by night and birds mostly by day. Both are preyed on by bat hawks.

Green tree python

SHREWS, SNAKES AND CATS
Green tree pythons loop themselves silently around tree branches to wait for prey, such as tree shrews, mouse deer, and civets, which they suffocate in their coils. The shrews feed on insects and fruit.

Tree shrew

Mouse deer

The tail is used to steer in the air.

Flying gecko
The gecko has flaps on its sides and its feet.

SUMATRAN TIGER
Sumatran tigers are the smallest of all tigers. They eat mostly sambar and other deer and wild pigs, but will occasionally kill a rhino calf. Like all tigers, they rely on ambushing their prey, so they prefer to live in the densest parts of the forest, where they can find cover. There are now only about 400 of them left in the wild in five national parks on Sumatra. There are just over 200 in zoos around the world.

SOUTH AMERICAN RAIN FORESTS

THE Amazon rain forest is by far the largest continuous area of rain forest in the world — and possibly home to a wider variety of creatures than all land-based habitats put together. There are tens of thousands of known species here — from soldier ants and hummingbirds to giant beetles and the biggest snakes in the world — and there are many more that are yet to be identified.

CHOCO-DARIEN

Separated by the Andes from the Amazon, this wet region has its own rich array of creatures, including Baird's tapir, Geoffroy's tamarin and the toucan barbet.

Pacific Ocean

Andes Mountains

Woolly spider monkey *(see p. 116)*

PRIMATES

The Amazon's monkeys include spider monkeys, capuchins, sakis, titis, howlers and uakaris, and over 40 kinds of small marmoset and tamarin. Monkeys of South and Central America have wide, flat noses.

Actaeon beetle *(see p. 146)*

INSECTS

More than one million insect species are thought to live in the Amazon, including ants, fireflies, cicadas and many kinds of colorful butterflies.

Three-toed sloth *(see p. 120)*

AMPHIBIANS

There is little standing water in the rain forest, yet many amphibians live here. Some frogs live by small puddles, and many tree frogs live by pools in treetop plants. Toads, such as the large cane toad and the Suriname toad, live in damp leaf litter, as do salamanders and legless caecilians.

Great curassow *(see p. 134)*

GROUND BIRDS

The dense vegetation on the Amazon forest floor provides good cover for a range of ground birds, including elegant sunbitterns, quail doves, quails, nightjars and at least eight kinds of tinamous. Waterbirds include cormorants, spoonbills and ibises.

HERBIVORES AND SMALL MAMMALS

Besides tiny deer and piglike peccaries and tapirs, there is an abundance of small mammals, including many rodents such as agoutis, capybaras, pacas and porcupines, a range of anteaters and sloths, the kinkajou and many bats, including the blood-drinking vampire.

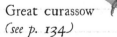

Golden poison arrow frog *(see p. 129)*

SOUTHWEST AMAZON
The forest has an extraordinary number of birds and mammals, including red uakari monkeys, ocelots, capybaras and giant otters.

NEGRO-BRANCO FORESTS
Here in the remote heart of the Amazon, saki monkeys, jaguars and many other rare animals survive — and even the giant ground sloth may not be a myth.

Amazon River

Paraná River

N

Electric eel

BIRDS OF THE AIR

The Amazon air is constantly filled with the sound of birds — colorful parrots, macaws and parakeets, noisy caciques, elegant hoatzins, quetzals, hummingbirds, giant-billed toucans, and numerous smaller birds such as antbirds and woodpeckers.

Toco Toucan
(see p. 143)

FISH

There are over 1,500 known species of fish in the Amazon — and many more as yet unidentified. They include piranhas, electric eels, knife fish and the pirarucu (one of the world's largest freshwater fish).

PREDATORY MAMMALS

The largest land predators are the big cats — jaguars, ocelots and pumas. Pumas are more common in areas closer to the Andes mountains. Smaller predators include raccoonlike coatis, ferretlike grisons and weasels.

Amazon river dolphin
(boto) *(see p. 111)*

RIVER MAMMALS

The Amazon river has its own unique range of mammals, including dolphins and sea cows (manatees), which look like seals but are unrelated. There are also rodents, such as the giant water rat and the capybara — the world's largest rodent, which weighs up to 145 pounds (66 kg).

REPTILES

The Amazon is one of the richest of all habitats for reptiles. Not only are there crocodilelike caimans and various turtles, such as the Arrau river turtle and the matamata, but also many snakes, such as the emerald tree boa, vine snakes and anacondas.

Ocelot
(see p. 117)

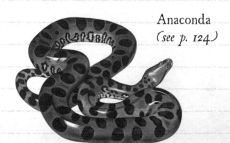

Anaconda
(see p. 124)

LIVING ON TREES

IT is a long way down from the tops of the trees in the Amazon rain forest — often 165 feet (50 m) or more — and the leaves and branches grow so densely that little sunlight ever penetrates to the ground. High in the treetop canopy, there is sun and rain and breezy air. Far below on the forest floor, it is still, humid, and perpetually gloomy. So striking is the difference in conditions that there are often distinct layers down through the trees. Each layer forms a different habitat, with its own range of plants and animals, each adapted to its own particular world.

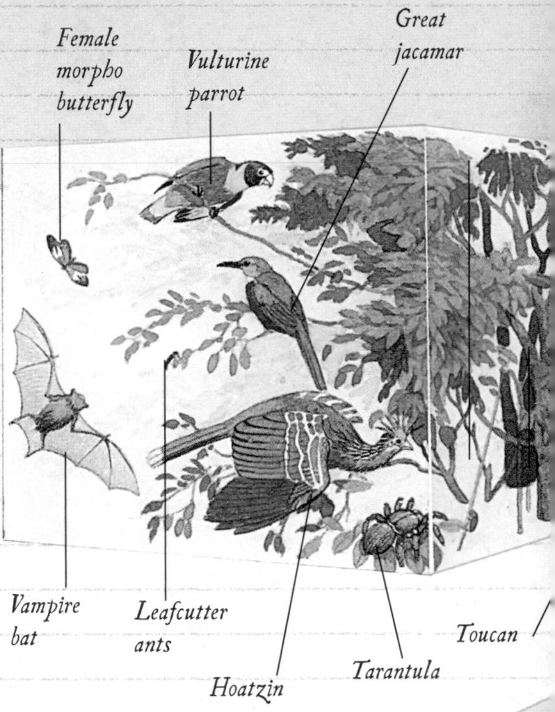

ADAPTATION: BRIGHT COLORS

Many of the world's most colorful birds live in rain forests. In the Amazon, there are exotic cotingas and macaws, jewellike hummingbirds and many others. Colored plumage may help birds find each other in dense jungle foliage. Male birds are especially vivid to attract females, which are often drab in comparison.

This brightly colored hummingbird is one of at least 360 species of hummingbird. So gemlike are these tiny birds that in the 1800s they were actually made into jewelry.

Macaws like the scarlet macaw are some of the biggest and most brightly colored of all parrots.

The Andean cock-of-the-rock is the best known of over 90 kinds of cotinga. The male is bright red, but the female is brown.

RAIN FOREST LAYERS

There are typically four layers in the rain forest: the forest floor; the "understory" of small trees, tree trunks and shrubs; the "canopy" of tree crowns; and the "emergent" layer of tall trees rising above the canopy. Sometimes this pattern is disturbed by natural events. As a tree grows old and falls, for instance, it may pull down many others tied to it by vines, creating a clearing; new trees will grow in the clearing, and the layers are eventually reestablished.

Female morpho butterfly

Vulturine parrot

Great jacamar

Vampire bat

Leafcutter ants

Hoatzin

Tarantula

Toucan

FOREST FLOOR

Large mammals such as peccaries, and birds such as curassows, feed on the vegetation on the forest floor, foraging over a wide area. Smaller mammals feed on insects and plant matter.

Worms, centipedes, ants, termites, cockroaches and a host of other tiny creatures live in the dank layer of rotting vegetation on the forest floor.

Pudu

Ruddy quail dove

White-lipped peccary

Sunbittern

28

Spider monkey

Harpy eagle

Male morpho butterfly

Two-lined bat

Howler monkey

Three-toed sloth

Prehensile-tailed porcupine

Emerald tree boa

Olingo

White-fronted nunbird

Hummingbird

Kinkajou

Poison arrow frog

St. Vincent Amazon parrot

Great curassow

Ocelot

Upper Amazon porcupine

Termites, cockroaches, beetles, centipedes, millipedes, earthworms

EMERGENT LAYER: 115–230 FEET (35–70 M)

The tallest trees may tower 230 feet (70 m) into the sunlight. Here flying creatures — mainly insect-eating birds and bats — swoop on their prey in midair. The birds and bats in turn are hunted by big birds of prey such as the harpy eagle. Spider monkeys may climb up for fruit.

CANOPY LAYER: 65–165 FEET (20–50 M)

The canopy is the lush green layer of tree crowns, bathed with sun and rain and teeming with life, nourished by the abundance of fruit and nuts that grow there. Most animals in the canopy spend all their lives up there, and are well adapted to treetop life. There are fliers, such as birds, bats and butterflies, gliders like some squirrels, and climbers, such as monkeys, sloths, ants and spiders.

UNDERSTORY LAYER: 15–65 FEET (4.5–20 M)

This is the lower layer of small trees, shrubs and tangled vines used by climbing creatures. Little sunlight gets down here and many leaves are colored dark green or red, to make the best use of the available light. Birds, bats, monkeys, squirrels and many kinds of snake live here. There are frogs, too, finding the water to lay their eggs in pools caught by plants high up in the trees.

BLUE MORPHO

The blue morphos that live in the forest canopy are large butterflies, up to 6½ inches (16.5 cm) across. The tops of their wings flash iridescent blue in the sunlight as they fly, but the undersides of the wings are brown, which keeps them hidden when they rest with their wings folded up.

AFRICAN RAIN FORESTS

ALTHOUGH the African rain forests have fewer species than those of South America and Asia, they are still an astonishingly rich habitat. Among the giant hardwood trees of the Congo rain forest lives a huge variety of creatures, including monkeys, apes and smaller primates that use their gripping hands and feet to move through the trees with amazing agility.

SMALL PRIMATES: PROSIMIANS

Relatives of monkeys and apes, prosimians are small primates with big eyes and long tails. Like all primates, they use their hands and feet to climb. Pottos and bush babies live in African continental rain forests, but lemurs, aye-ayes and indris live only in Madagascar.

Aye-aye (see p. 108)

EASTERN GUINEA

Much reduced in size, this forest is still home to many monkeys, such as sooty mangabeys and diana monkeys, and also rare pygmy hippos.

Zambezi River

Okapi
(see p. 117)

Royal
antelope
(see p. 108)

GRAZING MAMMALS

Africa's grassland grazers rely on speed and stamina to escape from predators. Rain forest grazers escape by being elusive. Antelopes are either small enough to dart into hiding, like royal antelopes and duikers, or are camouflaged like the bongos.

MONKEYS AND APES

Monkeys and apes are kings of Africa's forests, moving freely through the trees in search of fruit, leaves and insects. Here live three of the four great apes: chimpanzee, bonobo, and gorilla. (The fourth is the orangutan.) Monkeys include mona monkeys, mangabeys and colobus.

Colobus monkey
(see p. 116)

FORAGING MAMMALS

The largest animals in the African rain forest are okapis and elephants, both of which can browse on leaves some way above the ground. Small foragers include the pygmy hippo and hogs such as the red river hog and the giant forest hog, the world's biggest pig.

DZANGA SANGHA, CENTRAL AFRICA

One of the last areas of untouched rain forest, this is the home of rare forest elephants, bonobos and lowland gorillas.

REPTILES AND AMPHIBIANS

Africa's rain forest is home to the Goliath bullfrog, the world's biggest frog — with its legs extended it can be more than 30 inches (80 cm) long. There are also colorful sedge frogs, chameleons, and lizards such as Nile monitors. Snakes include pythons and tree cobras.

Eastern green mamba
(see p. 126)

Nile River

Red-crested turaco
(see p. 144)

PREDATORY MAMMALS

In treetops, crowned hawk eagles are major predators; in branches, pythons are. Only near the ground are mammals the main hunters. Here, the leopard is the top predator, hunting young antelopes, monkeys and apes.

MADAGASCAR

Cut off from mainland Africa 150 million years ago, this island has unique fauna, including lemurs and ayes-ayes.

BIRDS OF THE AIR

African rain forests are home to dozens of species of hornbills (Africa's equivalent of Amazonian toucans), scores of colorful parrots and lovebirds, plus African barbets and turacos.

African palm civet *(see p. 111)*

Armored shrew
(see p. 120)

SMALL MAMMALS

Among the many small mammals living in the rain forest are tree hyraxes, the African brush-tailed porcupine and tree pangolins. Tree pangolins look similar to anteaters, but are covered with an armor of scales. They spend most of their lives in trees.

INSECTS

Like all rain forests, Africa's teem with insects, including many species of beetle (such as the giant goliath beetle), ant, termite, fly and cockroach, including the huge Madagascar hissing cockroach that forces air out of its body noisily in order to alarm predators.

Oleander sphinx moth *(see p. 152)*

GROUND BIRDS

The largest birds in the African rain forest are those that forage on the ground for seeds, shoots, and berries. The biggest is the spectacular Congo peafowl, but red-necked francolin are also very large birds. Less obvious are ground-nesters such as the standard-winged nightjar.

Congo peafowl
(see p. 140)

31

MOVING THROUGH TREES

M OVING through branches high above the ground is very different from moving along the ground. Many rain forest animals have developed special skills for what zoologists call "arboreal locomotion," including leaping, climbing, swinging, and gliding. Tree frogs have special pads on their toes that help them as they climb. Woodpeckers, treecreepers and other birds have clawed feet for clinging. Squirrels and other small mammals climb with the help of claws, too. But the best climbers are monkeys, apes and smaller primates, which climb, leap and swing with astonishing agility.

GORILLA

The gorilla is the biggest of all the apes, standing 6½ feet (2 m) tall and weighing up to 500 pounds (230 kg). Despite its fierce appearance, it is a shy, gentle creature that eats only leaves and shoots. Males thump their chests to warn off intruders. Gorillas have long arms suitable for swinging, but they never do so, spending much of their time on the ground, walking on all fours on their knuckles. They climb trees at night to find a place safe from leopards, their only enemy apart from humans.

Capuchin: climbing and leaping

Black spider monkey: leaping and New World brachiation

ADAPTATION: GRIPPING HANDS

All primates are well adapted to living in trees and nearly all have hands with fingers and feet with toes for gripping branches — except for humans (whose feet cannot grip). American monkeys have a short thumb. But African and Asian monkeys and apes have opposable thumbs — that is, thumbs that can bend the opposite way to the fingers to provide a very precise grip. Some apes use precision grip to make and use tools. These include stripping small twigs and using them to fish ants out of their nests to eat.

AFRICA

Galago: leaping

Mangabey: climbing and leaping

Colobus: leaping and Old World semi-brachiation

Chimpanzee: Old World brachiation and running

Mandrill: quadrupedal on the ground

ASIA

Tarsier: leaping

Slow loris: slow climbing

Langur: semi-brachiation and leaping

Gibbon: brachiation

Macaque: quadrupedal on the ground

SOUTH AMERICA

All monkeys climb using their four limbs, which is called quadrupedalism. Capuchins and many other American monkeys, such as marmosets, move like this — climbing, springing and running along branches with amazing agility. Some American (New World) monkeys, like spiders and howlers, have extra help — a prehensile or gripping tail. This tail is like an extra limb, giving enough support for monkeys to swing from branch to branch on their arms, which is known as "New World semi-brachiation."

AFRICA

Like American monkeys, African monkeys move on all four limbs. Most African monkeys are more agile than American monkeys. The colobus is a great leaper and it will also swing using its arms ("Old World semibrachiation"). Prosimians (small primates) cling vertically to tree trunks and may leap. Apes, such as chimpanzees, have long arms and swing properly (brachiation), but won't climb very high. Gorillas rarely climb, and walk on their knuckles.

ASIA

Asian monkeys move on all fours like American and African monkeys. Some, like macaques, run on the ground, only rarely climbing trees. Others, like langurs, move easily through the trees using their tail as a balance, making leaps of 33 feet (10 m). Asia's two apes — the gibbon and orangutan — both brachiate. Gibbons are the greatest of all swingers, moving from branch to branch on their long arms with amazing agility.

New World monkey with short thumb

Short opposable thumb for branch swinging

Large opposable thumb for very precise grip

Short opposable thumb for walking on palms

Spider monkey

Ape: gibbon

Ape: gorilla

Monkey: macaque

DESERTS

MORE than one-fifth of the world's land surface is desert, where it hardly ever rains. There are deserts on all the continents except for Europe. There is a grandeur in the vast emptiness of these barren expanses, each with its own evocative name — Gobi, Sahara, Kalahari, Mojave.

The polar regions are called deserts because it is too cold to rain there. But the greatest deserts are those in the subtropics where the air is forever calm and clear. Here, cloudless skies allow daytime sun to beat down in relentless heat — then temperatures plummet at night. With no vegetation to break the flow, winds whip across the desert, blowing dust and sand in every eye and drying up the land.

Satellite pictures show deserts as great brown and yellow scars on Earth's rich, green continents — seemingly devoid of life. Even close up, they can appear barren. Yet this lifelessness is an illusion — an astonishing variety of both plants and animals survive there, using an extraordinary range of tricks to cling to life in extreme conditions.

WHERE ARE DESERTS?

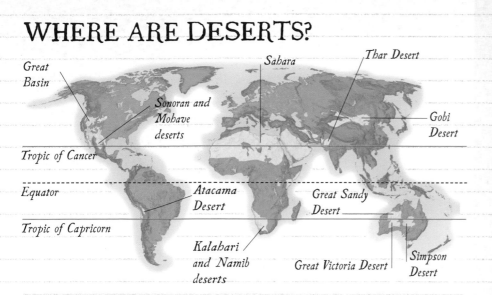

Great Basin

Sonoran and Mohave deserts

Sahara

Thar Desert

Gobi Desert

Tropic of Cancer

Equator

Atacama Desert

Great Sandy Desert

Tropic of Capricorn

Kalahari and Namib deserts

Great Victoria Desert

Simpson Desert

COMPARING DESERTS

NORTH AMERICA

North America's deserts have vast plains and towering cliffs. The Great Basin is sagebrush scrub. To the south, Joshua trees and creosote bushes punctuate the Mojave. Farther south, giant cacti like the saguaro stand like pillars in the Sonoran.

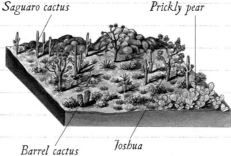

Saguaro cactus

Prickly pear

Barrel cactus

Joshua tree

AFRICA

Landscapes in the Sahara vary from rocky hamadas to seas of sand dunes (ergs). It is so hot that vast areas are barren and plants often grow only near oases, where date palms may also grow. The Namib has the world's biggest dunes — up to 1,300 feet (400 m) high.

Date palms

Oleander bush

Acacia bush

ASIA

Asia's Gobi Desert is hot in summer, but in winter there are no barriers to protect it from the icy air blowing in from Siberia to the north. Vegetation blooms briefly after the spring rains and survives through the early summer before the searing heat dries it out. The dominant plants are saxaul shrubs, and patches of low plants like saltwort and feather grass.

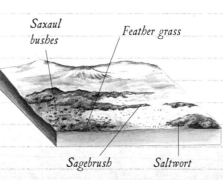

Saxaul bushes

Feather grass

Sagebrush

Saltwort

DESERT ENVIRONMENTS

The driest deserts get less than 4 inches (100 mm) of rain a year. Areas with less than 24 inches (600 mm) are said to be semiarid. In hot deserts, rain comes in showers that run off the land, or evaporate almost instantly.

SCORCHING SUN

All deserts are dry. Some are hot and daytime summer temperatures can soar to 122°F (50°C), although nights are cool. This graph shows conditions for In Salah, Algeria, in the Sahara.

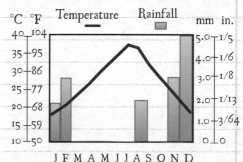

°C °F   Temperature   Rainfall   mm in.

J F M A M J J A S O N D

OASIS

Little rain falls on the surface, but there is often water below ground. Some is water left over from wetter times in the ancient past. Oases occur where this underground water gets to the surface.

DESERT BLOOM

Many desert plants lie dormant for months, apparently lifeless — then burst briefly into flower when it rains. They often germinate, bloom and die in just a few hours.

AFRICAN DESERTS

THERE are three great deserts in Africa: the Namib and Kalahari in the south, and the vast Sahara that covers almost all of northern Africa. The Sahara is not only the largest desert on Earth, but also the hottest. It is completely waterless over vast areas, yet many creatures can still survive here — tough-skinned lizards and snakes, rodents, goats and gazelles, and countless insects.

BROWSERS AND FORAGERS

Some of the biggest desert creatures are camels, which can survive a week without water and much longer without food. On the desert fringes, olive baboons and hamadryas baboons also manage to find enough to survive.

Dromedary camel *(see p. 110)*

KALAHARI DESERT

Although a desert, the sandy Kalahari has plenty of vegetation and is home to many large animals, including gemsbok antelopes, zebras, and cheetahs.

Zambezi River

GRAZING MAMMALS

Surprisingly, many grazing animals live in the Sahara. Grevy's zebras roam the fringes, while sheep, goats, ibexes and asses haunt mountain areas. Antelopes, such as the addax, and dama, dorcas and goitered gazelles live in the heart of the desert.

Springbok
(see p. 121)

Fat-tailed gerbil *(see p. 112)*

SMALL MAMMALS

Medium-sized mammals find it hard to cope with desert heat, but small ones can burrow and hide in the shade. The Sahara has 40 species of rodent, including gerbils, mice and jerboas. There are also long-eared hedgehogs and rock hyraxes.

BIRDS OF PREY

Birds can fly long distances in search of food and water, and have higher body temperatures than mammals. Many birds can survive in the Sahara. Large birds of prey include lappet-faced vultures, lanner falcons and African pygmy falcons.

Pale chanting goshawk
(see p. 136)

SAHARA
The world's largest hot desert is a mix of hamada (rocky uplands), reg (stones and gravel) and erg (seas of sand).

N

ARABIAN DESERT
Many larger animals here have been slaughtered by motorized hunting parties, but a few Arabian oryx survive and there are many rodents and lizards.

Mediterranean Sea

Nile River

Red Sea

Striped hyena
(see p. 114)

PREDATORY MAMMALS

Although there is little plant life for food in the desert, there are other animals to eat. There are many medium-sized predators in the Sahara, including dogs such as hyenas, jackals and fennec foxes, and cats such as the caracal and sand cat.

INSECTS

A tough outer skin, called an exoskeleton, protects insects and arachnids from drying out in desert habitats. Insects, such as flies, wasps, locusts, beetles (such as scarabs), ants and termites live alongside arachnids such as wolf spiders, jumping spiders and scorpions.

Courser
(see p. 133)

Darkling beetle
(see p. 146)

Arabian toad-headed agamid
(see p. 124)

BIRDS OF THE AIR

In fall, birds like warblers, swallows and martins fly south over the Sahara to escape the European winter, then fly north the following spring. Some birds, such as wheatears, even stay for the winter; others, like rock sparrows and weavers, live here all year.

GROUND BIRDS

With few trees, ground birds can cope better here than perching birds. Ostriches and guinea fowl are seen on the fringes, while houbara and Nubian bustards live farther in. Like many desert creatures, bustards get most of their water from the prey they eat.

Black-bellied sandgrouse
(see p. 142)

REPTILES AND AMPHIBIANS

Reptiles are well adapted to life in the desert. They have dry, scaly skins that prevent water loss. There are over 100 species in the Sahara, including lizards like the desert monitor, geckos and skinks, as well as snakes and tortoises.

DESERT SURVIVAL

LIFE in African deserts is life on the edge. The creatures that live here must be able to cope not only with the extreme heat and lack of water but also with the scarcity of food. Grazing animals and other herbivores often have to roam far and wide in search of plants to eat — and cope with the lean times when there is little growing anywhere. Predators, too, find prey scarce, and larger hunters can go many weeks without a kill.

AFRICAN DESERT FOOD WEB

The small range of creatures in the desert means food webs here are much simpler than elsewhere. Moreover, while in other habitats many species may feed on a similar range of food and occupy similar places in the food web, food in the desert is so scarce that each kind of food may support only a single species. Predators like big cats and dogs cannot afford to be too choosy about their prey when times are lean.

The fast-running caracal is the desert's biggest cat, hunting at dusk for reptiles, birds like sandgrouse, and mammals like the beira.

Spitting cobras live near oases where they can find prey. They hunt at night for rodents, lizards, and small birds, which they kill with their venom-injecting fangs.

Honey pot ants stroke aphids and cochineal insects with their antennae to collect honeydew — a sugary substance that these insects secrete.

Ant lions are large insects. Their larvae dig funnel-shaped pits to trap ants. They hide in the pits with only their jaws showing and flick sand to knock ants into the trap.

ADAPTATION: WALKING ON SAND

Walking on soft, scorching hot sand is not easy, so many desert mammals have specially adapted feet. Desert cats like the sand cat, for instance, have fur pads on the underside of their feet to protect them from the heat. The hooves of the Arabian oryx are unusually large to stop them sinking into soft sand. Camels' feet are both large and padded.

Antelope
Extra wide hooves spread the weight of the addax over a greater area.

Bactrian camel
Shaggy fur on the Bactrian camel's foot protects it from snow as well as sand.

The fat sand rat is a gerbil that feeds on seeds. It copes with lean times by living off the thick layer of fat all over its body, built up when food is plentiful.

The sand cat looks like a large domestic cat. It hunts at night for rodents, lizards and insects, sheltering in caves by day.

The lanner falcon often perches on dead trees at water holes looking for prey, or swoops down from heights of 1,640 feet (500 m). It often catches birds in flight, but if none are available it will eat lizards and small mammals.

Like other Uromastyx lizards of the Sahara, the mastigure has a spiny tail. It feeds on small mammals and eggs.

Small lizards like the spiny-tailed lizard get the fluids their bodies need from feeding on insects.

The beira antelope eats grass and the leaves of bushes, such as acacia, that grow in the stony hills.

During the day the pintail sandgrouse forages far and wide for seeds.

Dromedary camel
A thick pad of fat under the camel's foot helps it walk steadily on the sand.

DESERT LIZARDS
Lizards have thick skins that cut moisture loss to a minimum, and strategies to cope with desert conditions. Unable to make their own body heat, they control their temperature by basking in the sun until they are warm enough to hunt, or find mates. As temperatures soar they must find shade to avoid overheating, and hide under rocks or burrow into the sand.

ASIAN DESERTS

A SIA's Gobi Desert is one of the world's forgotten places — a vast, parched, windswept expanse stretching across southern Mongolia into China. Unlike the ever-hot Sahara, the Gobi swings from scorching summer days — over 113°F (45°C) — to icy winters — often below -40°F (-40°C). This harshness has made it a refuge for creatures hardy enough to survive, including some of the world's rarest animals, such as the Bactrian camel.

SOUTHERN DESERTS

No other deserts have such scorching summers and icy winters, yet many jerboas and reptiles, such as the huge gray monitor, live here. So too does the very rare Asiatic cheetah.

Caucasus Mountains

THAR DESERT

The Thar is home not only to desert foxes and to caracals, but also to large grazers, such as chinkaras and blackbucks, plus many rodents and about 300 species of bird, such as the rare great Indian bustard.

PREDATORY MAMMALS

The Gobi once had two big predators; the Gobi bear and the snow leopard, which used to venture down from the mountains of Tibet. These are now very rare, and the main hunting mammal is the marbled polecat, which hunts at night for lizards and small mammals.

Gobi bear (see p. 109)

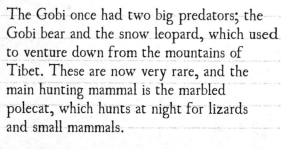

Bactrian camel
(see p. 110)

BROWSERS AND FORAGERS

There are no oases in the Gobi, and the Bactrian camel is the only large foraging animal able to stomach the sparse vegetation and cope with the extreme conditions. The camel is always on the move, seeking tough grass, leaves and thin branches for food.

Pallid harrier
(see p. 136)

BIRDS OF PREY

In summer, various birds of prey visit the Gobi, including spectacular golden and imperial eagles. All year-round, there are carrion-feeding vultures, such as the lammergeier and the giant Cinereous vulture (the Eurasian black), with its enormous 10-foot (3 m) wingspan.

BIRDS OF THE AIR

In summer, many birds visit the Asian deserts and surrounding dry steppes. They include wheatears, desert warblers, desert larks and stone curlews. Other birds such as the Mongolian accentor and the saxaul sparrow are here most of the year.

Desert lark
(see p. 138)

TAKLA MAKHAN

This giant high-altitude plateau is the largest sand desert in Asia.

GOBI DESERT

Covering over 500,000 square miles (1.3 million sq km), the Gobi is a vast expanse of dry, stony river valleys — home to numerous lizards and rodents, and rare Bactrian camels.

Ural Mountains

Altai Mountains

Mongolian
agama lizard
(see p. 126)

REPTILES

Many reptiles cope with the Gobi's extremes by burrowing. There are tortoises and many kinds of gecko and lizard, such as the gray monitor and Gobi racerunner. They are food for snakes like the lebetine viper and Tartar sand boa.

SMALL MAMMALS

Small animals cope with the Gobi's extremes by hiding underground — in summer to avoid the heat of the day and in winter to avoid the cold. Many kinds of jerboa live here, along with various hamsters and hedgehogs.

Desert hedgehog
(see p. 113)

GRAZING MAMMALS

In spring, places in the Gobi turn briefly green and grazing animals move in from the surrounding steppes. Besides wild equids, such as the kulan and Przewalski's horse, there are wild goats such as ibexes, and antelops including the saiga antelope.

Kulan (wild ass)
(see p. 114)

Common
earwig
(see p. 148)

INSECTS

The extremes of the Gobi make life difficult even for insects and other invertebrates. Even so, there is a range of insects in the desert, including ants, beetles, bees and earwigs, arachnids such as scorpions and sun spiders, and woodlice and centipedes.

GROUND BIRDS

The plants that spring up after winter in the central Asian deserts provide enough seeds to support a range of ground birds, including bustards such as the houbara, as well as Henderson's ground jay, Pander's ground jay, and various kinds of sandgrouse.

Pallas's
sandgrouse
(see p. 142)

WIDE-OPEN SPACES

THE deserts and dry steppes of central Asia are among the few places in the world where wild horses survive. They, and the African zebras, are the only remaining wild descendants of the first horselike creatures that appeared 50 million years ago. The world was wetter then, and these horse ancestors were small forest creatures. But as the world became drier and forests shrank, so bigger horses evolved that could live on dry grassland and even in deserts, where they still survive.

Hyracotherium
54–38 mya (million years ago)
Also known as the dawn horse, or eohippus, this was a forest dweller that fed on soft leaves and fruit. It was the size of a small dog, 8 inches (20 cm) high, and it scampered rather than ran.

Mesohippus
40–32 mya
Mesohippus appeared as large areas of forest turned to scrub. It was bigger – 24 inches (60 cm) high – and could run.

Anctitherium
25–5 mya
This successful offshoot from mesohippus survived until five million years ago in China. It browsed on soft forest leaves.

HORSE EVOLUTION

The horse's family tree dates back 50 million years to hyracotherium, fossils of which have been found in both North America and Europe. Since then it has grown bigger, longer legged, longer muzzled, developed hooves instead of toes, and changed from a browser to a grazer. But it was never a steady progression, and this illustration shows just a few major stages and branches.

Miohippus
36–24 mya
With miohippus, the evolutionary path of the horse began to branch. It was slightly bigger than mesohippus.

Parahippus
24–17 mya
Bigger – up to 40 inches (1 m) high – and faster, it had teeth better adapted for eating grass. The move out from forests had begun.

PRZEWALSKI'S HORSE

Most "wild" horses are descendants of escaped domestic horses — Przewalski's horse is the only truly wild horse. It was first identified in the 1880s by Russian explorer Nicolai Przewalski. There were very few and the last wild one was seen in the wild in 1969. Fortunately, over 1,000 survived in zoos, and in the 1990s some were reintroduced to the wild in Mongolia.

Hipparion
15–2 mya
This was one of the many successful branches of grazing horse, long surviving in Africa.

Dwarf
hamster

Dwarf hamsters live
in burrows in sand
dunes in Central
Asia, emerging at
night to feed.

Chinese hamsters are
very small hamsters,
barely 3 inches
(8 cm) long.

Chinese
hamster

Great
jerboa

Great jerboas are one
of several jerboa
species living in the
Gobi. They can jump
up to 10 feet (3 m).

ADAPTATION: BURROWING RODENTS

Few medium-sized mammals can cope with hot
deserts, but deserts are home to a huge variety
of tiny rodents. Rodents hide from the sun in
burrows during the day. Burrows retain the
moisture of the animal's breath and stay at a
steady 77–95°F (25–35°C). Some rodents have
huge back legs and leap around, barely touching
the hot ground when they come out at night.

Merychippus
17–11 mya
This was the first real
grazer, with a long neck
for reaching down to
graze and hooflike feet
for running on grass.

Hippidion
5 million–8,000 years ago
Hippidion was a large offshoot of
pliohippus, about 55 inches (1.4 m)
high, that developed when early horses
spread into South America from the
north five million years ago.

Equus
4 mya–present
The first modern horse,
Equus, appeared about four
million years ago. It gave rise
to six species: true horses,
asses, onagers, and three
kinds of zebra.

Zebras
There are three species
of zebra – the Plains
(E. quagga), Mountain
(E. zebra) and Grevy's
(E. grevyi). Each arose in
different parts of Africa.

Pliohippus
12–5 mya
An early hoofed horse,
it was once thought to be
the direct ancestor of the
modern horse Equus.

Przewalski's horse
(Equus ferus)
The only true horse left in the wild is
Przewalski's horse. Some experts think
it is the ancestor of the modern horse.
Others think they both descended from
a common ancestor, now extinct.

Onagers
(Equus hemionus)
With the Asian
onagers, well adapted
for life in the desert,
the horse moved
farthest away from its
damp forest origins.

Asses (Equus asinus)
Asses (or donkeys) are quite
similar to onagers but
originated in northern Africa.

43

AMERICAN DESERTS

THE southwestern corner of North America is a vast area of plains and mountains, rocky outcrops and canyons, encompassing four great deserts — the Great Basin, Mojave, Sonoran, and Chihuahuan. Each of these deserts has its own distinctive range of wildlife, from the Great Basin with its sagebrush and coyotes to the Chihuahuan with its mesquite scrub and tarantulas. This region is also home to the hottest place on the planet, Death Valley, where a record 134°F (56.7°C) was recorded in 1913.

Bobcat
(see p. 109)

Greater roadrunner
(see p. 142)

GROUND BIRDS

With so few trees, many desert birds nest or feed on the ground, including California quails, roadrunners, inca and mourning doves, and the common poorwill. Turkeys and ring-necked pheasants are visitors to the more moist parts of the desert.

REPTILES AND AMPHIBIANS

Besides lizards, the deserts are home to rattlesnakes, whip snakes, king, coral and gopher snakes, and also the rare desert tortoise. Amphibians like spadefoot toads and desert slender salamanders emerge from burrows only after rains.

Western diamondback rattlesnake
(see p. 126)

PREDATORY MAMMALS

Rodents, reptiles and birds are prey for a number of cats and dogs. Cats include bobcats and pumas. Dogs include gray foxes and coyotes. Efforts are under way to reintroduce Mexican gray wolves, hunted to extinction in the wild in the 1950s.

Chuckwalla (see p. 124)

SMALL MAMMALS

As in many hot deserts, there is a wealth of small mammals. Rodents such as kangaroo rats and ground squirrels stay cool by sheltering in burrows, and get their moisture from their food. Jackrabbits stay in the shade and lose heat through their big ears.

Desert kangaroo rat (see p. 114)

BIRDS OF PREY

Most small desert creatures are safe in their burrows, but when they come to the surface they make easy targets for birds of prey, such as prairie falcons, American kestrels, hawks, turkey vultures, golden eagles and owls like the great horned and burrowing owls.

Red-tailed hawk
(see p. 136)

LIZARDS

The many desert lizards include swift-moving zebra lizards, fearsome-looking desert horned lizards, pretty fringe-toed lizards, desert spiny lizards, banded geckos, iguanas and whiptails. The Gila monster and the Mexican beaded lizard are the United States' largest poisonous lizards.

INSECTS AND SPIDERS

The teeming insect life of the deserts includes fire ants, beetles, weevils, dragonflies, butterflies such as the western tiger swallowtail, and the Magicada cicada. Spiders include many large tarantulas.

Black widow spider (see p. 153)

Gila woodpecker (see p. 144)

BIRDS OF THE AIR

Despite the lack of trees, many birds may linger in the desert, including the crowned sparrow, the warbling vireo, the rock wren, thrashers, and warblers like the hermit. Birds like the cactus wren, gilded flicker, and Gila woodpecker live here all the time.

GRAZING ANIMALS

The deserts are one of the last refuges for the bighorn sheep. They keep cool here by staying in the shade, sweating and panting. Pronghorns live here too, and also white-tailed deer, which feed on guajillo brush, prickly pear cactus and other shrubs.

Shy mule deer (see p. 111)

GREAT BASIN
The Great Basin is a scrubland of sagebrush, roamed by pack rats, coyotes and bobcats and scanned by buzzards, hawks and owls.

DEATH VALLEY
Linking the Great Basin to the Mojave, Death Valley is the hottest, lowest place in North America — 282 feet (86 m) below sea level and sometimes reaching more than 130°F (54°C) during the day.

MOJAVE DESERT
The Mojave is a desert of Joshua trees and creosote bushes — the home of rattlesnakes, kangaroo rats, desert tortoises, cactus wrens and Gila monsters.

Sierra Nevada

Gulf of California

Gulf of Mexico

CHIHUAHUAN DESERT
In the Chihuahuan, mesquite scrub grows higher up, and opuntia and barrel cactus lower down. Tarantulas, scorpions and lizards lurk here. Antelope jackrabbits are also common.

SONORAN DESERT
The Sonoran is where saguaro cacti grow more than 50 feet (15 m) tall. Creatures like wood rats, elf-owls, Gila woodpeckers and hummingbirds live on the saguaro.

45

SCORCHING SUN

SURVIVAL in hot deserts is survival against the odds for the animals that live there. Not only is there an extreme scarcity of water to cope with, but blistering heat both directly from the sun and also radiating back off the sun-scorched ground. Facing these twin threats, desert animals have developed a range of tactics. Rodents like kangaroo rats shelter in burrows during the heat of the day and gain their water from the plants they eat. Snakes such as rattlesnakes have venom to make a kill quickly. Some animals have large ears for losing heat; others have wide mouths. Each creature has its own way of coping with the extremes.

ADAPTATION: BIG EARS

Desert animals have developed many techniques for losing heat. One of the most distinctive is to have large, thin ears filled with blood vessels: breezes blowing over the ears cool the blood. Black-tailed jackrabbits and kit foxes both have large ears like this.

Blood vessels come near the surface and cool the blood over a large area in the jackrabbit's giant ears.

Black-tailed jackrabbit

The blood is cooled as blood vessels come near the surface inside the cool shade of the kit fox's large ears.

Kit fox

The elf owl avoids the heat in a hole inside the saguaro cactus.

The dark plumage of the turkey vulture soaks up heat, so it urinates on its legs to keep cool, and soars up into cooler air on thermals.

Toads like the Sonoran green stay dormant in holes until the summer rains fill water holes. Then they emerge, breed, lay their eggs, and restock on food and water for another long wait.

Antelope jackrabbits have big ears filled with blood vessels that help the rabbit cool quickly when in the shade.

Common poorwills go into a sleep called estivation when very hot. When awake, they keep cool by gaping their beaks and fluttering their throats to evaporate water — but they must drink often to do this.

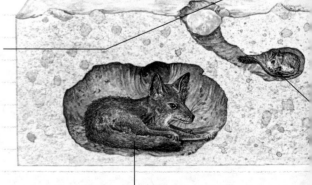

Kit foxes avoid the worst heat by curling up in burrows by day. Their paws are thickly furred to protect them from the hot ground and they have big ears to help keep them cool. They get water from their food.

JOSHUA TREE

The Joshua trees (yuccas) of the Mojave Desert are centers of animal activity, providing a home for many small creatures. The insects draw other animals to feed.

Cactus wren

Scott's oriole

LIVING WITH DROUGHT AND HEAT

Lack of water is a year-round problem in the desert, and for four or five months each year, temperatures on the desert surface are too high for any creature to survive for long. This illustration shows just some of the many ways in which desert wildlife manages to stay cool, and avoid dying of thirst.

Many birds are only active in the relative cool of dusk and dawn. The kingbird is active all day, but always perches in shade under bushes.

The noisy little Gila woodpecker is the desert's home builder, chipping out holes in the saguaro cacti and Joshua trees.

Night snake

Even lizards like Gila monsters avoid the worst of the heat — sheltering under rocks or in burrows. They also move quickly on hot ground, holding their bodies high on stretched legs.

Yuccaboris weevil

Yucca moth

Desert night lizard

The burrowing owl shelters underground.

Sonoran green toad avoids the hot sun in its hole.

The ant lion larva digs a pit to trap prey.

The trapdoor spider hides in a test-tube-shaped pit with a lid.

Kangaroo rats shelter by day in burrows, plugging the hole to retain moisture from their breath. Chemical processes in their bodies help them turn dry seeds into water.

The bull snake sleeps out the day in its tunnel.

The northern grasshopper mouse makes its cool hole under a rock.

TEMPERATE WOODLANDS

IN winter, many temperate woodlands are gaunt and cold. Deciduous trees lose their leaves to economize on the water that is hard to draw from the bitterly cold ground. Icy winds whip through bare branches, and snow may blanket the ground, leaving the wood apparently lifeless.

Yet come spring, the warmth of the sun starts to spread through the ground, leaf buds appear on the trees, and delicate flowers burst into bloom on the woodland floor. By summer, the trees are lush and green, and the woodland teems with life. Not all temperate woods are deciduous. Where winters are cool rather than cold — in California, around the Mediterranean and in Australia — trees are broad-leaved (not conifers) but also evergreen. Even here, the change from winter to summer is marked.

For creatures that dwell in temperate woods, survival means coping with the dramatic changing of the seasons — or, like many birds, leaving for the winter. Nevertheless, an amazing variety of animals do cope, by foraging what little food does exist or by hibernating. Temperate woods may not have as many animal species as tropical forests, but they are among the richest of all animal habitats.

WHERE ARE TEMPERATE WOODLANDS?

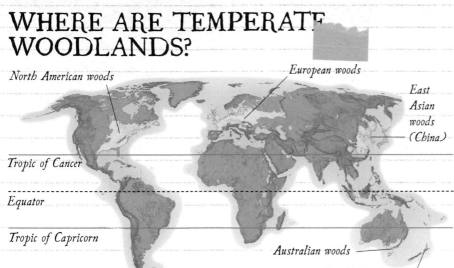

North American woods

European woods

East Asian woods (China)

Tropic of Cancer

Equator

Tropic of Capricorn

Australian woods

New Zealand woods

COMPARING TEMPERATE WOODLANDS

Shagbark hickory

Beech

Undergrowth of sassafras

Basswood

NORTH AMERICA

In the woods of eastern North America, trees such as oak and hickory spread their canopies over shrubs such as sassafras. Farther north, pine and redwood forests grow.

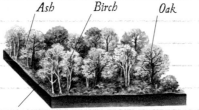

Ash

Birch

Oak

Undergrowth of ferns, bramble

EURASIA

European woods vary locally, from beech woods on lime soils to oaks on clay. A mixed wood may have oak, ash and birch, with an undergrowth of thorn and bramble.

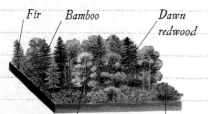

Fir

Bamboo

Dawn redwood

Maidenhair tree

Rhododendron, azalea bushes

CHINA

Today, only pockets of China's broad-leaved woodlands are left. In these grow maidenhair and dawn redwood trees, along with dense clumps of rhododendron and azalea.

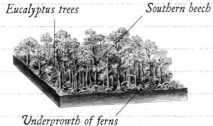

Eucalyptus trees

Southern beech

Undergrowth of ferns

AUSTRALIA

Dense woods of eucalyptus grow in South Australia. Farther south and at higher elevations where it is cooler and wet, woods include evergreen beech along with mountain ash.

TEMPERATE WOODLAND ENVIRONMENTS

Water is slow to evaporate in temperate woodland and there is always enough rain for trees to thrive — typically 30–60 inches (760–1,500 mm) a year. In some places, rainfall is so high the woods are called "temperate rain forests."

SUN AND RAIN

In a typical temperate wood, summers are warm, but winters chilly, with ground temperatures under 41°F (5°C). Frequent frosts make it hard for most trees to draw up water.

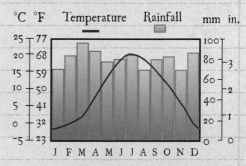

°C °F   Temperature   Rainfall   mm in.

WOODLANDS IN WINTER

In winter, deciduous trees are completely bare and the wood is open to the sky. But the air is cold, and food is hard for animals to find, so only the hardiest creatures stay.

WOODLANDS IN SPRING

In spring, various flowers including primroses and bluebells have a brief chance to bloom before the dense canopy of leaves closes in over them, shrouding them from the sun.

49

EURASIAN TEMPERATE WOODLANDS

THE supply of food in temperate woods is too seasonal for many large animals to live here. But there are many birds and small mammals — and an even greater abundance of insects and other small invertebrates. Each kind of woodland — beech, oak, mixed, pine, evergreen — attracts its own species. For example, some birds such as redpolls favor birch woods, while chaffinches prefer beech woods.

GROUND BIRDS

The woodland floor is rich in both seeds and invertebrate life, especially in summer, providing an abundant larder for birds such as nightingales, pheasants and woodcocks, which wade through leaf litter probing for worms.

Nightingale
(see p. 139)

Fallow deer
(see p. 111)

GRAZING MAMMALS

Often, only clearings have enough grass for grazing, but woodlands provide deer with shelter. Deer can also feed on tree shoots and shrubs. Woodland deer include native red, fallow and roe deer, and introduced species such as muntjac and Chinese water deer.

Gray wolf
(see p. 123)

PREDATORY MAMMALS

There is often too little prey in winter to sustain pure meat-eaters like big cats, though there are wildcats and lynxes. Most predators, such as wolves, foxes and weasels, can survive on a range of foods in hard times.

RODENTS AND SMALL MAMMALS

Leaves, fruit, nuts and seeds provide food for many small mammals, and for insects that in turn are food for mammals. A 1/4 square mile (0.65 sq km) of woodland can support more than 5,000 mice and voles, plus many others.

Fat dormouse
(see p. 112)

BIRDS OF PREY

Buzzard
(see p. 133)

With short wings for weaving through trees, small birds of prey like sparrowhawks hunt close to the ground, ambushing prey. Big birds like golden eagles glide over woods and swoop on prey in clearings. Tawny and long-eared owls hunt at night.

Great spotted woodpecker
(see p. 144)

BIRDS OF THE AIR

The profusion of insect life in the woodland spring draws a host of songbirds such as warblers and thrushes. The rich summer crop of berries, seeds and nuts provides food for birds such as tits and jays.

Puss moth and caterpillar
(see p. 152)

BROWSERS AND FORAGERS

Many woodland mammals mix their diet a little, and even carnivores, such as martens, often forage for fruits and nuts. The main foragers, however, are badgers and boars. Badgers feed mostly on earthworms, but also eat seeds, beetles and fruit in fall.

Wild boar
(see p. 109)

BUTTERFLIES AND MOTHS

The spring leaves of deciduous trees provide food for countless caterpillars, while adult moths and butterflies suck nectar from flowers. Purple hairstreaks flutter in oak treetops and emperors near willows. Fritillaries feed on violets on the ground.

INVERTEBRATES

In spring, there is an explosion of invertebrate life in the wood, thriving on the new growth. The leaf litter teems with creatures such as wood ants, centipedes, slugs and snails, while leaves sustain many kinds of beetles, may bugs and crickets. Some flies prey on other animals.

Ladybug
(see p. 150)

BIALOWIEZA
The Bialowieza on the Polish border is one of Europe's last great forests — home to wolves, bears, deer and now the European bison, or wisent, which has been reintroduced from zoos.

POCKETS OF WOODLAND
Much of Europe was once covered in deciduous woods, but the soil beneath the trees is so rich that much has now been cleared for farmland. Natural woods survive only in isolated pockets.

WARM, DRY WOODS
The woodlands around the Mediterranean are mostly evergreen, with trees such as the cork oak and pistachio.

WOODLAND LIFE

LIKE tropical forests, temperate woods have distinct layers, although the trees are not as tall or densely packed. The top layer is the canopy formed by the crowns of trees. Here numerous herbivores — birds, small mammals, and insects — feed on leaves and fruit. Lower down is the undergrowth of brambles and thorn, where ground birds and larger mammals find cover. The woodland floor is a deep layer of litter formed by fallen leaves, which rot slowly in the cool air. Here, voles and shrews dig covered runways and there is a teeming population of insects, woodlice, centipedes and other invertebrates.

ADAPTATION: BIRD SONG

In winter and spring especially, woods are filled with the songs of blackbirds, thrushes and warblers. All birds call to keep in touch with each other, but male songbirds like these sing to attract a female or to proclaim their territory. Each species has its own song, which often varies through the seasons. In winter, male blackbirds sing quietly to charm females, but in spring they perch on a song post (such as a high branch) and sing out loudly to announce their territory. After finding a mate, songbird pairs build a nest, often preferring particular heights.

Mistle Thrush above 65 feet (20 m)

Blackbird up to 32 feet (9.8 m)

Nightingale almost on the ground

Grasshopper warbler almost on the ground

Willow warbler up to 2 feet (0.6 m)

Garden warbler up to 2–3 feet (0.6–1 m)

Song thrush up to 5 feet (1.5 m)

WOODLAND FOOD WEB

Each tree in the wood is a world of its own, and each kind has its own range of creatures. A deciduous tree gives creatures both food and shelter and links them together in a living unit. Crucial to life in a tree are the countless insects and other small creatures in the crown that feed on the leaves and fruit, and form the base of the complex web of food dependency between the animals.

Peppered moth caterpillars eat the spring leaves of many deciduous trees. The adult is camouflaged by day against the lichen-covered bark.

Pheasants birds are opportunist feeders, and eat not only seeds and insects, but also lizards, small snakes and small mammals, such as mice.

EURASIAN BADGER

Badgers like to live in woods with good cover and soft, dry soil in which they can dig their setts. These huge burrow networks have a dozen or so entrances and provide a home for a male, a female or two, and cubs. Setts are passed on through the generations, and many are a century or more old. The badgers emerge at dusk to forage for food. They will even eat small mammals. In winter when food is scarce they may eat carrion.

Long-eared owls spend the day in the abandoned nests of others, such as crows. At night they hunt for voles, shrews and other small nocturnal mammals, and birds.

Sparrowhawks are agile fliers that use the cover of trees to ambush birds varying in size from tiny blue tits to larger birds, such as common pheasants.

Blue tits relish the variety of food in the wood, eating all kinds of insects in summer, including caterpillars, and insects and seeds in winter.

The larvae of longhorn beetles can damage trees as they tunnel through them, feeding on the living wood. Adult beetles feed on sap, pollen, nectar or leaves.

Shrews scurry through tunnels in the leaf litter, searching for woodlice and beetles.

Woodlice are crustaceans, like crabs and lobsters, and have adapted to life on land. They feed on rotting wood and vegetation.

Red foxes feed mainly on rabbits, hares and small mammals like shrews and mice, but will eat almost anything – beetles, birds, frogs and even garbage.

Pot worms are tiny white worms that play a key role in the soil by digesting dead organic matter. Up to 30,000 worms may be present in 1 square yard (1.8 sq m) of soil.

Wood mice eat berries, fruit, seeds, mushrooms, worms and insects. They go into a torpid state in winter when food is scarce.

NORTH AMERICAN TEMPERATE WOODLANDS

WHEN European settlers arrived, the eastern United States was covered by a vast deciduous forest, in which roamed mountain lions and wolves. Much of the forest has gone, along with the lions and wolves, but pockets survive. These are home to a host of small mammals, birds and insects. Some are able to cope with the harsh winter, often by sleeping or varying their diet. Others arrive in spring to make the most of the summer.

Cascades

Rocky Mountains

Missouri River

Great Plains

Rio Grande

Sierra Madre

BIRDS OF THE AIR

Even in winter, the woods echo with the calls of birds like chickadees, woodpeckers and even cardinals. In spring, migrants such as warblers and redstarts wing in from the south to make the most of the feast of insects and new plant growth.

Blue jay *(see p. 137)*

Eastern box turtle
(see p. 128)

REPTILES

Areas of wetland and fields in the woods of eastern North America provide prey and shelter for many reptiles, including wood turtles, skinks, and snakes, such as the garter snake, the rough green snake, and the copperhead.

Common
sawfly
(see p. 152)

AMPHIBIANS

Many frogs, toads, newts and salamanders lay eggs in woodland streams and ponds and live as adults among the trees — oak toads in South Carolina, gray tree frogs in southern Canada, and many more.

Spotted salamander
(see p. 131)

Raccoon
(see p. 119)

SMALL MAMMALS

In summer, there is a plentiful supply of invertebrates, fruit and nuts for many small mammals such as eastern chipmunks, voles and Virginia opossums. They in turn are food for small carnivores such as long-tailed weasels.

INSECTS, INVERTEBRATES

Spring leaves sustain an army of weevils and gall wasps, while a host of beetles feed on the wood of trees. But the thick leaf litter on the forest floor is one of the world's richest microhabitats, teeming with small creatures such as ants, centipedes, slugs and snails.

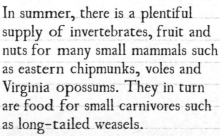

ADIRONDACK MOUNTAINS

In the valleys of the north, forests of sugar maple, birch and pine are home to more than 50 species of mammal, including beavers, coyotes, moose and pine martens as well as eagles and ospreys.

ALLEGHENY MOUNTAINS

One of the few remaining pockets of the forests that once stretched right along the Appalachians. The Alleghenies provide a refuge for many creatures such as bears, Indiana bats and Allegheny wood rats.

GREAT SMOKY MOUNTAINS

This is one of the last great stands of virgin deciduous wood, where tall and stately basswood, beech and hickory trees grow.

Black bear (see p. 109)

PREDATORY MAMMALS

In summer, woodland rabbits and hares are targets for both red foxes and bobcats. Gray foxes prey on insects and rodents — and climb with catlike agility. In hard times all three hunters turn to foods such as fruit. In North Carolina woods, rare red wolves may be seen.

Wild turkey (see p. 144)

GROUND BIRDS

Game birds, such as ruffed grouse and introduced pheasants grow large on seeds and berries pecked off the woodland floor and need to take off only for short flights. Ruffed grouse nest in aspens, where the female feeds on catkins as she incubates her eggs.

BROWSERS AND FORAGERS

North America's only large deciduous woodland browser is the white-tailed deer. But because they feed on such a wide range of food — from leaves to fallen fruit — they can survive anywhere from the cold pine forests of Maine to the warm swamps of Florida.

White-tailed deer (see p. 111)

BIRDS OF PREY

Woodland trees provide perfect perches for agile raptors that make sudden sallies to snatch birds and mammals. Cooper's hawks prey on bats, squirrels and chipmunks. Sharp-shinned hawks grab small birds. Larger northern goshawks may pounce on hares.

Eastern screech owl (see p. 140)

THE WOODLAND YEAR

FOR the creatures of temperate deciduous woods, life is dominated by the seasons. No other habitat changes as much through the year, from almost Arctic desolation in winter to almost tropical abundance in summer. Each creature copes in its own way, but there are four main strategies: some animals can vary their diet and lifestyle with the seasons; many birds migrate in winter; some small creatures sleep through the winter; and many insects put their development on hold until spring.

Swainson's hawk

Black-and-white warbler

Others

Swainson's hawk

Scarlet tanager

ADAPTATION: MIGRATION

Most of the birds of the deciduous forest avoid the chill of winter by migrating south every fall. The route and destination vary between species, but most migrate between the same localities, using the stars and their own internal magnetic compasses to guide them with astonishing accuracy.

Red-eyed vireo

WINTER SLEEP

Winter cold means animals need extra energy to function — yet food is scarce. Many small mammals survive by hibernating, as do some reptiles, amphibians and insects. Hibernation means winding down body processes until the animal slips into a dormant state in which it uses barely any energy. Most hibernate in holes safe from predators.

Red foxes vary their diet, making the most of any food available.

Wild turkeys visit the wood in winter for shelter and to feed on acorns.

Porcupines gather in dens and come out when the weather is dry to make a short foray for bark, their winter food.

Ruffed grouse

Gray squirrels stay active all winter, relying on caches of nuts buried in fall.

White-tailed deer huddle together in areas called "deer yards" and feed on acorns.

Wood frog

Long-tailed weasels turn white in winter, becoming almost invisible against the snow.

Spotted salamanders hibernate in holes in the soil.

Snapping turtle

WINTER

As the cold of winter really takes hold, warm-blooded animals can generate their own heat to avoid freezing. Cold-blooded animals must use other strategies. Some insects flood their bodies with antifreeze proteins and the antifreeze fluid, glycerol. Many frogs and turtles hide in ponds under the ice, absorbing oxygen through their skins. Wood frogs actually freeze, and survive.

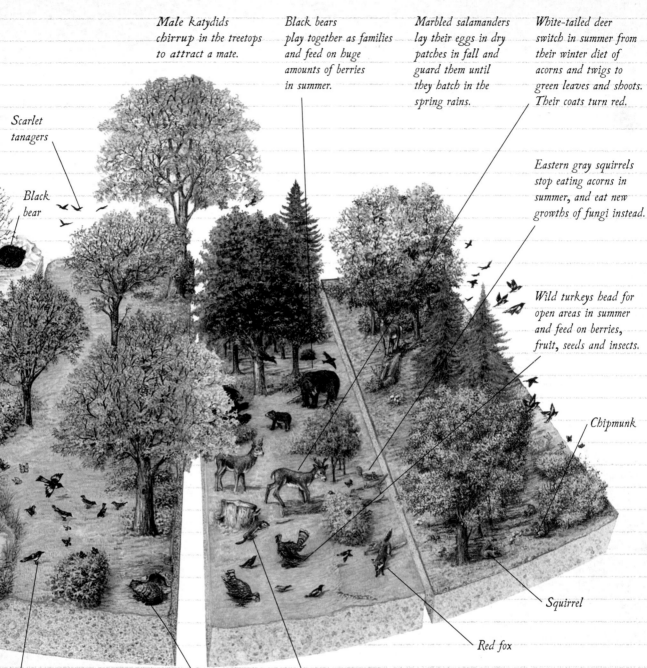

Male katydids chirrup in the treetops to attract a mate.

Black bears play together as families and feed on huge amounts of berries in summer.

Marbled salamanders lay their eggs in dry patches in fall and guard them until they hatch in the spring rains.

White-tailed deer switch in summer from their winter diet of acorns and twigs to green leaves and shoots. Their coats turn red.

Scarlet tanagers

Black bear

Eastern gray squirrels stop eating acorns in summer, and eat new growths of fungi instead.

Wild turkeys head for open areas in summer and feed on berries, fruit, seeds and insects.

Chipmunk

Squirrel

Red fox

Redstarts

Monarch butterfly

Groundhog

Weasel

SPRING

As spring arrives, buds appear on trees, flowers bloom and insects multiply. Spring azure butterflies sip on butterfly weed and monarchs lay eggs on milkweed. Birds that winter in the south, such as redstarts, vireos, tanagers and warblers, fly in to feed on insects.

SUMMER

In summer, every square yard of woodland grows 2 pounds (1 kg/sq m) of plant matter. Both the plants and the insects that feed on them provide abundant food. Fledgling birds begin to take to the air. Mammals born in spring grow and begin to learn how to fend for themselves.

FALL

Leaves turn gold, red, yellow, and brown. Songbirds flock together for the migration, as do monarch butterflies. Animals that are staying begin to build up winter food reserves — either by eating, like deer, or by burying food "caches," as do squirrels, chipmunks, jays and even foxes. Deer bucks seek out does and engage in fierce battles with rivals.

ASIAN TEMPERATE WOODLANDS

A VAST temperate forest once stretched right across the center of China through Korea and into far eastern Siberia. Most of the forest was cleared by farmers 4,000 years ago, but the remnants that survive are some of the richest and most diverse temperate forests in the world — home to a phenomenal range of plants and a host of unique animals, including the rare giant panda.

DABA SHAN
The mixed evergreen and oak forests that cloak Daba Shan are home to rare golden snub-nosed monkeys, leopards and musk deer, as well as Reeves's pheasant and wild pigs.

Mole shrew
(see p. 120)

Golden monkey
(see p. 116)

PRIMATES

There are about 18 species of monkey living in forest trees in China. Many of these, almost uniquely, live in the temperate zone, including the rare Yunnan snub-nosed, which lives in evergreen forests over 10,000 feet (3,000 m) up, where snow lies most of the winter.

BIRDS OF THE AIR

Many woodland birds fly far to avoid the winter cold, but eastern woods are often so mountainous that many need only move to warmer places in the valleys as winter sets in. Among the vast range of woodland birds here are rosefinches, tits, crows and woodpeckers.

Asian fairy bluebird
(see p. 132)

SMALL MAMMALS

A huge range of small mammals are sustained by the fruits, nuts and abundance of insect life in the forests of the Far East, including mice, rats and voles. These in turn provide prey for sables, minks, weasels and martens.

Red panda
(see p. 118)

FORAGING MAMMALS

China's most famous native animal is the giant panda, which survives now only in Sichuan, Gansu, and Shaanxi provinces, where it feeds mostly on bamboo – unlike the more omnivorous red panda.

INSECTS

In every eastern forest, the ground and trees are teeming with ants, beetles and many other insects. But China's glory is its butterflies, including the orange oakleaf (a perfect mimic of withered oak leaves), the Chinese gifu, common clippers and the rare golden kaiser.

Bombycidae moth (silkworm)
(see p. 151)

Oriental fire-bellied toad
(see p. 131)

REPTILES AND AMPHIBIANS

The diversity of China's woodland is matched by its amphibians and reptiles. In one area, 73 kinds of reptiles and 35 amphibians have been noted. Reptiles include Reeves's turtles, krait snakes, and Amur and red-backed ratsnakes.

WOLONG

The moist mountains of Wolong are the last refuge of the giant panda, as well as home to more than 90 mammal species including clouded leopards and white-lipped deer, and also 300 bird species including rare pheasants.

SICHUAN

Very little of the vast broad-leaved evergreen forests remain, but along the rivers black kites hunt by day and bats hunt by night. Stump-tailed macaques cling to the trees on Emei Shan mountain.

USSURI FORESTS

Here, on cool, low coastal hills, pine grows alongside oak and walnut. This remote world is a refuge for rare Amur tigers and leopards, as well as black bears, goatlike gorals, and unique snakes like the Ussurian mamushi.

KOREAN WOODS

In oak and birch woods surviving in Korea, black bears, mandarin voles and wolves roam. This is the home, too, of the white-bellied black woodpecker.

Takin
(see p. 121)

GRAZERS AND BROWSERS

The forests of East Asia were once so dense and so steep that the deer living here, such as sika and eld's deer, Reeves's and Fea's muntjacs, and Siberian musk deer, had to be small. On open slopes high up, there are bigger white-lipped deer, blue dwarf sheep and goatlike serows.

GROUND AND WATER BIRDS

Three of the world's 15 crane species – including the Eurasian crown crane, famed for its spectacular courting dance – hunt for fish by the rivers of the East Asian forests. Here, too, live crested shelducks, mandarin ducks and Chinese mergansers.

Pheasant
(see p. 141)

Amur tiger
(see p. 122)

PREDATORY MAMMALS

The rich prey of the forests supported many large predators in the past: tigers, clouded leopards, wolves and black bears. But the shrinking of the forests, and the activities of poachers who trap the animals to use their body parts in a variety of products, have put them in grave danger.

THE LOST FOREST

AT the western edge of China, in Sichuan, the soaring Himalayas drop away into a startling landscape of high plateaus, flat basins and deep ravines. The steep slopes are perpetually shrouded in mist, providing ample moisture for thick forests to grow. Remarkably, the special climatic conditions mean that as they climb each slope these forests vary as much as forests do from Florida to Alaska — ranging from subtropical in the valleys to alpine high up. This unique variation provides niches for the extraordinary range of animals that make western China one of the world's most special habitats.

ADAPTATION: THUMB PADS

The rare giant panda is a member of the bear family, but unlike its close cousins it lives almost entirely on a vegetarian diet. It lives in bamboo forests above 4,500 feet (1,400 m) and feeds almost exclusively on bamboo shoots, which it grips in its forepaws to eat. To help it hold the stems, the panda's forepaw has developed an extra thumb pad.

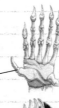

In most animals, this bone is just a wrist bone, but in the panda it has grown into an extra thumb.

The panda's extra thumb allows the panda to grip bamboo firmly while eating and to snap off shoots from the plant.

Since they spend between 12 and 14 hours a day eating, pandas sit or lie on their backs to eat. This enables them to use their paws to hold the bamboo as they chew it.

LIVING LEVELS

Everywhere in the world, temperatures steadily fall as hillsides rise. But two things make Sichuan particularly special. The first is the sheer range of the changing conditions. The second is that Sichuan stands at an animal crossroads, where creatures that evolved in Tropical Asia meet those that evolved in the Palearctic – northern Eurasia and North America. Moreover, the isolation of the deep valleys has allowed some cold-climate animals, such as mole shrews, to avoid competition and survive long after they have disappeared elsewhere in the world.

The various forest levels ensure there is a suitable niche for this huge range of creatures. The illustration shows some of the animals that live at different levels. Some, such as lovebirds, are limited to just one level.

MUSK DEER

The musk deer is a small animal barely 40 inches (1 m) tall that lives in bamboo forests. Males have long canine teeth instead of antlers and these are used for fighting. Musk deer have been poached heavily for the scented musk oil that male deer secrete, which is used to make perfume.

South China tiger (probably extinct)

Monal pheasant

Tufted deer

Black-necked crane

Reeves's pheasant

Red-crowned crane

Lynx

Tufted deer

Reeves's pheasant

Takin

Asiatic black bear

Lynx

Tufted deer

Muntjac deer

Goral

Serow

Silver pheasant

Tragopan

Giant panda

Lovebird

Goral

Merganser

Demoiselle crane

Serow

Golden snub-nosed monkey

ALPINE ZONE:
above 12,000 feet (4,000 m)
Right at the top are open alpine meadows, thinning out to bare rock just below the permanent snow line.

RHODODENDRON SCRUB:
9,000–12,000 feet (3,000–4,000 m)
Near the tops of the slopes, it is too cold and dry even for conifers to survive, and the forest opens out into a scrub of rhododendron.

COOL TEMPERATE FOREST:
6,000–9,000 feet (2,000–3,000 m)
At this level, the bamboos are replaced by thickets of rhododendrons and azaleas, and the conifers thin out and begin to become stunted.

CLOUD FOREST:
4,500–9,000 feet (1,400–3,000 m)
This zone is cooler and wetter and frequently shrouded in a damp mist of low cloud. Here the oaks give way to dense groves of pines and fir trees mixed with tall stands of fast-growing bamboo.

THE LOWER SLOPES:
2,000–4,500 feet (600–1,400 m)
The foothills support a mix of broad-leaved evergreen and deciduous trees, mostly oaks. Here and there are uniquely primitive trees: ginkgoes and dawn redwoods.

AUSTRALASIAN TEMPERATE WOODLANDS

THE far south of Australia, the island of Tasmania and north New Zealand are so wet in places that rain forests grow, even though this is the temperate zone. Near sheltered east coasts, however, the land is warmer and drier, and here dry eucalyptus forests grow. Each area has its own range of wildlife, and isolation has made the creatures of Tasmania and New Zealand especially distinctive.

Gulf of Carpentaria

Arnhem Land

Barkly Tableland

Kimberley Plateau

MacDonnell Ranges

Simpson Desert

Great Sandy Desert

Gibson Desert

Great Victoria Desert

N

SOUTHWEST AUSTRALIA

The warm, wandoo tree woods of the southwest are filled with birds such as ringneck parrots and spinebills. They are also home to rare kangaroolike bettongs and tiny, ferocious little mouselike phascogales. Rarest of all is the western swamp turtle.

Koala (see p. 114)

Kookaburra
(see p. 138)

TREE-BROWSING MAMMALS

In among the branches of the gum trees of southern Australia and Tasmania clamber and jump many agile marsupials including brush-tailed possums, phalangers and greater gliders, which can glide 330 feet (100 m) between trees.

REPTILES AND AMPHIBIANS

New Zealand's frogs belong to an old group called Leiopelma, and have changed little in 70 million years. Eastern snake-necked turtles, tiger snakes and eastern brown snakes slither through the forest in southeast Australia.

Tuatara
(see p. 128)

BIRDS OF PREY

New Zealand has very few birds of prey, apart from the karearea falcon, but introduced ravens take nestlings. The open gum tree forests of southern Australia and Tasmania provide good hunting for wedge-tailed eagles, whistling kites and other raptors.

BIRDS OF THE AIR

In gum tree forests, honey-eaters are the equivalent of northern songbirds. Other birds include tiny pardalotes, dusky robins and black currawongs.

Crimson rosella
(see p. 142)

GROUND BIRDS

The absence of predators has meant that many New Zealand birds, including the brown kiwi, kakapo and takahes, have lost the power of flight. Most ground birds in Tasmania are introduced, as they could not fly there themselves.

Superb lyrebird
(see p. 138)

Potoroo
(see p. 118)

GROUND BROWSING MAMMALS

In New Zealand, the only browsing mammals are introduced species, such as deer and chamois. But in Tasmania and southeast Australia, marsupials including kangaroos, wallabies and potoroos, hop around drier woodland floors.

NORTH ISLAND

In among soaring kauri trees live rare kokako birds, kiwis, and kakapo and kaka parrots.

New Zealand

SOUTH ISLAND

Woods here are filled with birds such as bellbirds, tuis, the Okarito kiwi and the tiny rifleman.

SOUTHEAST AUSTRALIA

In among the scribbly gum and stringybark trees live extraordinary birds such as lyrebirds and kookaburras, and many kinds of marsupial, such as koalas, quolls, bandicoots and wombats.

TASMANIA

Cut off from the rest of Australia, this is home to unique creatures such as Tasmanian devils and thornbills, and rare creatures such as pygmy possums and duckbilled platypuses.

Blue-black spider wasp (see p. 155)

INSECTS

New Zealand has over 20,000 insect species; many are native, including thousands of kinds of beetle. But many species have been blown over by high-altitude winds from Australia, including butterflies like the Australian painted lady.

PREDATORY MAMMALS

New Zealand's only native mammal predators are bats. Tasmania has had only a handful of small marsupial hunters, such as quolls, since wolflike thylacines were wiped out in the 1930s.

Tasmanian devil
(see p. 122)

Weta
(see p. 155)

GRASSHOPPERS

New Zealand has no native mice, so their niche in the forest habitat is taken by large grasshopperlike insects called weta, and by grasshoppers, which are common in the mountain forests of the South Island. Mountain grasshoppers can grow to 1¼ inches (3 cm).

SAFE ON THE GROUND

THE two most remarkable features of New Zealand's wildlife are its lack of native mammals, apart from two bat species, and its abundance of flightless birds, such as kiwis and kakapos. There were no other mammals because the islands of New Zealand broke away from the rest of the world's continents and became isolated 190 million years ago — long before mammals really developed elsewhere. Without mammals to prey on them, New Zealand birds had much less need to fly — and so flightless birds either survived or evolved there. New Zealand remained a safe haven for flightless birds until humans arrived bringing predatory animals, such as cats. Now most of these birds are extinct or endangered.

FLIGHTLESS BIRDS

Each of the southern continents has its own large flightless bird — the South American rhea, the African ostrich, the Asian cassowary, the Australian emu, and the New Zealand kiwi, along with its now extinct giant moa. These birds, called ratites, are probably similar because they all descended from a flightless bird that evolved when the continents were joined together 100 million years ago. But some experts believe that the New Zealand birds are unique and lost the power of flight only after the islands became isolated.

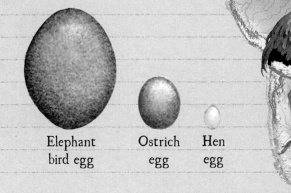

Elephant bird (extinct)

Rhea

BIG EGGS

The heaviest bird that ever lived was the elephant bird or *Aepyornis maximus* of Madagascar. This giant flightless bird, which survived on the island until humans arrived, was 9 feet (2.7 m) tall and weighed 1,000 pounds (450 kg). Its fossilized eggs are huge.

Elephant bird egg

Ostrich egg

Hen egg

ADAPTATION: EGG LAYING

Like New Zealand, Australia's isolation has endowed it with unique creatures, such as the duckbilled platypus with its ducklike beak, webbed feet and beaverlike tail. Two species of echidna and the platypus are the only monotremes, or egg-laying mammals. Monotremes evolved from the same ancestors as other mammals but were isolated in Australia, while mammals that give birth to fully developed babies took over elsewhere.

The platypus's ducklike bill is used to probe the mud on riverbeds for insect grubs and crustaceans.

Platypuses lay their eggs in a long burrow dug in riverbanks.

The platypus's front feet are completely webbed.

GONDWANALAND

The world's continents are not fixed in one place but moving slowly around the world. About 150 million years ago, when dinosaurs ruled the Earth and birds were beginning to evolve, all the southern continents were joined in a huge landmass that scientists call "Gondwanaland."

Gondwanaland breaking up about 60 million years ago.

CONFUCIUS BIRD

One of the earliest birds with a beak, dating back 130 million years, is *Confuciusornis*. Its fossils were found in Liaoning, China.

Confucius bird

NEW ZEALAND'S FLIGHTLESS BIRDS

Until humans arrived, New Zealand had flightless moas, such as *Dinornis maximus*, which grew to 15 feet (4.5 m) tall, and the smaller *Emeus crassus*. The modern kiwi is the last surviving moa. New Zealand also has other unrelated flightless birds including the kakapo (the world's only flightless parrot), the weka and the takahe.

Giant Moa (extinct)

Moa (extinct)

Ostrich

Cassowary

Dodo (extinct)

Emu

Kakapo

Takahe

Kiwi

KOALA

An exception to Australia's many ground dwellers is the koala. Although it is sometimes called a koala bear, it is not even closely related to bears. In fact, it is a marsupial and female koalas have a pouch. Although this opens downward, young koalas never seem to fall out, even though koalas are climbing animals and the mother clambers around trees energetically. Koalas feed entirely on the leaves of gum trees (eucalyptus), sleeping by day and feeding at night. They get all their water from their food, so seldom need to come down from the branches.

TEMPERATE GRASSLANDS

WIDE, open, natural grasslands once stretched far across the interiors of North America and Asia. Here, well away from coasts and their moisture-laden winds, it is too dry for many trees to grow, yet there is enough rain and snow to nourish a rich growth of grass each spring. Vast tracts have been taken over for farming, but a great deal of the natural habitat remains.

From a distance, grassland can appear to be a monotonous, bleak place for animals to live. Even on calm summer days, a breeze usually ripples through the grasses; in winter, when snow falls, blizzards can roar unhindered across the plains.

But grass has hidden advantages. While most plants grow from their tips, grass grows from near the ground, so it can be grazed with minimal damage. Grazing animals, which cope with the lack of shelter by gathering in huge herds, find plentiful food. Grass puts down deep roots, too, softening the soil and making it perfect for burrowing creatures. So, while the surface is placid, there may be a hive of activity underground as little creatures sleep, eat and dig.

WHER[ ]RE TEMPERATE GRASS[ ]NDS?

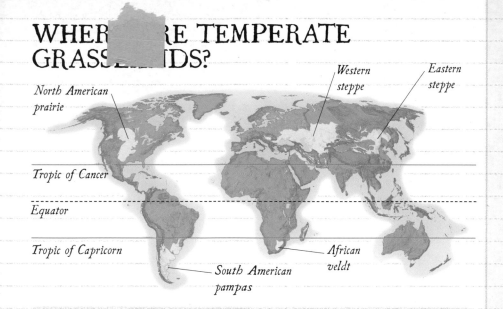

North American prairie

Western steppe

Eastern steppe

Tropic of Cancer

Equator

Tropic of Capricorn

African veldt

South American pampas

COMPARING TEMPERATE GRASSLANDS

Short grasses, such as buffalo and blue grama, on drier sites

Wooded steppe with birch, wild apples on wetter sites

Medium grasses, such as Junegrass and western wheatgrass

Tall grasses, such as Indiangrass and big bluestem, on wetter sites

Laburnums, dwarf almonds on less dry sites

Steppe with grasses such as crested hair-grass, and sedges

NORTH AMERICAN PRAIRIES

Hundreds of kinds of grass grow in the prairies, and as rainfall decreases to the west, so the grasses change. On the high, dry western plains, short grasses such as buffalo grass and blue grama grow. These are under 20 inches (50 cm) tall, which is why it is called shortgrass prairie. Farther east is mixed grass prairie — grasses like Junegrass grow up to 5 feet (1.5 m) tall. In the moist east some tallgrass prairie remains, where Indiangrass and big bluestem grow 10 feet (3 m) tall.

ASIAN STEPPE

The grasslands of Eurasia are commonly called steppes and the vast region of grassland here is the largest in the world. Much of the Eurasian steppe is semiarid because it is far from the coastal winds that bring rain. Short grasses such as steppe feather grass and fescue grasses thrive where many other types of plant cannot survive. In wetter areas, small trees such as laburnums and dwarf almonds grow, and in the moister west, clumps of fruit trees and birch create wooded steppe.

TEMPERATE GRASSLAND ENVIRONMENTS

Temperate grasslands have "continental" climates. Summers are warm and humid, with an average temperature of 64°F (18°C); winters are cool and dry, averaging 50°F (10°C).

RAIN AND SNOW

Most rain falls in the summer, but a great deal of the grassland's moisture comes from the snow that falls in winter. This acts as a reservoir to start the growing season.

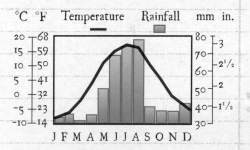

°C °F Temperature Rainfall mm in.

20 — 68
15 — 59
10 — 50
5 — 41
0 — 32
-5 — 23
-10 — 14

80
70
60
50
40
30

3
2½
2
1½

J F M A M J J A S O N D

RUSSIAN STEPPES

Like the prairies, the steppes are places of unforgettable beauty in the spring. At this time, flowers begin to cover the ground — countless tulips, Russian sage and anemones turn the land into a patchwork of colors.

THE GREAT PLAINS

Thunderstorms are frequent in late summer on the prairies. But more frightening still are the tornadoes, the violent corkscrew winds that often whirl beneath them.

NORTH AMERICAN TEMPERATE GRASSLANDS

BEFORE the Europeans came, the mid-American prairies and the Great Plains to the west were an endless sea of rippling grass, roamed by huge herds of bison. Although much of the prairie is now farmland, especially in the east, large wild areas remain. Here, although the bison and other large animals are mostly gone, there is an abundance of small mammals, birds and insects.

CALIFORNIA CENTRAL VALLEY

This area is known for its blooms of California poppies. Large herbivores such as pronghorn antelopes, tule elk and mule deer live here along with small animals, such as kangaroo rats and ground squirrels.

Greater prairie chicken (see p. 133)

GROUND BIRDS

With little cover in the prairies, most birds fly to escape predators, so there are only a few ground birds, such as prairie chickens and sage grouse. In recent years, farming has reduced their numbers greatly.

REPTILES

The cold winters on high prairies limit reptiles, most of which live in burrows to avoid predators. There are short-horned, sagebrush and northern prairie lizards. Snakes include copperheads and blue racers.

Gopher snake (see p. 127)

THE WESTERN SHORTGRASS PRAIRIE

This stretches from Nebraska to New Mexico and is home to a wealth of butterflies, birds and mammals such as prairie dogs.

Black-tailed prairie dog (see p. 118)

SMALL MAMMALS

Little shelter means the prairie's small mammals are nearly all burrowers. These include white-tailed jackrabbits and many other rodents, such as ground squirrels, gophers and voles.

BIRDS OF THE AIR

In summer, many birds, including yellow warblers and vesper sparrows, fly in from the south to feast on the insects and other invertebrates that appear above ground. Others, like chickadees, stay all year.

Eastern meadowlark (see p. 139)

Golden eagle (see p. 134)

BIRDS OF PREY

Small mammals have to come to the surface from their burrows every now and then. With no vegetation to hide in, they make easy targets for birds of prey, such as prairie falcons, Swainson's hawks, Mississippi kites, northern harriers and golden eagles.

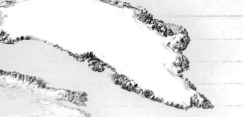

Harvester ant
(see p. 145)

INVERTEBRATES

The prairie soil teems with microlife such as ants and worms. In summer, the surface buzzes with insects. Honeybees hum, silver-spotted skippers and other butterflies flutter, and crickets chirrup. In winter, bees huddle in hives, butterflies migrate or stay as pupae, while other insects hide in the soil.

Western spadefoot toad (see p. 131)

AMPHIBIANS

The melting of the winter snow and the first spring rains leave shallow sheets of water in tallgrass and mixed-grass prairie. Here, amphibians like the plains leopard frogs, Wyoming toads and Great Plains narrow-mouthed red toads, can lay their eggs.

THE NORTHERN SHORTGRASS PRAIRIE

This stretches from Alberta to Wyoming. It is the largest grassland in North America, home to a rich variety of animals, including mammals like white-tailed deer, cougars and bobcats, and birds such as ferruginous hawks, sharp-tailed grouse and mountain plovers.

THE FLINT AND OSAGE HILLS

Covered in large areas of tallgrass prairie, these were once home to vast herds of bison and elk. Greater prairie chickens are still common.

N

Bobcat
(see p. 109)

PREDATORY MAMMALS

The bison herds that once dominated the prairies were too intimidating for even a big predator to tackle, and today most prairie predators are small. Swift foxes, coyotes and bobcats grab rodents as they emerge from burrows, but black-footed ferrets chase them right inside.

Pronghorn
(see p. 118)

GRAZING MAMMALS

Once, 70 million American bison roamed the prairies in huge herds, but their numbers have fallen dramatically. Other prairie grazers include the agile pronghorns and white- and black-tailed deer, which rely on speed rather than bulk and numbers for escape.

PRAIRIE PREY

LIFE is not uniformly spread across the prairies. Instead, it clusters around hot spots, such as streams and springs, isolated trees or sheltered valleys. But the busiest spots of all are prairie dog colonies. The prairie dog is what is called a "keystone" species — a species that is central to the well-being of the other animals in the habitat — and they have done more to shape the prairie's wildlife than perhaps any other creature. More than 200 other wildlife species have been seen on or near the colonies, and many depend on the prairie dogs for their food or habitat.

ADAPTATION: FLOWER CHOICE

The spring and summer flowers of the prairie attract a host of butterflies, including skippers, blues and red admirals. While most caterpillars eat leaves, often from one type of plant, adults are less fussy. They fly to a range of flowers where they can find the sweet nectar they need to mate or migrate.

One of the most common butterflies on the prairie, the silver spotted skipper, sips on the flowers of knapweed, butterfly weed, and joe-pyeweed.

Buckeye butterflies usually feed only on plantain as caterpillars. As adults, they prefer aster, knapweed and chicory.

Clouded sulfur butterflies feed on aster, morning glory and lantana, while their caterpillars feed on plants of the pea flower.

PRAIRIE DOG CENTRAL

A prairie dog "town" is an elaborate burrow of tunnels where thousands of animals live together. The burrows are so big that all kinds of creatures find homes within them, from deer mice to salamanders. The prairie dogs' tireless burrowing also works over the soil, so that plants grow better. Their foraging activities and droppings promote plant growth still further, so that a rich green mix of grasses and forbs (broad-leaved plants) grows up, providing a feast for grazers such as bison. The prairie dogs are also prey for hunters, from swift foxes to hawks.

Hawks hover over prairie dog colonies and try to catch them above ground.

Prairie dogs feed above ground during the day but use the burrows as a bolthole to escape predators, as a place to sleep at night, and to rear their young.

Highly endangered black-footed ferrets feed almost exclusively on prairie dogs and, being so slender, can easily slip in and drag a victim off to their own part of the burrow.

70

AMERICAN BISON

These massive grazing animals feed on wheat grass, buffalo grass, and other similar grasses. They got the name "buffalo" from French explorers who called them *les boeufs* when they saw them in herds of 100,000. Tens of millions of bison perished after the Europeans arrived, and by the mid-1800s the bison was close to extinction. Moves to protect them succeeded, and wild herds have become reestablished.

American bison like the fresh plant growth stimulated by the prairie dogs' constant clipping of the grass. They wallow in the dust to get rid of insect pests.

Swift foxes prey on prairie dogs if they are still out eating as night falls.

Mountain bluebirds feed in winter on beetles and flies that live in prairie dog colonies. They hover over the burrows to spot their prey, or perch nearby.

Coyotes often lie in wait at the prairie dogs' backdoor escape when a badger starts digging at the front.

American badgers dig into prairie dog burrows at night to catch them sleeping. The prairie dogs have a backdoor escape route.

Mountain plovers like to nest in the short grass created by prairie dog grazing, especially on bare soil where the prairie dogs dig.

Badgers may often take up residence once they have dug into a burrow to get at the prairie dogs.

Cottontail rabbits often live in abandoned prairie dog burrows. Both rabbits and prairie dogs eat the same plants, so if the rabbits come out during the day, the prairie dogs chase them away.

Eastern tiger salamanders are one of many amphibians happy to take advantage of the shelter provided by the township.

Burrowing owls make their nests in old prairie dog burrows. When alarmed, their young make sounds like rattlesnakes.

Prairie rattlesnakes occasionally move into prairie dog burrows. They sometimes prey on young prairie dogs, but adults gang up and chase the snakes away.

EURASIAN TEMPERATE GRASSLANDS

THE steppes of Asia form a huge band of feather and fescue grass stretching a quarter of the way around the world. Bleaker still in winter than the prairies — especially on the high Eastern Steppe beyond the Altai mountains — they bloom profusely in summer. Countless small mammals last out the winter under the ground to make the most of the summer bounty. Many more birds and grazing animals arrive in spring.

BIRDS OF PREY

So exposed are grassland rodents and reptiles on the surface that many birds of prey hunt here, including pallid harriers, white-tailed hawks, rough-legged hawks and lesser kestrels. The growth of farming has made all of these rarer.

Pallid harrier
(see p. 136)

PREDATORY MAMMALS

Wolves are less common than they once were, but many smaller predators, including pine martens and Siberian polecats, feed on the abundance of rodents. Rare snow leopards inhabit the high steppes of Central Asia.

Pallas's cat
(see p. 110)

European water vole (see p. 122)

SMALL MAMMALS

There is little shelter on the steppes for small mammals, but a host of rodents such as ground squirrels, marmots and pikas, live in the soil. Voles, rabbits and hares scamper through scrub and forest steppe.

UKRAINIAN STEPPE

Here, where forest mixes with grass in the damp climate, much grassland has been lost to farming. But surviving pockets are home to a host of animals from roe deer to meadow vipers.

THE KIRGHIZ-KAZAKH STEPPE

This is the world's largest area of dry steppe, home to steppe marmots and pikas, saiga antelopes and corsac foxes, as well as many birds such as pallid harriers.

Caspian Sea

Aral Sea

Pamir Mountains

Golden oriole (see p. 139)

BIRDS OF THE AIR

In spring, many birds wing into the steppes to feed on the spring explosion of insect life: they include crested larks, chaffinches, starlings and golden orioles. Great tits and Eurasian rollers nest here all year-round.

Locust (see p. 150)

INSECTS

For most insects, grass provides quite enough shelter from the elements, and the steppes are home to a huge range of them including ants, stag beetles, and blister beetles. The spring flowers attract thousands of species of bee and butterfly, such as swallowtails.

GRAZING MAMMALS

European bison are few and rarely seen, but moose venture in from the north. Every year, winter sees a migration of Mongolian gazelles down from the high plateaus of Tibet. On the high steppes, ibex, argali sheep and mountain goats clamber over slopes.

Saiga antelope (see p. 119)

FORAGING MAMMALS

The steppes are one of the last strongholds of the wild boar, which forages over wide areas, digging up the ground with its nose to find bulbs and tubers. Boars live mostly in forest steppes where the food is more varied. Here, too, live Eurasian badgers.

Eurasian badger (see p. 108)

QINGHAI-TIBET PLATEAU
Too cold and remote for farming, the high mountain steppe is one of the world's few large intact ecosystems. Here live large herds of grazers such as Tibetan antelopes (chiru), Tibetan gazelles, argali sheep and kiang horses, as well as rare predators such as snow leopards and lynxes.

MONGOLIAN-MANCHURIAN STEPPE
The vast steppes of East Asia are one of the world's largest areas of grassland. Huge herds of Mongolian gazelle still roam here, along with birds such as bustards and plovers. In the marshes and reedbeds breed huge flocks of Oriental white storks and demoiselle cranes.

GROUND BIRDS

There are few trees to nest in on the steppes, but bustards and quails nest in the grass, where there is a good supply of foods such as insects, seeds, roots and shoots. At lakesides, white-naped cranes, flamingoes, curlews, white-headed ducks and many others gather.

Great bustard (see p. 133)

REPTILES AND AMPHIBIANS

Rodent burrows are often taken over by reptiles such as vipers. Briefly in spring, pools teem with frogs such as the Asiatic grass frogs, which then go to ground in the heat of summer.

Altai Mountains

Lake Baikal

Gobi Desert

N

Smooth snake (see p. 127)

LIFE UNDER GRASS

HERDS of large herbivores such as saiga and deer are a conspicuous feature of the steppe landscape, but much of the grazing is done by unseen mouths — countless small burrowing mammals that emerge each day to feed on grass, shoots, and buds. These small mammals — mostly rodents such as marmots, ground squirrels and hamsters — play a crucial part in the steppe's ecosystem by bringing millions of tons of fresh soil to the surface each year as they burrow. These small mammals in turn are kept in check by predators such as polecats and eagles.

ADAPTATION: DOWNWARD NOSTRILS

The saiga antelope evolved to cope with the extreme steppe weather, from icy winters to hot, dusty summers. Its downward-pointing nostrils warm frosty air before it reaches the lungs, and filter out summer dust. Despite this adaptation, saigas are critically endangered following human interference, which has brought death and disease to their habitat.

The saiga has a thick, wiry coat to shield it from the elements.

Nasal chamber

Nostril

Golden hamsters live alone in a burrow they dig 6¹/₂ feet (2 m) or more down. They are aggressive toward other hamsters and only rarely come out of their burrows to feed on seeds, nuts and insects.

Steppe lemmings have long, waterproof fur, even covering their feet and ears, which keeps them warm when they have to emerge to forage occasionally in winter.

DEMOISELLE CRANE

Early on summer mornings, demoiselle cranes are sometimes seen striding over the ground near marshes and rivers, snapping up seeds and insects with their beaks. Demoiselles mate for life and are renowned for graceful courtship dances that strengthen the bonds between mated pairs. They are still abundant worldwide, but farming and hunting have reduced their numbers in the western steppe.

Common hamsters collect seeds in their cheek pouches to survive when food is hard to find. They store them in their burrows. By the end of summer, there may be 22 pounds (10 kg) of food in the larder.

74

LIFE UNDERGROUND

For many animals in grasslands, underground is the safest place to be. Here they are not only sheltered from the elements, especially the worst winter weather, but hidden from most predators. Rodents are the chief grassland burrowers, but there are also a few amphibians and reptiles and a huge number of insects such as ants, as well as earthworms and nematode worms.

European susliks are small mammals related to squirrels that make nests by digging deep tunnels into the soil. They feed mainly on roots, seeds and leaves.

Bobak marmots hibernate in deep burrows all winter. Before they go to sleep, they feed intensively to build up their body fat. This keeps them alive through the winter.

Steppe lemmings dig shallow temporary burrows in summer 1 feet (30 cm) deep. In winter, they live in much deeper permanent burrows, up to 3 feet (1 m) below the surface.

Northern mole voles are well adapted for digging, with blunt snouts and tiny ears and eyes to keep out sand. When digging, they use their teeth to loosen the soil, and their strong paws to push it out of the way.

Scheltopusiks are legless lizards. When attacked, they break off their tails – which make up two-thirds of their length – in several pieces. Predators are confused by all the wriggling pieces, unable to tell which is the body.

75

TAIGA AND TUNDRA

STRETCHING right around the world in the far north of North America and Eurasia is a vast expanse of conifer forest. Known in Russian as "taiga," and scientifically as "boreal" forest, this cool, dark green forest is one of the world's largest habitats. Beyond it to the north is open, treeless "tundra" bordering the Arctic Ocean — vast, windswept expanses of grasses, mosses, bog and stunted trees.

Winters are long and severe in both taiga and tundra. Snow falls thickly in fall and never melts until spring, and in the long winter night, temperatures can plunge to -48°F (-45°C). Beneath the surface, the tundra soil stays permanently frozen, even during summer.

Amazingly, many creatures stay in both taiga and tundra all year-round — not only bulky, thick-coated mammals like caribou, but even tiny birds like tits — relying on the shelter and sustenance provided by the evergreen conifers. In the brief summer, snows melt, days are long and the winter residents are joined by less hardy creatures such as songbirds and insects, emerging from winter dormancy or moving up from the south.

WHERE IS TAIGA AND TUNDRA?

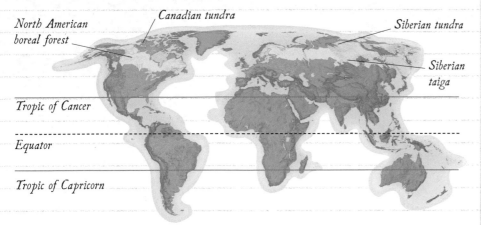

North American boreal forest

Canadian tundra

Siberian tundra

Siberian taiga

Tropic of Cancer

Equator

Tropic of Capricorn

COMPARING TAIGA AND TUNDRA

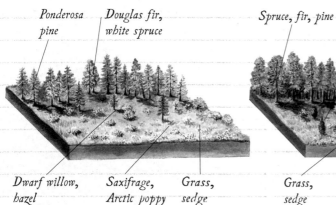

Ponderosa pine

Douglas fir, white spruce

Spruce, fir, pine

Smaller pines, birches

Dwarf willow, hazel

Saxifrage, Arctic poppy

Grass, sedge

Grass, sedge

Juniper

Saxifrage, Arctic poppy

NORTH AMERICA

In the south of the boreal forest, conifers are mixed in with deciduous trees such as sugar maples and American beech. Farther north, the forest is closely packed with conifers, such as jack pines, balsam firs and white spruce. Unlike deciduous trees, the conifers in these northern forests have branches that slope down to shed snow easily without breaking. In the far north, the trees become sparser and more stunted, opening out into grass and moss tundra where the only trees are tiny Arctic willows, dwarf spruces and dwarf hazels. There are bogs and lakes in both taiga and tundra.

EURASIA

As in North America, deciduous maples, lindens and ash grow alongside pines in the southern part of the Eurasian forest. Farther north, the deciduous trees disappear. Here, winters are so cold that only a handful of tree species can survive, creating a vast expanse of conifers — mainly larch in Siberia, but also fir, spruce, pine and occasionally birches and willows. This is the true taiga, which covers vast areas of Siberia. To the north is the tundra, where little covers the ground but mosses and lichens. In places, though, junipers and dwarf willows grow.

TAIGA AND TUNDRA ENVIRONMENTS

The climate of the taiga and the tundra is severe. Average temperatures are below freezing for up to six months of the year. Summers are often warm but usually short.

SUN AND RAIN

Average temperatures hover around freezing, but while winter days can fall below -40°F (-40°C), summer days may rise over 104°F (40°C). Most precipitation falls as snow.

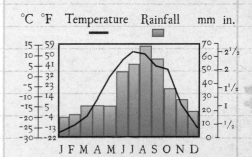

°C °F   Temperature   Rainfall   mm in.

J F M A M J J A S O N D

TUNDRA IN SUMMER

As the snow melts in spring, the tundra becomes boggy. But the ground turns green with moss and grass, while here and there a patchwork of wildflowers emerges.

TAIGA IN WINTER

Snow is universal in taigas and the ground is frozen, making it hard for trees to draw up water. But the needlelike leaves of conifers lose little water and so stay green on the tree.

EURASIAN TAIGA AND TUNDRA

STRETCHING from Scandinavia right across Siberia, the Eurasian taiga is the world's largest forest, with open tundra to the north. Winters here are colder than anywhere on Earth except Antarctica. However, many animals survive the cold, including large, thick-coated mammals, small mammals like voles that keep warm by burrowing, and predators such as wolves that kill for food to keep them warm.

BIRDS OF THE AIR

Pinecone seeds and berries allow small birds such as tits, wrens, nutcrackers and crossbills to survive in the taiga all winter. The summer eruption of insects and berries draws in migrants from the south, like waxwings and spotted woodpeckers.

Pine grosbeak
(see p. 136)

REPTILES

Very few reptiles can survive in the cold of the taiga and tundra, as they depend on the sun's warmth for energy. Nevertheless, viviparous lizards, sand lizards, adders and grass snakes survive in some areas.

Slow worm
(see p. 127)

Midge (see p. 151)

INSECTS

The springtime melting of the snow in the tundra creates bogs perfect for hatching the larvae of insects that have stayed dormant through the winter. Summer sees hordes of blackflies and mosquitoes rising from pools and tormenting the animals from which they suck blood.

Western capercaillie
(see p. 133)

GROUND BIRDS

In the taiga, grouse feed on pine needles and berries on the forest floor. In the tundra, willow ptarmigans and snow buntings peck on the ground for buds and seeds and burrow into the snow to avoid the cold.

SCANDINAVIA-RUSSIA TAIGA

Many of the forests here have been threatened by logging, but they are still home to huge numbers of creatures, including mammals such as wolves, bears and caribou, and birds such as gyrfalcons, ospreys and Siberian jays.

Mediterranean Sea

Red Sea

Wolverine
(see p. 123)

PREDATORY MAMMALS

Though plant food is scarce in winter, there is enough prey for both large predators like wolves and bears, and smaller mustelids. Wolves can kill animals much larger than themselves, like moose, by hunting in packs.

KOLA PENINSULA TUNDRA

Only the toughest survive in this bleak northern tundra, where polar bears, wolverines and Arctic foxes hunt in winter, and reindeer and elk raise their young in summer.

BIRDS OF PREY

There is ample prey in the taiga, even in winter, for many birds of prey. Black kites are widespread, and northern goshawks and sparrowhawks are often seen darting through trees ambushing birds. Above, golden eagles scan the ground for small mammals, while ospreys dive for fish in taiga lakes.

Snowy owl
(see p. 140)

WEST SIBERIAN TAIGA

Almost half of West Siberia is bog, and many creatures here depend on water for food, including water voles, beavers, muskrats, and countless waterbirds such as ducks and cranes.

Reindeer
(see p. 110)

GRAZERS AND FORAGERS

Big animals have the bulk to cope with winter, and the taiga has many deer — roe, sika, musk deer, red deer and elk that move to the tundra in summer to breed. In winter, deer rely on bark, stripping it from saplings.

AMPHIBIANS

Like reptiles, amphibians are few and far between in the extreme conditions of the taiga. Siberian salamanders are able to survive the winter by hibernating in a frozen state. Their body tissues defrost in the spring as temperatures rise.

Natterjack toad
(see p. 131)

NORTHEAST SIBERIAN TAIGA

This vast forest gets some of the world's coldest winters, with temperatures dropping to -58°F (-50°C). But many animals can endure the cold — mammals such as moose, bears, red squirrels and wolverines, and birds such as hazel grouse, ospreys and golden eagles.

N

Sea of Okhotsk

Himalayas

Tibetan Plateau

LIVING ON PINES

COMPARED to broad-leaved trees, conifers are hard trees for animals to live with. Not only are their needlelike leaves tough and sharp, but both leaves and wood contain an oily resin that is difficult for animals to digest. Yet many animals have managed to find a way to feed on them, eating their seeds, buds or even their bark. Often their feeding habits have become highly specialized to make the most of the conifers. Conifers also provide shelter from the northern cold. What they lack in quality they more than make up for in quantity — conifer forests provide a vast home for those that live there.

Siberian jays are omnivorous birds, eating insects, mushrooms and berries. In winter they often rely on pinecone seeds, which they pry out with their strong beaks.

Pine grosbeak male

Pine grosbeaks depend heavily on conifers in winter and spring, eating pine and fir tree needles and buds, as well as extracting seeds from cones.

BROWN BEAR

Few creatures are better adapted to cope with winter on the taiga than the bear — with its thick fur and bulky body, the animal has become Russia's national symbol. Although bears eat most things, they eat mainly grass in spring and fruits and berries in fall. In winter, food is scarce, so bears feed themselves well in fall, then retire to the shelter of a cave or a hole where they sleep for most of the winter.

Nutcrackers, like many other taiga birds, have strong beaks for cracking open cones to get at the seeds. Nutcrackers sometimes hoard stores of seeds for hard times.

ADAPTATIONS: LAKE BAIKAL

Baikal is the deepest lake in the world. It is also the oldest — it formed more than 25 million years ago in a deep crack in the Earth's surface. This, combined with its long isolation from the rest of the world, has meant Baikal has developed its own unique range of creatures, such as the Baikal whitefish and the Baikal seal, the world's only freshwater seal — maybe stranded here 500,000 years ago.

Lake Baikal is more than 5,315 feet (1,620 m) deep in places.

Baikal holds a fifth of the world's fresh water.

There are at least 36 species of fish in the lake, including the golomyanka, which unusually gives birth to live young.

Sables have been hunted in the wild for their warm fur, essential to their survival in the Siberian winter. They climb trees well, but hunt for small animals mostly on the ground.

Baikal seals are small and have only little flippers since they have no need to swim fast.

Baikal seal

Baikal whitefish

Ural owls sleep in holes in pine trees by night, and hunt during the day for small daytime-active rodents.

Common crossbills have unique crossed beaks that allow them to extract seeds from spruce cones. Two-barred crossbills have longer bills for dealing with larch cones.

Common crossbill

Flying squirrels nest and roost in tree cavities and eat pine buds as well as deciduous leaves.

Male

Female

Siberian tit family

Siberian tit

Siberian tits and crested tits nest in holes in pines and survive through winter by eating insects that are dormant in the bark.

Goosanders are ducks that fly and swim fast. They hunt for fish in the taiga's many lakes and rivers, but often nest in holes in pine trees.

Red-backed voles eat seeds and berries under the trees, while wood lemmings feed on moss, rushes, sedges, stems, and bark.

Goldeneye are ducks that nest in holes in conifers, and have suffered as trees have been cleared from some areas.

Hazel grouse are among the many grouse that peck for seeds on the forest floor.

Capercaillies have strong digestive systems that allow them to survive almost entirely on pine needles in winter.

NORTH AMERICAN TAIGA AND TUNDRA

NORTH ALASKA COAST
NORTH ALASKA COAST
This plain is famous for the great caribou herds that arrive here each summer to raise their young.

IN North America, boreal forest stretches in a broad band some 500 miles (800 km) wide, south of the tundra across Canada into Alaska. Winters here are bitter, and it is a vast, barely disturbed wilderness. In the far northwest, huge herds of caribou trek north in spring to their summer breeding grounds on the tundra, while the forest is home to many small mammals, birds and insects.

Brooks Range

Cascade Range

PREDATORY MAMMALS

With warm fur and food from prey to maintain body heat, predatory mammals are well equipped to get through winter, although they often have to range far to find prey. Besides lynxes and wolves, there are many mustelids such as martens.

American marten
(see p. 116)

Gray squirrel
(see p. 121)

SMALL MAMMALS

Cone seeds, bark and buds sustain many rodents, including chipmunks and deer mice, that survive the winter by hibernating in burrows or tree holes. Snowshoe hares eat grass in summer but live on pine buds in winter.

NORTHWEST TAIGA
Otters and beavers, moose, wolves and bears are among the many creatures that make their homes in the mountain forests of the northwest.

REPTILES

Reptiles cannot function without heat, so very few reptiles live in the boreal forest, and none live in the tundra. Turtles survive the winter under the ice in frozen ponds; eastern garter snakes go to sleep underground.

Wood turtle
(see p. 128)

Grizzly bear
(see p. 109)

FORAGING MAMMALS

The scant undergrowth of the forest provides little food for foragers. Even so, raccoons find food by eating almost anything, while porcupines climb trees to find new shoots in summer, and survive on soft bark and conifer needles in winter.

BIRDS OF THE AIR

In summer, wood warblers arrive with other birds such as thrushes and grosbeaks to feed on insects and berries. Other birds such as chickadees survive through winter with fluffy plumage and by gorging on seeds.

Black-capped chickadee
(see p. 133)

NUNAVUT TUNDRA

Considered a cold desert because of its lack of plants, Nunavut's tundra is still rich in wildlife. Polar bears and Arctic foxes hunt across the ice, while herds of musk oxen, caribou and moose graze.

Northern leopard frog
(see p. 130)

AMPHIBIANS

Although amphibians find it hard to cope with the cold of the northern winter, there are frogs hardy enough to survive in the taiga's lakes and the tundra's bogs, including tiny boreal chorus frogs and mink frogs that hibernate underwater.

INSECTS

Conifer leaves are hard to eat, and the wood oozes sticky resin that traps insects. Nevertheless, many insects thrive in the forest, including gypsy moths and woodwasps. Gypsy moth caterpillars eat needles. Woodwasp grubs bore into the wood.

Crane fly (see p. 148)

Mackenzie

Hudson Bay

Rocky Mountains

Lake Superior

GRAZERS AND BROWSERS

Caribou and moose are large deer that venture north on to the open tundra in summer, then retreat to the forests in winter. But even they are not as tough as musk oxen — shaggy cows that brave the northern tundra all year around.

MID-CANADA TAIGA

This is one of the world's last great wildlife refuges — home to countless animals, including moose, caribou, black bears, wolves, lynxes, muskrats, snowshoe hares and many others.

Moose
(see p. 117)

BIRDS OF PREY

Birds of prey can survive the winter cold by feeding on meat, and the boreal forest is home to owls such as the great horned and snowy owls, and raptors such as bald and golden eagles and red-tailed hawks. Ospreys hunt fish in the forest lakes and rivers.

Osprey
(see p. 139)

N

BEAVER HOME

BEAVERS are rodents, like prairie dogs, that are no bigger than a small dog — less than 3 feet (1 m) long. Yet, despite their size, they make a bigger impact on the northern forest environment than perhaps any other creature. They are what zoologists call a "keystone" species — a creature whose effect on the lives of others in the habitat is crucial. Beavers cut down trees with their teeth and use the logs to dam streams and create lakes where they are safe from attack. The changes they make to the environment have crucial benefits for other mammals, birds, reptiles, fish and insects.

Carpenter moth caterpillars move into the rotting wood and logs.

Woodpeckers like the insects in exposed wood.

ADAPTATION: CONE EATERS

All rodents have sharp, tough incisor teeth for gnawing into nuts, but conifers pose special problems, even for rodents. The seeds of most conifers are enclosed deep inside woody cones, protected by tough scales. The scales are open when the cones are new, but once the seeds are fertilized the scales close up, making them hard to get at. Squirrels have become adept at finding the seeds in cones and they store up hoards of cones to help them through the winter.

Beaver dams are sticks cemented with grass and mud.

Water voles like the grassy edges of the pond.

The edible seeds in a cone are protected by tough wooden scales.

Red squirrel

Douglas fir cone

The squirrel has sharp incisors for gnawing into the cone.

Nimble hands allow the squirrel to turn nuts and cones to find the best angle of attack with its teeth.

Golden-mantled ground squirrel

Pondskaters skim across the still lake.

FELLING AND DAMMING

Beavers' impact on the forest works in two ways. First, they fell trees with their teeth both to use as sticks for the dam and to feed on the bark and leaves. This creates clearings and also, because beavers prefer to cut down trees like willows and aspens, they allow other trees to flourish. Second, as they dam the streams, beavers create large pockets of deep, still water, and also produce new wetland sites along the shore of the lake behind the dam.

Sawfly larvae are caterpillarlike and feed on leaves.

Pike prey on the bottom-feeding fish.

Mallard, teal, and goldeneye ducks find the ideal nesting sites around beaver ponds.

Otters find good hunting in beaver ponds. The pond also provides stable water for making a den and otters may move into burrows left by water voles.

Green darner dragonflies benefit from the widening of the water surface.

Mergansers are attracted by the fish in the slow-moving pond water.

Pumpkinseeds feed on bottom-dwelling insects that like slow-moving water.

A beaver lodge is typically 6–10 feet (1.8–3 m) across, but may be up to 20 feet (6 m) long.

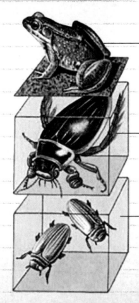

Bronze frogs and other frogs benefit from the wetland shores.

Diving beetles find new prey, such as tadpoles and small fish.

Whirligig beetles feed on insects that fall on the wide pond surface.

CANADIAN BEAVER

Beavers are well adapted for life in the water with their webbed feet and paddlelike tails. Their eyes and nose close off so they can stay underwater for 15 minutes or more. They are also master engineers. Once they have cut down all the lakeside trees, beavers dig canals to bring logs from farther afield.

The mud they plaster over the lodge and dam freezes like concrete in winter to make a very solid structure. They also build up the inside of the lodge with mud so that their young are kept clean and dry, even though lodge entrances are underwater. They even make a ventilation shaft!

WETLANDS

WETLANDS vary tremendously — from the bleak marshes of northern Europe, where little is heard but the sigh of the wind and the haunting cry of the curlew, to the lush, steamy mangrove swamps of southern Asia, filled with the noise of animals.

Every wetland is an area that is neither all water, nor all land. In swamps, there is a lot of water and very little land. In marshes, there is slightly less water and more land. Bogs are essentially waterlogged land. This balance between land and water is constantly shifting, as floods cover some of the dry places and droughts leave other areas high and dry.

Wetlands cover no more than 6 percent of the world's land surface. Yet their importance to wildlife is out of all proportion to their size and they teem with plant, fish and bird life. Wetlands have been drained in some areas, but, because they are often hard to exploit commercially, they have become priceless refuges for many of the world's most endangered species of animals.

COMPARING WETLANDS

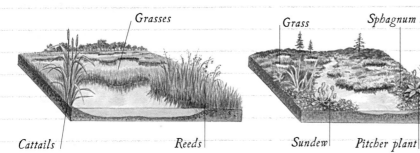

MARSHES

Marshes can be either fresh or saltwater. Freshwater marshes typically develop where rivers and lakes flood low-lying land. There are usually patches of grass, reed and cattail, with pools of standing water.

BOGS

Bogs develop in cooler places, where rain falls on soft, spongy ground but does not drain away. Often only sphagnum moss grows on the damp, acid soil, and organic matter does not decay but accumulates as peat.

SWAMPS

Swamps can be either fresh or saltwater. They are much wetter than marshes and there are pools and inlets for much of the year. Unlike marshes with their grasses and reeds, the main plants in swamps are trees.

MANGROVE SWAMP

Mangrove swamps develop in the saltwater along tropical coasts. Here mangrove trees put down their buttresslike roots in pure sand, gradually spreading farther out into the water and building up the land area.

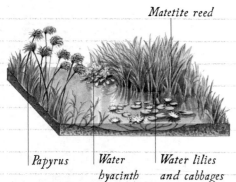

TROPICAL MARSHES

The term tropical marshes refers to treeless swamps in the tropics, such as Africa's Okavango. They develop inland where rivers seasonally flood vast, badly draining areas, yet there is too little rain for trees to grow. Tall papyrus reeds and other water plants choke meandering channels.

WETLAND ENVIRONMENTS

Wetlands stay wet because they are constantly topped up with water. Even in cool parts of the world, they would eventually dry out if the water was not replenished. Northern bogs are kept wet by melting snow. Tropical marshes are filled by seasonal rivers.

ESTONIAN BOG

The world's largest areas of wetlands are in the cold tundra of northern Eurasia and North America. Here, every hollow in the ground becomes waterlogged each spring as snow melts.

MARSH IN WINTER

The moisture in the air over wetlands means they are often enveloped in mist. In cooler marshes in winter, the air cools quickly at night. By morning, moisture in the air has condensed to form a lingering mist.

REED BEDS

Few plants can survive with their roots and stems mostly underwater. The few that can, like tall reeds and tiny duckweeds, grow in wetlands throughout the world. In shallower water, sedges and rushes grow.

NORTH AMERICAN WETLANDS

HUMAN activity has already destroyed half of North America's natural wetlands, and a further area the size of Chicago is lost each year.

Yet there are still huge areas of wetland in the continent — from the vast bogs of northern Canada to the Florida and Georgia swamps of Okefenokee and the Everglades. Here, in these precious, watery refuges, survive a host of rare snakes, frogs, turtles, beavers, otters and birds.

ALASKA BOGS
Alaska has huge areas of wetland which cover almost half the state.

SAN FRANCISCO BAY
Salt marshes are home to rare species including salt marsh harvest mice and Ridgway's rails.

Rocky Mountains

Rio Grande

Sierra Madre

Spring peeper (see p. 131)

AMPHIBIANS

Wetlands are perfect for amphibians. Many frogs, toads and newts breed in marshes and temporary ponds, then feed on dry land as adults. Bogs are home to four-toed salamanders and carpenter frogs.

BIRDS OF PREY

Large raptors, such as bald eagles and ospreys, fly over marshes scanning for fish to scoop up. Merlins and northern harriers search the land for prey, such as mice and frogs. Great blue herons wade through the water, spearing fish with their long beaks.

Belted kingfisher (see p. 138)

INSECTS

Few adult insects live underwater, but mayflies, caddisflies, mosquitoes, dragonflies and damselflies develop in the water as larvae — many breathing with gills like fish. They then emerge from the water as adults.

Adult

Diving beetle (see p. 146)

Larva

WATERFOWL

Many ducks, geese and other waterfowl breed and feed in wetlands. Dabbling ducks like mallards upend in the shallows to filter feed tiny animals from the mud. Geese graze on grass on the shore.

Pied-billed grebe (see p. 136)

STILL WATER FISH

Freshwater habitats for fish vary a lot, from reed-choked shallows to clear deeps. Pumpkinseeds live in vegetation near the shore. Largemouth bass and walleyes live in deeper water.

Pumpkinseed

Alligator snapping turtle *(see p. 128)*

REPTILES

North America's wetlands are home to many snakes such as garter and ribbon, and species of freshwater turtle from bog turtles to box turtles. Nearly all these turtles are endangered, partly because they are hit by cars when they move on land.

HUDSON BAY BOGS
One of the world's largest wetlands, these are famous for their caribou, as well as fishers, minks and snowshoe hares.

Hudson Bay

PRAIRIE POTHOLES
Appearing every spring, these marshes are home to more than 100 species of birds and many rare frogs.

GREAT LAKE MARSHES
These are a key bird habitat, not only for waterfowl, such as ducks and herons, but also for songbirds and hawks.

GREAT DISMAL SWAMP
(see p. 91)

CHESAPEAKE BAY
This vast area of creeks and marshes is home to mammals such as muskrats, raccoons and beavers, and birds such as herons and egrets.

MISSISSIPPI SWAMPS
One of the world's richest freshwater fish habitats.

Gulf of Mexico

N

FLORIDA SWAMPS
Besides the Everglades, Florida has the Okefenokee cypress swamp — home to more than 200 kinds of birds, about 50 mammals, nearly 70 reptiles and almost 40 amphibians including gopher tortoises.

Common muskrat *(see p. 117)*

WATER MAMMALS

Many mammals live in the cold and wet of a marsh. Most are herbivorous rodents such as lemmings, voles and beavers, which feed on plants. There are also predators such as mink and otters.

RIVER FISH

Rivers can be fast or slow flowing and have wide variations in temperature. Brook trout and sculpin live in cold, fast-flowing streams. Paddlefish prefer warmer, slower-flowing rivers.

Paddlefish

WADING BIRDS

American golden plover *(see p. 141)*

Wading birds find rich pickings in wetland mud. Every fall countless waders fly from the Arctic to spend winter in American marshes — black-necked stilts, avocets, plovers and sandpipers.

WETLAND SURVIVAL

WETLANDS are biological superstores, providing huge quantities of food for wildlife. Billions of microscopic algae and larger plants flourish here. Dead plant leaves and stems break down in the water to form detritus. In rivers, detritus is washed away, but in wetlands it accumulates to provide a source of food as rich for animals as living plants. Detritus and living plant matter are eaten by countless tiny water insects and their larvae, shellfish and other fish, and these in turn provide food for larger animals.

Otters' main prey is fish, caught by day. But they also eat frogs, crayfish, snakes and insects.

WETLAND FOOD WEB

At the bottom of the wetland food chain are tiny creatures like mayfly larvae, which feed on detritus on the bottom. They in turn provide food for free-swimming creatures such as dragonfly and damselfly nymphs. All the other creatures in the wetland benefit from the sheer abundance of these minute creatures — whether they feed on them directly, like ducks, or feed on another animal that feeds on them.

Narrow-winged damselflies prey on small insects such as caddisflies and insect larvae.

Water boatmen skate across the water, feeding on algae and reeds.

Mallards eat algae and also bottom-dwelling insect larvae.

Minnows feed on algae and insects like caddisflies and water boatmen.

Sunfish feed on algae.

Crayfish eat dead insects and fish.

ADAPTATION: NYMPH TO ADULT

Dragonflies and damselflies have an unusual life cycle that is perfectly suited to their life as aquatic predators. Eggs are laid on water plants and hatch into nymphs. The nymphs are wingless and live under water, gradually growing bigger by preying on insects, tadpoles and small fish. Eventually, after two or more years, the nymphs are ready to surface and emerge as winged adults.

When it is ready to emerge, the nymph crawls out of the water on a plant stem.

The adult gradually breaks out of the nymph's skin.

Eventually, the adult emerges fully and leaves the nymph's skin behind.

The wings gradually strengthen and the adult color develops.

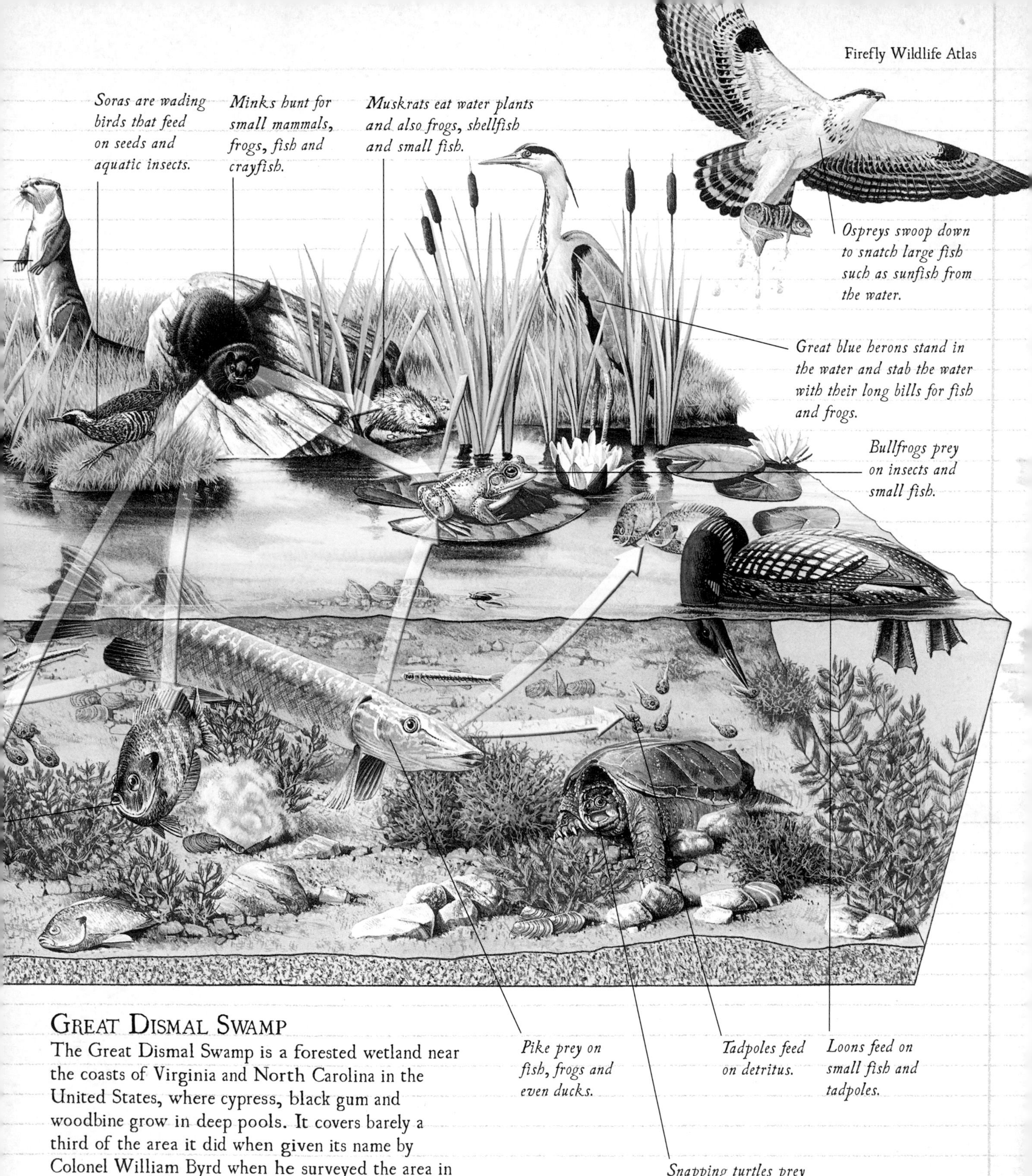

Soras are wading
birds that feed
on seeds and
aquatic insects.

Minks hunt for
small mammals,
frogs, fish and
crayfish.

Muskrats eat water plants
and also frogs, shellfish
and small fish.

Ospreys swoop down
to snatch large fish
such as sunfish from
the water.

Great blue herons stand in
the water and stab the water
with their long bills for fish
and frogs.

Bullfrogs prey
on insects and
small fish.

GREAT DISMAL SWAMP

The Great Dismal Swamp is a forested wetland near
the coasts of Virginia and North Carolina in the
United States, where cypress, black gum and
woodbine grow in deep pools. It covers barely a
third of the area it did when given its name by
Colonel William Byrd when he surveyed the area in
1728. It was once the habitat of many rare birds,
including the endangered ivory-billed woodpecker,
and remains an important wildlife refuge — home to
deer, raccoons, bears and opossums.

Pike prey on
fish, frogs and
even ducks.

Tadpoles feed
on detritus.

Loons feed on
small fish and
tadpoles.

Snapping turtles prey
on small mammals,
fish and birds.

EUROPEAN WETLANDS

EUROPE has lost many of its wetlands over the centuries as marshes and bogs have been reclaimed for farming and building. But it still has over a fifth of the world's most important wetland wildlife sites — rare wilderness refuges in this crowded, highly developed part of the world. These are the haunts of vast flocks of wintering birds, countless frogs and toads, many water rodents, and an unimaginable number of invertebrates.

Club-tailed dragonfly
(see p. 148)

INSECTS

Marshes and bogs are breeding grounds for insects. Some — caddisflies, mayflies and dragonflies — live as larvae underwater then surface as adults. Water boatmen hunt on water surfaces; diving beetles and saucer bugs hunt underwater.

RIVER FISH

The rich plant and insect life in smooth-flowing lowland rivers and creeks is food for a wealth of fish — chub, bleak, carp, roach and bream. In faster rivers, dace and barbel feed on insects. In upland streams, trout, salmon fry and minnows are common.

Bream

Common frog
(see p. 129)

AMPHIBIANS

Amphibians are well adapted to make the most of the wetlands habitat, living as tadpoles in water and on land as adults. Newts such as the smooth and palmate spend much of their lives in water. Frogs like the huge marsh frog and common toads live more on land.

REPTILES

Northern marshes are too cold for reptiles except for a few, such as grass snakes and pond turtles, that live in the water. Many snakes and lizards live on dry ground in the warmer south.

Grass snake
(see p. 127)

THE CAMARGUE
Although much reduced, the Camargue still has its famous herds of wild horses and cattle, and is a precious refuge for flamingoes, egrets, night herons and many other birds.

WATERFOWL

With their network of creeks and gentle shores, marshes make an ideal habitat for waterfowl. Snow and white-fronted geese graze on shore. Dabbling ducks like teal and divers like pochards feed in the water.

THE COTO DONANA
A haunting wilderness of marsh, heath and dunes, this region is home to more than 200 bird species and a refuge of two very endangered species: the Spanish imperial eagle and the Iberian lynx.

Moorhen *(see p. 139)*

N

Mediterranean Sea

WATER MAMMALS

The huge bulk of plants in a marsh, and the insects around them, draw many small mammals to live here, including brown rats, bank and water voles, muskrats and water shrews. Predators such as red foxes and wild cats roam the shores.

Eurasian otter
(see p. 117)

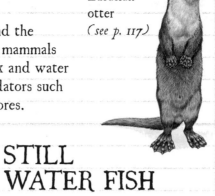

WADING BIRDS

Wetlands are home to many long-legged birds that wade through water to hunt fish and frogs, such as cranes, herons and bitterns. In winter, huge flocks of smaller waders walk along shores, probing the mud with long bills for food such as curlews, godwits, lapwings and plovers.

Buzzard
(see p. 133)

BIRDS OF PREY

Wetlands see a constant battle of wits as birds of prey swoop low and small creatures dive into the water. Voles are food for Montagu's harriers and rough-legged buzzards; small birds are prey for hen harriers and, in winter, merlins.

STILL WATER FISH

Lakes, pools, and backwaters are home to fish, such as tench, which cruise slowly on the bottom, hunting for small creatures. Pike also live here, lying in wait among reeds for prey such as bleak and rudd.

Great egret
(see p. 135)

Pike

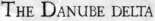

THE PRIPET MARSHES
On the Ukraine–Belarus border remains one of the largest marshes in Europe, home to elk, wild boar, lynxes, beavers and many other mammals, and a host of birds such as black and hazel grouse, orioles, woodpeckers, owls, blue tits and ducks.

THE VOLGA DELTA
This is a huge wetland of creeks and lakes — a feeding ground for millions of migratory birds such as swans, herons and ibises, and rarer species such as great white egrets and penduline tits.

THE DANUBE DELTA
A maze of creeks, lakes and marshes, this region is home to many kinds of frog, over 300 species of bird (including pelicans, water rails, cormorants and pratincoles), and countless fish, such as sturgeons, eels and Tyulka sprats.

Baltic Sea

Carpathian Mountains

Ural Mountains

Adriatic Sea

Danube

Volga River

Caucasus Mountains

Black Sea

LIVING IN DAMP PLACES

THE wetlands of Europe are among the most important of all habitats for birds in this part of the world. No creature is better able to take advantage of the mix of land and water, nor cope so well with the frequent flooding. Although wetlands vary widely, a huge range of waterfowl and wading birds make their homes here. Many others find safe resting places during migration. Wetlands can look like quite uniform habitats — just grass, mud and water — but every bird has its own special niche, exploiting a particular aspect of the habitat, and each has its own chosen nesting site.

Snipe make a cup-shaped nest on dry, grassy spots.

ADAPTATION: BILLS FOR MUD

Shorebirds walk along the shore, probing the mud and sand for food with their long bills. Each species of bird has a slightly different length and shape of bill, so that they can reach different foods and not compete. They range from plovers with short bills for feeding near the surface, to godwits with long bills that probe deeply for prey such as lugworms.

Bar-tailed godwits dig deep for small crabs, shrimps, sandhoppers, insects and lugworms.

Lapwings feed on a wide range of insect larvae and worms, a little way below the surface.

Ringed plovers feed on small shrimps, snails, worms and insects near the surface.

Harriers make a large dish-shaped nest of reeds amongst sedges.

Redshanks make a cup-shaped nest from grasses and sedges, hidden in shoreline grass.

Crakes make a thick nest on grassy shores of grass and sedge knitted into a cup-shaped cluster.

Avocets nestle down in open hollows on islands.

Gadwalls find a hollow hidden by plants on an island and line it with duck down and leaves.

Pochards scrape out a shallow cup on an island and line it with grass.

Shovelers look for shallow scoops on islands and stuff them with grass, feathers and down for warmth.

Black-tailed godwits nest in hollows hidden by thick grass on islands.

GRAY HERONS

These birds make colonies of nests called heronries at the tops of trees or in reed beds. Each nest platform is 3 feet (1 m) or so across and is made of sticks and twigs.

OSPREYS

These birds of prey make big nests on top of pine trees.

Mallards nest in hollows in waterside trees.

Yellow wagtails nest in drier scrubland in cup-shaped nests. They build their nests in a dip in the ground from grass and plant stems and line the nests with hair and fur.

Garganeys nest on the ground in drier scrubland near tussocks of grass, building their nest from twigs and grasses.

Water rails make a large nest in reeds over mud using dead stalks and leaves.

Reed warblers nest in a deep cup of grasses woven around reed stems over the water.

Moorhens make a floating nest platform of dried water plants.

Great crested grebes make their nest on a floating platform of weeds anchored among reeds.

Bearded tits nest in lined reed baskets woven into reeds well above the water.

Coots build floating nests of reeds, often with a ramp leading into the water.

95

AFRICAN WETLANDS

AFRICA is well endowed with wetlands. Over 4 percent of its area is covered with permanent wetlands and many large areas become swampy after heavy rain. Many animals live on the fringes of these swampy areas, while countless birds, reptiles and insects live deep in these wetlands.

NIGER DELTA

The mangrove swamps of the Niger delta are home to pygmy hippos, manatees, otters and over 150 species of fish.

Damselfly
(see p. 148)

INSECTS AND OTHERS

The most spectacular swamp insects are large, colorful dragonflies. Warm water and dense vegetation attract mollusks and worms, including the swamp worm, which has a snorkel for breathing in the thick mud.

THE OKAVANGO DELTA

This is one of the world's most important animal habitats *(see p. 98–99)*.

Congo River

Lake Tanganyika

Lake Nyasa

FISH

African swamps are home to myriad fish, many of them huge. The Okavango has more than 100 species, including catfish, African pike and African lungfish. In the Nile swamps lives one of the world's biggest freshwater fish, the Nile perch, 6 feet (1.8 m) long and weighing 280 pounds (130 kg).

African lungfish

Flamingo
(see p. 135)

WADING BIRDS

Among the most spectacular sights of African wetlands and lakes are huge flocks of large wading birds stepping through shallows, feeding on fish, frogs and snails. Among them are night herons, sacred ibises, shoebills, spoonbills, egrets, marabou storks and hamerkops.

PREDATORY MAMMALS

Lions and hyenas, and occasionally wild dogs and cheetahs, roam through the woods surrounding swamps. Sometimes leopards and smaller cats called caracals will prowl at night. However, few of them venture right into the swamp.

Caracal
(see p. 110)

Nile crocodile
(see p. 125)

LAKE CHAD

This is a remarkable wetland on the fringes of the Sahara, where millions of birds such as ibises and spoonbills live or stop over.

CONGO BASIN

The Congo has about 700 species of fish, and the flooded forests are home to unique animals like the water genet, Congo clawless otter and Ruwenzori otter shrew.

Nile River

EAST AFRICAN MANGROVES

Among the mangrove roots live animals such as dugongs and sea turtles, as well as many fish.

THE SUDD

Every year a vast area of southern Sudan floods to form the Sudd, providing water and food for huge numbers of migrating birds and mammals such as antelopes, lechwes, kobs and Mongalla gazelles.

REPTILES AND AMPHIBIANS

African swamps are warm enough for reptiles, including lizards like monitor lizards and snakes like green water snakes and olive grass snakes. The land and water combination draws frogs, too, such as snoring puddle frogs and reed frogs.

Common kestrel
(see p. 137)

BIRDS OF PREY

Abundant fish make wetlands a paradise for birds of prey, such as fish eagles and Pel's owls that use their amazing night vision to hunt. There is plenty of prey for other predators, too, such as the spotted eagle.

Great crested grebe
(see p. 136)

BIRDS OF THE AIR

African swamps are visited by a huge number of birds. The Okavango delta has nearly 500 bird species — not only water birds like pelicans and pygmy geese, but birds drawn to the wooded areas, such as bee-eaters, honeyguides and shrikes.

GRAZING MAMMALS

At certain times of year, huge numbers of grazing animals including kudu, impala and buffalo move in from the surrounding savanna to take advantage of the water and lush grazing. Some antelopes like waterbucks and lechwes are adapted to moving around in the wetlands all year-round.

Impala
(see p. 114)

Hippopotamus
(see p. 113)

LARGE MAMMALS

Many large mammals migrate in and out of swamps in response to seasonal fluctuations in the water level. During the dry season in the surrounding grassland, the swamps may still be swollen from floods in the mountains. Herds of elephants are joined in the swamps by giraffes and rhinos.

97

HIPPO WORLD

BOTSWANA'S Okavango delta is one of the world's biggest swamps, a placid expanse of winding channels, papyrus-fringed lagoons and open grasslands, stretching over 5,000 square miles (13,000 sq km). The extent of the delta varies through the year, peaking during the rainy season and when the rains reach the Okavango River in Angola. Larger animals, such as elephants come and go with the changing of the delta, but all year-round there is an abundance of wildlife — over 400 species of bird can be found here, and mammals from lions to bush babies. The Okavango is the kingdom of one animal more than any other, however — the hippopotamus — and it plays a key role in the life of the swamp.

ADAPTATION: SWAMP FEET

There are many places in swamps where the surface is very soft, and often consists of little more than soggy vegetation. To walk over these safely, some swamp creatures have developed big feet to spread their weight. Sitatunga and lechwe antelopes have splayed hooves to help them move over boggy ground, while the lily trotter has splayed toes for walking on lily leaves.

Jacana — *The toes splay out wide to spread the bird's weight, perhaps over several leaves.*

Sitatunga — *The splayed hooves are perfect for boggy ground, but make the antelope awkward on solid ground.*

Hippos often deal with biting insects by wallowing in mud. The wallowing helps stir up nutrients that benefit other water creatures.

Saddlebilled storks feed on water snails, which feed on the water plants that grow richly on hippo dung.

Most hippos are born underwater, so to reach the surface for their first breath, they must be able to swim from birth. They are naturally buoyant and often gallop gracefully along the bottom at high speed.

HIPPOPOTAMUS

Hippos are huge animals, with males weighing up to 7,000 pounds (3,200 kg). They stay semi-submerged in water during the day because of their sensitive skin, and feed on grass at night. Hippos once lived across most of southern Africa but they are now confined to small areas.

As they stand in water, hippos drop vast piles of dung that enrich the water, providing vital nutrients for both plants and microorganisms. This benefits fish, which in turn provide food for larger fish, reptiles and birds.

Hippos climb out of the water at dusk to feed on grass. They consume up to 80–100 pounds (36–45 kg) of grass a night. The paths they make through the bush, as they search for their favorite short grass, allow other animals easy access to the water. Their grazing keeps the grass trimmed, stimulating new growth and stopping shrubs and trees from taking over.

Hippos spend the day resting in water to keep cool and protect their skin from the sun. On overcast days, they often leave the water to bask on the bank. Hippo skin produces a special liquid that acts as a sunblock.

Hippos often stay in the water with just their nostrils, eyes and ears above the surface. They can submerge completely for half an hour by closing their nostrils and slowing their heart rate.

With their huge bulk, hippos have no problem trampling down patches of papyrus reeds as they climb out. In doing so, they provide clear spaces for crocodiles to make their nests among the reeds.

When a male hippo gives its huge yawn, it may be showing off its big canine teeth to frighten off a trespasser. Occasionally, the males fight and try to bite each other.

Hippos feed mainly on grass, but every now and then they feed on water lettuce and so help keep the water clear. The cabbage and lettuce grows so densely over water that from a distance it can look like a lawn. As the hippos move through swamps, they break through the vegetation to create new channels or lakes.

For hammerhead storks (hamerkops), the hippo's broad back makes the perfect feeding station as they sift the water at dawn and dusk for fish, amphibians, insects and crustaceans.

99

MOUNTAINS AND POLAR REGIONS

MOUNTAINS and polar regions are the world's coldest, most extreme environments. The heart of the polar regions and the highest mountains are so cold that they are permanently covered in ice and snow. They are also frequently covered in fog, or blasted by howling winds and blizzards.

Climbing a mountain in the tropics is a little like journeying from the Equator to the Poles. Temperatures drop 1.8°F (1°C) every 650 feet (200 m) up the mountainside, and the vegetation changes from tropical forest to mixed temperate and boreal forest, before the climber emerges on high alpine tundra and finally reaches the snowy summit.

A few creatures, such as polar bears in the Arctic and yaks in the Himalayas, survive close to the ice-covered poles or high peaks. But most polar and mountain wildlife finds a way to live around the seasonally shifting edge of the ice — on the windswept tundra or farther down in the boreal forest.

WHERE ARE MOUNTAINS AND POLAR REGIONS?

ALPS

The Alps are in the temperate zone, where the permanent snow line is reached quite low, at 8,850 feet (2,700 m). Below that, vegetation descends in ever warmer zones down to mixed deciduous forest. These zones vary depending on how directly a slope faces the sun.

above 8,850 feet (2,700 m)
— bare rock and snow

up to 8,850 feet (2,700 m)
— grass and alpine flowers

up to 7,870 feet (2,400 m)
— dwarf shrubs, such as juniper

up to 6,560 feet (2,000 m)
— coniferous forest, such as spruce and larch

up to 3,280 feet (1,000 m)
— mixed deciduous forest

AFRICA

In tropical Africa, the permanent snow line is much higher. It is at about 16,400 feet (5,000 m) on east Africa's highest peaks — at 19,340 feet (5,895 m) on Mt. Kilimanjaro and 17,058 feet (5,199 m) on Mt. Kenya. Below the snow line, vegetation descends through alpine tundra to savanna. The alpine tundra is exposed to hot sun during the day and icy cold at night, producing plants that are unique to the region.

above 16,400 feet (5,000 m)
— bare rock and snow

up to 16,400 feet (5,000 m)
— Afro-Alpine plants including giant lobelia and senecioee

up to 13,120 feet (4,000 m)
— dwarf shrubs and tree heaths including erica arborea and erica philippia

up to 10,820 feet (3,300 m)
— bamboo

up to 8,850 feet (2,700 m)
— montane forest

up to 7,220 feet (2,200 m)
— savanna grass and scrub

HIMALAYAS

The Himalayas are the world's highest peaks, with Mt. Everest at 29,029 feet (8, 848 m) the highest of all. Above 15,000 feet (4,572 m), all the range's peaks are covered in permanent snow. Below that the vegetation descends through alpine tundra to subtropical forest. Tibet, which lies in the Himalayas, has vast, high-altitude plateaus where it is too cold and dry for anything but short alpine grasses to grow. This region is often called mountain steppe.

above 14,760 feet (4,500 m)
— bare rock and snow

up to 14,760 feet (4,500 m)
— grassland with Alpine flowers

up to 12,470 feet (3,800 m)
— dwarf shrubs, such as rhododendrons

up to 10,500 feet (3,200 m)
— coniferous forest including cedar trees

up to 6,560 feet (2,000 m)
— broad-leaved forest

up to 3,280 feet (1,000 m)
— subtropical forest

MOUNTAIN AND POLAR ENVIRONMENTS

Mountain and polar habitats have much in common. The same extreme habitat is found only on the very highest mountain summits at the Equator. In the temperate zone, it is found lower down. At the Poles, it is found at ground level.

THE HIGH PEAKS

Steep crags, precipitous slopes and constant cold make it hard for any plants but lichens to gain a foothold on the very tops of mountains. Mountain peaks are cold wastelands.

ALPINE FLOWERS

In the temperate zone, there are marked seasonal changes. In spring, snow that may have fallen all over the mountain melts up to the snow line. Up on the high meadows just below the snow line, tiny, hardy "alpine" flowers bloom. Spring in the Arctic brings similar flowers.

CLOUD FOREST

In the tropics, the lower mountain slopes are often wrapped in clouds. Thick "cloud forest" grows here, home to many unique plants and providing a refuge for some of the world's most endangered animals, including gorillas.

MOUNTAINS

LIFE at high altitudes is tough, with icy winds, thin air, steep slopes and scant vegetation. Some creatures such as mountain goats have adapted to these conditions. Many mountain inhabitants, like deer, are migrants, only moving up in summer. Others are refugees, like pumas, forced up because humans have eroded their natural habitat.

PREDATORY MAMMALS

The mountains of North America are some of the last refuges for predators that once roamed widely, including wolves, coyotes, bears, lynxes and mountain lions. In the Andes, the mountain lion is the only large predator apart from the mainly vegetarian spectacled bear.

Spectacled bear
(see p. 109)

THE ROCKIES

These mountains stretch from the chill Brooks Range in Alaska, home to wolves and caribou, to the tropical Sierra Madre of Mexico with its parrot-filled valley forests.

Brooks Range

Rocky Mountains

Sierra Madre

Atlas Mountains

Andes Mountains

BIRDS OF PREY

Few creatures cope better at high altitudes than birds, with their warm feathers, and lungs ideal for thin air. Birds of prey can range far up and down mountains to find food. American mountains are home to many birds of prey — including hawks (such as Cooper's), golden eagles and falcons.

California condor
(see p. 135)

Bighorn sheep
(see p. 120)

LARGE MAMMALS

A number of grazing animals are well equipped to take advantage of the fresh plants that grow on almost inaccessible slopes. Ibex and bighorn and Dall sheep in North America and vicuña in the south are all agile climbers and have extra red blood cells, that help them to absorb more oxygen from thin air.

Snowshoe hare
(see p. 113)

SMALL MAMMALS

For small mammals, the cold of mountain peaks presents special problems. Many small mammals, such as marmots, retreat to burrows and hibernate in winter. Those that stay active, like pikas, often rely on food stores built up during the fall.

INSECTS AND OTHERS

High up, springtails, coccinellid beetles and apollo butterflies gather to feed where alpine flowers and spores of lichen and moss lie in rock crevices. When not feeding, the springtails and flies shelter under rocks alongside centipedes, earwigs and jumping spiders.

Common earwig
(see p. 148)

SMALL MAMMALS

In the Himalayas and other Eurasian ranges, little rodents such as pikas and mountain voles stay active through the year, surviving through winter by building up stores of hay in dry places under rocks. Alpine, black-capped and other marmots hibernate.

Himalayan marmot
(see p. 115)

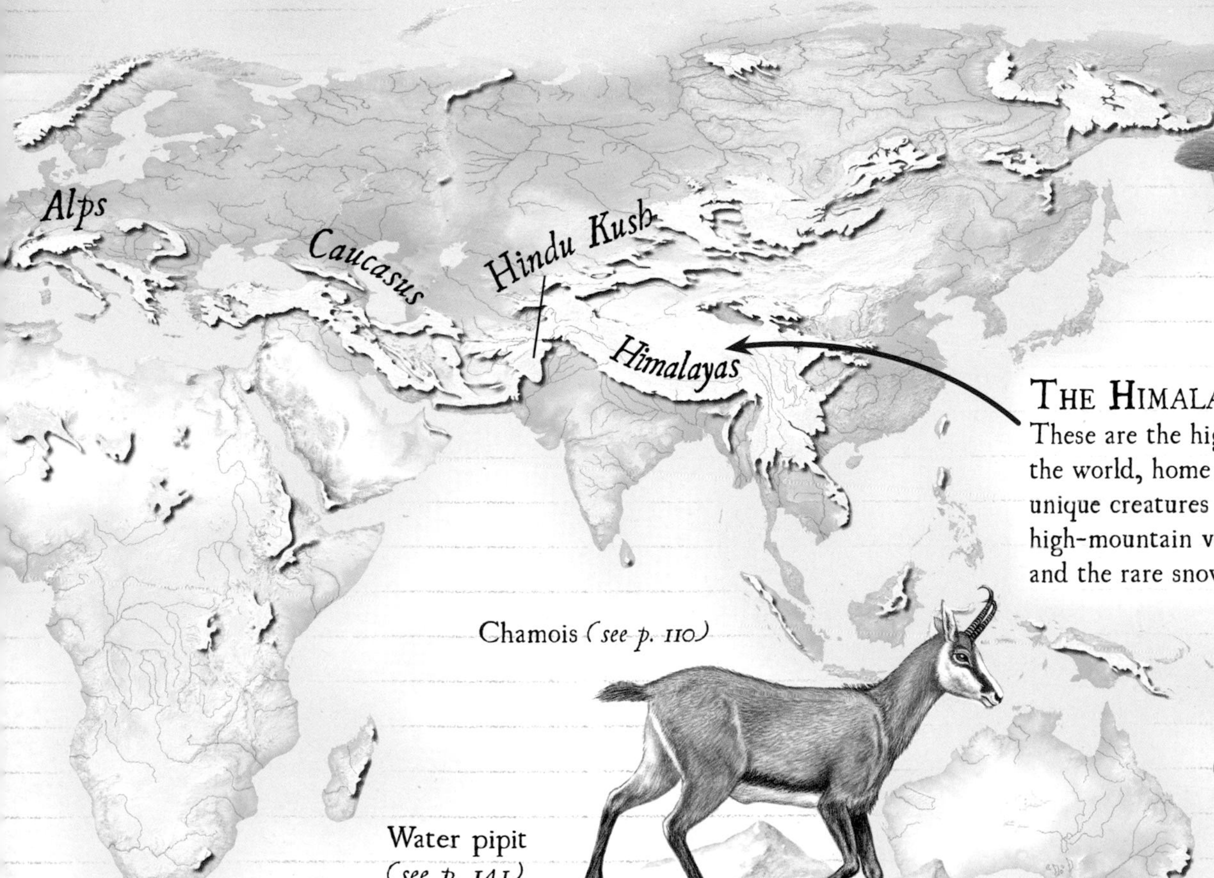

Alps

Caucasus

Hindu Kush

Himalayas

The Himalayas

These are the highest mountains in the world, home to a number of unique creatures such as the high-mountain vole, the goatlike tahr and the rare snow leopard.

Chamois (see p. 110)

Red-tailed hawk
(see p. 136)

Water pipit
(see p. 141)

BIRDS OF THE AIR

Some birds, like choughs, snowcocks and ptarmigans live high up in mountains all the time, making the most of the seeds and insects, which are surprisingly abundant. Ravens and geese fly up in summer. Migrating snipe and geese may fly far overhead.

LARGE MAMMALS

Many sheep- and goatlike animals climb up to graze on the high meadows in spring, including the tahr, the huge-horned Siberian ibex and the argali, the largest of all wild sheep. Shaggy oxlike yaks live at heights of 19,700 feet (6,000 m) up in the Himalayas.

BIRDS OF PREY

The exposed slopes of the mountains are an ideal hunting ground for birds of prey, and the Eurasian mountains are home to many rare birds of prey such as golden eagles. There are also many carrion-feeders such as the Himalayan griffon.

POLAR ICE

THE Arctic and Antarctic are the world's most difficult habitats. For half the year, each is unimaginably cold and almost perpetually dark. But there is a brief summer when plants bloom and insects multiply, and many birds fly in to make the most of the feast. A few hardy animals, like polar bears, stay all year, and there is always abundant life in the sea.

Wandering albatross
(see p. 132)

PENGUINS

Penguins cope with the cold, snug inside waterproof feathers and layers of blubber. They cannot fly but are superb swimmers, well adapted to catching fish, the most abundant food here. There are seven Antarctic species, (including Adelie and Gentoo).

Adelie penguin
(see p. 140)

Antarctic cod

FISH

Long summer days generate lots of plankton for food, so despite the cold, the Southern Ocean teems with fish — plunder fish, ice fish, Antarctic cod and dragonfish. There are few species, but shoals are huge — and there are swarms of krill so large they can be seen by satellites.

SEA BIRDS

Penguins are Antarctica's only year-round residents, but 35 other seabird species visit in summer, including terns, petrels, gulls and cormorants — and skuas that scavenge penguins' breeding grounds for their eggs and young.

Midge (see p. 151)

INSECTS

Antarctica's largest land animal is the wingless midge, only 1/2 inch (1 cm) long. Its largest predator is a mite. There are only a few insect species, but they live in huge numbers under rocks in soil and lichens. Springtails are common around penguin colonies, feeding on plants.

WHALES AND SEALS

The Antarctic's big predators are not land mammals, but seals and whales. Leopard seals prey on penguins, and toothed whales prey on seals. The abundance of fish means there are more seals in the Antarctic than in the Arctic, including the elephant seal — the world's biggest.

Blue whale
(see p. 123)

INSECTS

As lakes and bogs thaw in spring, countless insects emerge from winter dormancy. Springtails and beetles crawl over the tundra. Butterflies and bees sip on Arctic flowers. In summer, huge swarms of mosquitoes and blackflies erupt to pester animals.

Bumblebee
(see p. 147)

Rock ptarmigan
(see p. 141)

BIRDS OF THE AIR

As spring arrives, millions of birds flock to breed in the Arctic. Wagtails and pipits catch insects on the ground. Songbirds like wheatears feed on seeds too. Sand martins snatch insects in the air. As these birds fly north, predatory merlins and falcons are on their tails.

WHALES AND SEALS

The Arctic winter is hard for seals and whales because the sea freezes over, stopping them from coming up for air. Some migrate in winter. Seals that stay gnaw through the ice to make breathing holes, but they must keep working to keep the holes open as the ice thickens.

Harp seal (see p. 120)

PREDATORS

With so little cover in the exposed Arctic landscape, predators rely on camouflage to make attacks. In winter, Arctic foxes, ermines and least weasels all turn white to disguise themselves against the snow, turning brown again in spring. Even wolves are paler in winter.

Polar bear
(see p. 109)

Tundra swan
(see p. 143)

SEA BIRDS AND SHORE BIRDS

In summer, the fringes of the ice melt, exposing vast areas of sea. Many birds arrive to breed on the Arctic shores, including shore birds (such as dunlins, turnstones, and knots), water-fowl (such as Brent geese) and seabirds (such as puffins, jaegers and gulls).

GRAZING ANIMALS

Every spring, huge herds of caribou wander north through the tundra to feed on the fresh growth, led by pregnant females. They move north each day, swimming across rivers and inlets, trekking over 600 miles (1,000 km). Calves are born en route.

Moose
(see p. 117)

ANIMAL CLASSIFICATION

The animal kingdom is divided into groups called *phyla*. One of these is called chordates. Chordates are animals that have backbones, such as tigers and tortoises. Animals without backbones, such as snails, starfish and scorpions, are invertebrates. Nearly all the animals on Earth are invertebrates, which includes at least 1,000,000 kinds of insect.

Animals are organized, or classified, into several different groups. A brown bear, for example, is one of eight kinds or *species* of bear. Brown bears belong to the bear *family* and to the *order* of carnivores. The carnivores belong to the *class* of mammals, and mammals belong to the *phylum* of chordates. This chart shows the main animal groups.

ANIMAL KINGDOM

Waterbears	Sea anemones, Jellyfish, Corals and Hydras	Flatworms and Leeches	Comb jellies	Spiny-headed worms
Horseshoe worms			Lampshells	Segmented worms
Roundworms			Sponges	Velvet worms
				Other Phyla

Mollusks

ARTHROPODS

Horseshoe Crabs	ARACHNIDS *(103,000 species)*		CRUSTACEANS *(70,000 species)*		Octopuses and Squids
Millipedes	Camel spiders Harvestmen Micro-whip scorpions Mites and ticks Pseudoscorpions Scorpions Spiders Tailless whip scorpions	Tick spiders Whip scorpions	Horseshoe Shrimps	Branchiopods	Solenogasters
					Bivalves
		Scorpion	Barnacles	Copepods	Chitons
Sea Spiders					Snails
Centipedes			Mussel Shrimps		Tusk shells
			Crabs, Lobsters and Shrimps		Deep-sea Limpets

Moss animals

Rotifers

Echinoderms

INSECTS *(at least 1 million species)*

Ants, bees and wasps Beetles Booklice Bristletails Bugs Butterflies and moths	Caddisflies Cockroaches Diplurans Dragonflies Earwigs Fleas Flies Grasshoppers and crickets	Grylloblattids Lacewings and ant lions Lice Mantids Mayflies Scorpion flies Silverfish Springtails	Stick and leaf insects Stoneflies Stylopids Termites Thrips Web spinners Zorapterans	Sea Urchins Starfish Brittlestars Sea Cucumbers Crinoids

Beetle

Wasp

KEY TO THE MAIN ANIMAL GROUPS

Kingdom is the largest grouping of animals. Plants, fungi and protists belong to separate kingdoms.

Phylum is a main division in the animal kingdom. Chordates are a phylum. The plural of phylum is phyla.

Sub-phylum is a sub-division within a phylum. Crustaceans are a sub-phylum.

Class is a division of a phylum. Reptiles, birds, amphibians, fish and mammals are classes.

Order is a division of a class of animals. Bats, rodents, marsupials and primates are orders of mammals.

CHORDATES *(45,000 species)*

REPTILES *(10,000 species)*

*Crocodiles and
  alligators
Lizards and snakes
Tuatara
Turtles, tortoises
  and terrapins*

Snake

Crocodile

MAMMALS *(5,500 species)*

*Aardvarks
Anteaters,
  armadillos
  and sloths
Bats
Carnivores
Dugongs and
  manatees
Elephants*

*Elephant shrews
Even-toed hoofed
  mammals
Flying lemurs
Hares, rabbits
  and pikas
Hyraxes
Insectivores
Marsupials (pouched
  mammals)*

*Monotremes (egg-
  laying mammals)
Odd-toed hoofed mammals
Pangolins
Primates
Rodents
Seals, sea lions and walruses
Tree shrews
Whales and dolphins*

Primate

Elephant

AMPHIBIANS *(7,300 species)*

*Caecilians
Frogs and toads
Newts and
  salamanders*

Caecilian

Toad

BIRDS *(10,420 species)*

*Albatrosses, petrels
  and shearwaters
Cassowaries and emus
Cranes, rails, coots
  and bustards
Cuckoos and
  roadrunners
Divers or loons
Ducks, geese, swans
  and screamers
Eagles, hawks, kites,
  vultures, falcons
  and buzzards
Grebes
Herons, storks, ibises
  and flamingoes*

*Kingfishers, bee
  eaters and
  rollers
Kiwis
Mousebirds
Nightjars and
  frogmouths
Ostriches
Owls
Parrots
Pelicans, gannets,
  cormorants, darters
  and frigatebirds
Perching birds, such as
  robins and crows
Penguins*

*Pheasants, jungle fowl,
  grouse, partridges,
  turkeys and quails
Pigeons and doves
Rheas
Sandgrouse
Swifts and
  hummingbirds
Tinamous
Trogons
Turacos
Wading birds, gulls,
  terns and auks
Woodpeckers, barbets,
  toucans, jacamars
  and honeyguides*

Parrots

European
robin

BONY FISH *(31,000 species)*

*There are
48 orders
including:*

*Carp
Cod
Eels*

*Dragonfish
Flatfish
Lanternfish*

*Salmon and
  trout
Toadfish*

Salmon

SHARKS, SKATES and RAYS *(1,200 species)*

*Includes eight shark orders
and three orders of ray*

Rays

JAWLESS FISH *(43 species)*

SEA SQUIRTS *(2,813 species)*

MAMMALS

MAMMALS range in size from tiny shrews to gigantic blue whales. They have found a way to live in almost every habitat on Earth, because they are warm-blooded or "endothermic." This means they keep their bodies at the best temperature for body processes, whatever the conditions. A puma can live anywhere from tropical forests to snowy mountains. Even so, each mammal has its own preferred habitat.

Anteater, Giant
Range: C. and S. America
Habitat: Forest, savanna
Like all anteaters, the giant anteater has no teeth. Instead it has a very long snout and a 2 foot-long (60 cm) tongue for sucking termites and ants from their nests.

Antelope, Royal
Range: W. Africa south of the Sahara
Habitat: Forest, forest clearings
The royal antelope of the west African rain forest is the world's smallest hoofed animal — less than 12 inches (30.5 cm) high and with pencil-thin legs. It is a shy creature, able to vanish quickly — and can bound 10 feet (3 m). It is famed in local folklore for its speed and its wisdom.

Ape, Barbary
Range: Gibraltar and N. Africa
Habitat: Rocky areas, forest clearings
The Barbary ape is not actually an ape, but a monkey with no tail. It was once found over much of southwest Europe as well as Africa, but now its only European home is Gibraltar. It forages in trees and on the ground for leaves and fruit.

Armadillo, Nine-banded
Range: Tropical America
Habitat: Dry grassland, forest
Armadillos dig for ants and spiders at night. When threatened they curl up into a ball so that only their armor-plated back is exposed.

Aye-aye
Range: Madagascar
Habitat: Forest
The Madagascan aye-aye is a nocturnal creature with long, slender fingers. It uses its long third finger to tap on tree trunks to find insects, listening for movement with its super-sensitive ears. It then probes with the same finger to draw out the insect. During the day, aye-ayes hide in treetop nests of twigs.

Baboon, Olive
Range: C. Africa
Habitat: Savanna, forest
The olive baboon is a large, ground-living monkey with a doglike muzzle. It eats mostly grass, fruit and insects, but sometimes hunts small mammals.

Badger, American
Range: S.W. Canada to C. Mexico
Habitat: Open grassland, arid land
The American badger is a solitary hunter that digs out ground squirrels and prairie dogs at night. It can dig with amazing speed.

Badger, Eurasian
Range: Europe and Asia
Habitat: Forest, grassland
The Eurasian badger lives in families in huge burrows called setts. It emerges at dusk to play and hunt for worms and also small animals, fruit and nuts.

Bandicoot, Brown
Range: Australia
Habitat: Scrub, forest
Bandicoots are small marsupials that dig for insect larvae and plant roots. The brown bandicoot lives in dense scrub and eats fungi and scorpions.

Bat, Common long-eared
Range: Europe and N. Asia
Habitat: Forest
This bat's huge, highly sensitive ears help it to fly in pitch dark and also to locate its insect prey by using sound echoes.

Bat, Common vampire
Range: C. and S. America
Habitat: Forest caves, tree holes
The vampire bat lives only on blood, sucking it from its victims through its tongue. The victim loses only a small amount of blood, but the bat's bite may transmit diseases.

Bat, Ghost
Range: Australia
Habitat: Caves, old mine tunnels
This is a large carnivorous bat that feeds on insects, frogs, birds, lizards and small bats. It uses both ears and eyes to locate prey when hunting.

Bat, Greater fruit
Range: S. and S.E. Asia
Habitat: Forest
This bat has some of the largest wings of any bat, up to 5 feet (1.5 m) across. It roosts by day in large trees in flocks, which take to the air at night to hunt for fruit such as bananas.

Bat, Greater horseshoe
Range: Europe, Asia, N. Africa
Habitat: Forest, caves
Horseshoe bats get their name from the horseshoe-shaped rim on their noses which helps them amplify and direct the ultrasonic cries that they use to locate prey. The greater horseshoe catch moths in flight and beetles on the ground.

Bat, Spear-nosed
Range: Tropical America
Habitat: Forest
This bat feeds on mice, birds and insects, as well as flowers and pollen.

Bear, Black
Range: Asia, N. America
Habitat: Forest
There are black bears in both America and Asia. The American black bear eats very little meat, living mostly on grasses and fruits in summer and nuts in fall. In October these bears retreat to their dens and sleep through the winter, though they do not go into true hibernation.

Bear, Spectacled
Range: S. America
Habitat: Forest, savanna, mountains
The spectacled bear is the only South American bear. It lives mainly in forests, feeding on leaves, fruit and roots, but also sometimes preys on deer and vicuña. It is a good climber and sleeps in a tree in a large nest made from sticks — either alone or in a family group.

Binturong
Range: S.E. Asia
Habitat: Forest
This is a small carnivorous mammal related to the civet. It is the only carnivore besides the kinkajou to have a prehensile tail, which it uses as an extra limb when climbing.

Bobcat
Range: N. America
Habitat: Swamp, forest
The bobcat is the most common North American wildcat. It is about twice the size of a domestic cat and feeds mainly on rabbits and hares, but also catches ground birds. It hunts by slowly stalking its victim. It gets its name from its stubby, "bobbed" tail.

Bear, Brown/Grizzly
Range: Europe, Asia, N. America
Habitat: Forest, tundra
The American grizzly and Kodiak bears are two of the various subspecies of brown bear, which also include the Siberian bear and the Gobi bear. They are very strong and among the largest of all carnivores.

Bear, Gobi
Range: Gobi desert
Habitat: Desert
The Gobi bear is the world's only desert bear, living in southwestern Mongolia, where the local people call it Mazaalai. It is actually a type of brown bear, like the North American grizzly, but is adapted to coping with the arid conditions of the Gobi. It is now very rare and close to extinction, with only 30 or so animals surviving.

Bison, American
Range: N. America
Habitat: Prairie, open woodland
This huge, shaggy, cowlike creature can grow up to 10 feet (3 m) tall at the shoulders. It used to roam the American prairies in herds many thousands strong, and make annual migrations in search of good pasture. But mass slaughter by European settlers brought it almost to extinction. Now, about 20,000 live on reserves.

Bongo
Range: C. Africa
Habitat: Tropical forest
The bongo is the largest forest antelope, growing up to 7 feet (2.1 m) tall. It hides among bushes during the day and comes out at dawn and dusk to feed on leaves, fruit and bark. At night it grazes on grass. When a bongo runs, it tilts its head back to prevent its horns catching on branches.

Bear, Polar
Range: Arctic ocean
Habitat: Coasts, ice floes
The polar bear is the top predator of the Arctic region. It lives mainly on fish, seabirds, caribou, seals and other animals, but in the summer it also feeds on berries and leaves. Polar bears are excellent swimmers.

Beaver
Range: N. America
Habitat: Rivers and lakes
Beavers are large rodents that gnaw down trees with their powerful teeth to build dams across streams and make lodges to live in during the winter. They feed on bark and twigs in winter and other plants in summer.

Boar, Wild
Range: Europe, N. Africa, Asia
Habitat: Forest, woodland
The wild boar is the ancestor of the farmyard pig, but has bristly hair and males have tusks. It roots around woodland floors for plants and insects and also digs up bulbs and tubers. Wild boars are surprisingly fast, agile creatures and they can become quite aggressive if frightened.

Buffalo, Asian water
Range: India, S.E. Asia
Habitat: Forest, wetland
American bison are sometimes called buffalo, but true buffalo live in the tropics and have thinner coats and flattened horns, which Asian water buffalo use to defend themselves against tigers. The Asian water buffalo lives in southern Asia where it spends much of the day wallowing in muddy rivers. Most water buffalo are now domesticated.

Bush baby, Thick-tailed Greater
Range: S. Africa
Habitat: Forest, wooded savanna
This is the largest of the small African tree-dwelling primates known as galagos, or bush babies. These night hunters have huge eyes and ears for finding insects and reptiles in the dark.

Camel, Dromedary
Range: N. Africa, Middle East, Australia
Habitat: Dry grassland, desert
Camels are superbly adapted to life in hot deserts, with an amazing capacity to drink enough water to last for days, and the ability to let their body temperature climb during the day.

Camel, Bactrian
Range: China, Mongolia
Habitat: Desert, steppe
Bactrian camels have two humps, unlike the African dromedary, and a shaggy coat to cope with icy Gobi winters. They were tamed 4,000 years ago, and it was once thought all Bactrians in the wild were feral — that is, descendants of domesticated beasts. But in the late 1800s truly wild camels were found in central Asian deserts. This wild population is small.

Capybara
Range: S. America
Habitat: Forest, grassland, wetland
The capybara is the largest of all rodents — the size of a sheep. It eats mainly water plants, and is a superb swimmer, with partly webbed feet.

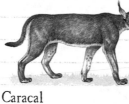

Caracal
Range: Africa, S.W. Asia
Habitat: Dry grassland, desert
Sometimes known as the desert lynx, the caracal hunts jerboas and ground squirrels at night and can bring down a bird just after takeoff.

Caribou
Range: N. Europe, Asia, N. America
Habitat: Tundra, taiga
Known in Europe as the reindeer, the caribou lives on the tundra and feeds mainly on grass in summer and lichen in winter, which it obtains by digging through snow. It is the only deer in which females as well as males have antlers. Caribou are often seen in huge herds on migration.

Cat, Pallas's
Range: C. Asia
Habitat: Desert, steppe, mountains
This is a small desert cat that lives in caves or burrows taken over from other animals such as marmots. It hunts small animals, such as mice and hares, at night.

Cat, Wild
Range: Europe, Africa, S.W. Asia
Habitat: Grassland, forest
The wild cat is an ancestor of the domestic cat and looks similar, but is bigger and has a shorter, thicker tail. It climbs trees well, but stalks most of its prey on the ground, catching small rodents and ground birds. Courting males howl and screech to attract females.

Chamois
Range: Europe, W. Asia
Habitat: Mountains
The chamois is the nimblest of all mountain goats, nipping easily from crag to crag. Its hooves have special spongy pads to help them grip on slippery rocks. In summer it feeds on herbs and flowers high up; in winter it moves down to feed on lichens and pine shoots.

Cheetah
Range: Africa, S.W. Asia
Habitat: Grassland
The cheetah is the fastest land animal, able to sprint at more than 60 miles per hour (100 kmph) for short distances. When hunting, it stalks as close as possible to its prey, then moves in for the kill with an explosive burst of speed — knocking over the victim and killing it with a bite to the throat. If the attempt fails, it usually gives up. Its prey are typically small antelopes, hares and birds.

Chevrotain, Water
Range: W. Africa
Habitat: Rain forest
This tiny mouse deer, about the size of a hare, lives in African rain forests. It rests during the day in undergrowth or a hole in the riverbank, then ventures out at night to forage.

Chimpanzee
Range: C. Africa
Habitat: Rain forest, wooded savanna
Chimps are quick and very clever apes. They are very expressive and use many noises and gestures to communicate with each other. They can also use simple tools, such as sticks, to get food.

Chinchilla
Range: N. Chile
Habitat: Rocky mountains
The chinchilla is a small rodent, with large eyes, long ears and a bushy tail, that lives in colonies in rock crevices. It eats plants, typically sitting up to eat with the food held in its front paws.

Chipmunk, Eastern
Range: N. America
Habitat: Forest
This little squirrel-like rodent lives in leafy forests in eastern North America. It is a lively animal, always on the move gathering seeds, nuts and berries, which it stores for winter.

Civet, African palm
Range: Africa south of the Sahara
Habitat: Forest, savanna
The civet is a small carnivorous animal
with a doglike muzzle and a long,
bushy tail. It lives in forests and
grasslands and feeds at night on
small lizards and rodents.

Coati
Range: Tropical America
Habitat: Forest
The coati belongs to the same family as
raccoons, but lives in packs in the forests
of tropical America. It has a long, very
sensitive nose, and snuffles in the
undergrowth for small animals, fruits,
and seeds.

Colugo
Range: Philippines
Habitat: Rain forest
Colugos, also known as flying
lemurs, are the world's largest gliding
mammals. They can glide 425 feet
(130 m) on the flaps of skin between their
limbs. There are two species: one from
Indonesia and one from the Philippines.

Coyote
Range: N. and C. America
Habitat: Prairie, open woodland
Known by American tribes as the "trickster"
for its cunning, the coyote has been poisoned
and shot by farmers for years, but still
survives. Females give birth to litters of about
six pups in a burrow in the spring. The male
brings the family food, including snakes,
rabbits, rodents, insects and fruit.

Deer, Fallow
Range: W. Eurasia
Habitat: Grassland, open woodland
Fallow deer spend the night and most
of the day under the trees or in thick
undergrowth, emerging at dusk and dawn
to graze. Fall is rutting time. Bucks (males)
herd the does (females) together and rivals
fight furiously with their antlers until
one retires defeated. The victor can now
mate with the females.

Deer, Red, or Wapiti
Range: Mainly N. America, Eurasia
Habitat: Temperate woodland, moors
Known as the red deer in Europe, the
wapiti is very common. Stags have antlers
up to 5 feet (1.5 m) long.

Deer, Mule
Range: N. America
Habitat: Prairie, open woodland
The nimble, shy mule deer is related to the
white-tailed deer, and migrates into the
desert from forest areas in the winter. The
deer move around mostly at dawn and
dusk, and on moonlit nights. In the heat
of the day, they bed down in cool places.
Bucks prefer to bed down on rocky ridges.
Does and fawns like flatter places.

Deer, White-tailed
Range: The Americas
Habitat: Forest, swamp, grassland
The adaptable white-tailed deer lives in
every habitat from the Arctic to the tropics
— partly because it browses on everything
from grasses to nuts and lichens.

Dhole
Range: S. Asia
Habitat: Rain forest, woodland,
mountians
The dhole is a wild dog that lives
in packs of up to 30. Dholes are
not fast runners, but they can chase prey
for long distances until they finally
tire. A pack can pull down a buffalo
or even a tiger.

Dingo
Range: Australia
Habitat: Dry grassland
The dingo was introduced to
Australia by people from Asia some
3,000 years ago as a hunting dog.
As well as kangaroos, dingoes attack
and eat sheep.

Dog, African hunting
Range: Africa
Habitat: Savanna, dry grassland
Hunting dogs live and hunt in huge packs,
preying on animals as large as wildebeests,
seizing their legs and dragging them to
the ground.

Dolphin, Common
Range: Worldwide
Habitat: Tropical and temperate oceans
Dolphins are actually a type of whale, but
they are smaller and incredibly agile. They
are acrobatic and playful, and can burst
right out of the water. They are also
extremely intelligent.

Dolphin, Amazon
River (boto)
Range: Amazon and Orinoco rivers
Habitat: Freshwater
The Amazon river dolphin or boto is
the largest freshwater dolphin, reaching
8½ feet (2.6 m) in length. As it matures,
it often turns vivid pink in color, but
it is usually blue-gray like other dolphins.
Unusually, for a dolphin, it can bend its
neck to turn its head in any direction.
It often swims upside down to see
the riverbed.

Dormouse, Fat

Range: Europe, Asia
Habitat: Forest

The fat or edible dormouse has a bushy tail like a squirrel's. It even sits up to eat like a squirrel, but keeps its tail laid flat. During summer days, it sleeps in its nest high in tree branches, and comes down only to forage for nuts, seeds and berries in the darkness. In winter, it hibernates in tree hollows or even in buildings.

Eland

Range: Africa south of the Sahara
Habitat: Savanna

The eland is the largest of the antelopes. Big bulls can weigh up to 1 ton (0.9 tonne). Both males and females have long, straight horns up to 28 inches (70 cm) long, with a spiral twist. They are browsing animals, feeding at dusk and dawn in open country with scattered trees. They not only eat leaves, but also dig up roots with their hooves.

Fox, Fennec

Range: N. Africa, S. W. Asia
Habitat: Desert

The fennec fox is the smallest dog, but has the largest ears in proportion to its body. Its big ears help it to keep cool and also locate the small rodents, birds and insects that it hunts at night. By day it shelters from the heat of the desert in small burrows. Fennec foxes are sociable animals and mate for life.

Gelada

Range: Ethiopia
Habitat: Mountains, grasslands

The gelada is a monkey that lives far away from trees. It feeds on plant material on the ground and even sleeps on bare rock. It has three areas of bare red skin which the male swells up when threatened.

Dugong

Range: Indian Ocean, western Pacific
Habitat: Coastal waters

The dugong is also known as the sea cow because it feeds on sea grass, and has a long hind gut to digest grass just as cows have a rumen. Dugongs lie quietly on the seabed for most of the time, coming up occasionally for air.

Elephant, African

Range: Africa south of the Sahara
Habitat: Rain forest, savanna

The African elephant is the biggest land animal, weighing up to 6 tons (5.4 tonnes). It needs to eat up to 660 pounds (300 kg) of food a day and drink more than 26 gallons (100 liters) of water. Males have tusks up to 10 feet (3 m) long.

Fox, Red

Range: N. America, Eurasia, introduced Australia
Habitat: Woodland, grassland

Red foxes hunt at night alone and come together only to breed and rear young. They feed on a wide range of food. Their natural habitat is forest and grassland, but many have managed to adapt to suburban gardens and even city centers.

Genet, Small spotted

Range: S.W. Europe, Africa, S.W. Asia
Habitat: Savanna, scrub

Genets are small carnivores related to civets. They stalk their prey stealthily, crouching almost flat before pouncing. They catch most victims, such as rodents and reptiles, on the ground.

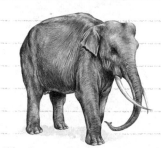

Echidna, Long-nosed

Range: New Guinea
Habitat: Rain forest

Echidnas are, along with platypuses, the only egg-laying mammals, or monotremes. Female echidnas usually lay one egg at a time, which they incubate inside a pouch until the eggs are ready to hatch. The long-nosed echidna is also known as the spiny anteater and feeds on ants and termites.

Elephant, Asian

Range: S. Asia
Habitat: Rain forest

The Asian elephant is smaller than the African, has smaller ears and just one fingerlike tip to its trunk — the African has two. Asian elephants live mostly in forests, feeding mainly on grass and leaves, using their trunks to pull up plants. Most Asian elephants are domesticated.

Gazelle, Thomson's

Range: E. Africa
Habitat: Savanna

Gazelles are graceful, fast-running antelopes with slender legs. Thomson's gazelles live in large herds in open grassland, and have to be almost constantly on the watch to avoid predators like cheetahs.

Gerbil, Fat-tailed

Range: Africa south of the Sahara
Habitat: Sandy desert

Like many desert rodents, this gerbil escapes the heat by resting in burrows and comes out in the cool of night to feed on seeds and insect grubs. It gets its name because it stores fat in its stubby tail. When food is plentiful, the tail swells up so much that the gerbil can barely drag it along. Then, when food is scarce, the fat is used up and the tail slims down.

Gerbil, North African
Range: N. Africa
Habitat: Desert
The North African gerbil lives in rough burrows dug in sand where it hides during the day, emerging at dusk to forage.

Gibbon, Lar
Range: S.E. Asia
Habitat: Forest
Lar gibbons are great acrobats, using their long arms to swing through the forest canopy with amazing speed.

Gibbon, Pileated
Range: Thailand, Cambodia
Habitat: Forest
The pileated gibbon has a black cap of hair on its head. It is born white, and turns black from the head down as it grows older. It is strongly territorial and a male will scream and shout abuse at other males.

Giraffe
Range: Africa south of the Sahara
Habitat: Savanna
The giraffe is the world's tallest animal, growing up to 16 feet (5 m). Half of its height is its incredibly long neck which enables it to reach the leaves and buds of acacia and thorn trees far above the ground. But it has to splay its long front legs in order to drink. Giraffes live in small groups of females and young led by a male.

Glider, Greater
Range: E. Australia
Habitat: Forest
The greater glider is the biggest of Australia's gliding possums, able to glide 330 feet (100 m) or more from tree to tree. Like all possums, it is a marsupial.

Glider, Sugar
Range: N.E. Australia, New Guinea
Habitat: Forest
The sugar glider is a gliding possum that feeds on the sugary sap oozing from wounds on the bark of wattle and gum trees.

Gopher, Plains pocket
Range: N. America
Habitat: Desert, grassland
The pocket gopher gets its name from its cheek pouches, which can be crammed full of food to take back to its burrow.

Gorilla
Range: C. Africa
Habitat: Rain forest
The gorilla is the largest primate and the largest of the great apes, weighing up to 440 pounds (200 kg). Gorillas live in forests in groups led by a large male, or silverback. Despite their size, they are gentle creatures, feeding on leaves and stems which they snap off with their hands.

Guanaco
Range: S. America
Habitat: Grassland, mountains
The guanaco is related to the camel and, like camels, it kneels when lying down. It is a very hardy creature, able to survive in the scorching Atacama Desert and on snowy mountains.

Guinea pig
Range: S. America
Habitat: Grassland, rocks
Guinea pigs, or cavies, are small rodents that feed on grass and leaves. Cavies are the ancestors of pet guinea pigs.

Hamster, Common
Range: Eurasia
Habitat: Grassland, farmland
Hamsters are small burrowing rodents with large cheek pouches that they use for carrying food back to their burrows.

Hare, Snowshoe
Range: Alaska, Canada, N. U.S.
Habitat: Forest, swamps, thickets
This animal has a dark-brown coat in summer that turns white in winter, except for black edges to the ear tips. It is usually active at night and in the early morning. It feeds on juicy green plants in summer and twigs, shoots and buds in winter.

Hedgehog, Desert
Range: N. Africa, Middle East to Iraq
Habitat: Arid scrub, desert
Hedgehogs cope with the desert heat by digging short burrows to shelter in during the day. At night, when the air is cool, they emerge to search for invertebrates such as scorpions, and the eggs of ground-nesting birds.

Hippopotamus
Range: Africa south of the Sahara
Habitat: Rivers or lakes in grassland
The hippo is a huge creature, weighing up to 3 tons (2.7 tonnes), with huge jaws. It lounges in water by day and emerges at night to feed on grass and other plants.

Hippopotamus, Pygmy
Range: W. Africa
Habitat: Rain forest
The pygmy hippo is a small hippo with a narrower mouth and thinner body. It lives mainly on land and feeds on leaves and fallen fruit, which it forages for at night.

Hyrax, Rock
Range: Arabian Peninsula, Africa
Habitat: Rocky hillsides
Hyraxes live in colonies of 50 or more individuals. They feed on leaves, grass and berries close to the ground, but can also climb trees to eat fruit such as figs.

Hyena, Striped
Range: Africa, S.W. Asia
Habitat: Dry savanna, desert
Hyenas look like dogs, but are an entirely separate family. The striped hyena feeds on carrion and also preys on small animals, such as sheep.

Impala
Range: Africa south of the Sahara
Habitat: Savanna
The impala is perhaps the most agile of all antelopes, bounding 33 feet (10 m) in a single leap — just for fun as well as to escape predators. Typically, impalas live in large herds in the dry season.

Indri
Range: Madagascar
Habitat: Forest
The indri is the largest of the lemurs, Madagascar's unique primates, though unlike the other lemurs it has only a stumpy tail. It is also the noisiest. To claim its territory it sings a weird song, audible more than 1½ miles (2 km) away. Indris live in family groups and forage through the trees by day for leaves, shoots and fruit.

Jackrabbit, Black-tailed
Range: U.S., Mexico
Habitat: Grassland, desert
The jackrabbit has long ears that help to keep it cool. It also has long, powerful back legs and bounds along at tremendous speed, up to 37 miles per hour (60 kmph). In summer it eats green plants and grass; in winter, more woody plants.

Jaguar
Range: C. and S. America
Habitat: Rain forest, savanna
The jaguar is the biggest South American cat. It mainly hunts deer, peccaries and capybaras, but swims well and often hunts otters, turtles and snakes in rivers.

Jerboa, Great
Range: C. Asia
Habitat: Steppe, desert
Jerboas are small, mouselike creatures with long tails and very long back legs that allow them to jump 10 feet (3 m) in a single leap. They live in burrows by day and emerge at night to feed on seeds and insects.

Kangaroo rat, Desert
Range: S.W. U.S., N. Mexico
Habitat: Desert
Kangaroo rats are rats with long tails and very long legs that help them jump like kangaroos, up to 6½ feet (2 m) in a single leap. They get most of the water they need from plants and avoid the desert heat by coming out of their burrows only at night. They can travel great distances to find food.

Kangaroo, Musky rat
Range: Australia
Habitat: Rain forest
Rat kangaroos are tiny kangaroos that live in Australian rain forests and feed on leaves, fruit and small animals. Unlike other kangaroos, they often move around on all four legs.

Kangaroo, Red
Range: C. Australia
Habitat: Dry grassland, desert
This is the largest and fastest marsupial. Bounding along on its huge back legs, it can reach 37 miles per hour (60 kmph). Females give birth to babies called joeys, which stay in the pouch for two months.

Kinkajou
Range: Tropical C. and S. America
Habitat: Rain forest
The kinkajou is a small tree-climber related to raccoons and coatis. It uses its prehensile tail to cling on while it is grabbing food. It feeds mainly on fruit and insects.

Koala
Range: E. Australia
Habitat: Eucalyptus forest
Sometimes incorrectly called a koala bear, the koala is actually a marsupial. It feeds entirely on the leaves and shoots of gum trees (eucalyptus). After emerging from the pouch, baby koalas ride on their mother's back.

Kulan (wild ass)
Range: C. and S. Asia
Habitat: Desert, steppe and grassland
There are five kinds of wild donkey or kulan found in central and southern Asia. Also known as onagers, these include the onager, Mongolian kulan, Turkmen kulan, Khur and the Syrian wild ass. Females live in small herds with their young and a single male. Other males live in bachelor groups.

Langur, Hanuman
Range: India, Sri Lanka
Habitat: Forest, scrub
Langurs are agile monkeys that live in the tropical forests of southern Asia. The Hanuman of India happily lives near houses and raids them for food, but is considered sacred so it is rarely hunted.

Lemming, Norway
Range: Scandinavia
Habitat: Tundra
Lemmings are said to commit mass suicide. In fact, when food is plentiful in the harsh tundra, lemming numbers rise sharply and they are forced to migrate. During their mass migration, some drown while crossing rivers.

Lemur, Ring-tailed
Range: Madagascar
Habitat: Rocky woods
Lemurs are agile, tree-climbing primates that live on Madagascar. The ring-tailed lemur has a catlike face with dark eye rings and a long, bushy, upright tail with dramatic gray and black rings. It also has glands that emit a strong scent when it is excited or disturbed.

Leopard
Range: Africa southern Asia
Habitat: Most tropical environments
The leopard is the most adaptable big cat, living everywhere from dense forest to open desert. A leopard has spots; a panther is a leopard that is entirely black. The leopard is a good climber and immensely strong. It often hauls kills as large as antelopes into trees out of the reach of scavengers, such as hyenas. It typically ambushes its prey, often leaping straight out of trees.

Lion
Range: Africa south of the Sahara, N.W. India
Habitat: Savanna
The lion is the second largest cat after the tiger, typically 6½ feet (2 m) long excluding the tail. Lions mostly live in groups called prides, consisting of about 15 animals, with three males and the rest females and their young. Prides hunt together, but it is usually the lionesses (females) that do most of the hunting.

Lion, Mountain
Range: N., C. and S. America
Habitat: Forest, grassland, mountains
Also known as the puma or cougar, the mountain lion mainly hunts deer. Unlike lions, mountain lions hunt on their own and purr instead of roar.

Llama
Range: Andes (S. America)
Habitat: Mountains
The llama is a relative of the guanaco, domesticated long ago, perhaps by the Incas of Peru. Unlike the alpaca, the llama is used for meat and for carrying goods.

Loris, Slender
Range: S. India, Sri Lanka
Habitat: Forest
Unlike most primates, the slender loris is very slow moving, creeping along branches on its spindly legs and ambushing insects, such as grasshoppers.

Lynx
Range: N. America, Eurasia
Habitat: Coniferous forest, scrub
The lynx lives alone in forests and hunts hares, rodents, young deer and birds. The North American lynx depends especially on snowshoe hares. It also has big paws for walking on snow. The tufts on the lynx's ears help it hear in dense pine forests.

Macaque, Japanese
Range: Japan
Habitat: Forest
The Japanese macaque is one of the few primates apart from humans to live outside the tropics, living high up in cold mountain forests. It has unusually thick fur. In especially cold, snowy winters it sometimes lounges up to its neck in hot springs to keep warm.

Manatee, American
Range: Atlantic and Caribbean coast of N. and C. America
Habitat: Warm coastal waters

The manatee looks a little like a seal but, like the dugong, it grazes on sea grass. For much of the day it lies on the seabed, just coming up to the surface every few minutes to breathe. Manatees live in family groups and often gather in large herds.

Mandrill
Range: W. Africa
Habitat: Rain forest
The mandrill has a flaming red nose and blue cheeks. It is also the heavyweight of the monkey world, weighing up to 120 pounds (55 kg). It feeds mostly on plants, but may kill small animals.

Mangabey, Agile
Range: C. Africa
Habitat: Rain forest
The agile mangabey is a better climber than its white-cheeked cousin, but mangabeys are actually slower moving through the trees than other African monkeys.

Marmot, Himalayan
Range: Himalayas
Habitat: Alpine grassland

About the size of a large cat, this mammal lives in large colonies that dig deep burrows in which they can hibernate. It is found in the high grasslands at altitudes of up to 17,100 feet (5,200 m).

Marten, American
Range: Canada, Alaska, N.W. U.S.
Habitat: Taiga/pine forest
Martens are small, tough carnivores that live in pine forests. They are skillful climbers and adept at catching red squirrels, which they chase through the treetops. They live in dens in hollow trees or logs.

Meerkat
Range: Southern Africa
Habitat: Savanna
The meerkat is a small mammal that lives in burrows, linked to form a colony. It feeds on insects, spiders, scorpions and small mammals. When above ground, some of the group always act as lookouts, sitting upright. When cool, the meerkat sits up sunning itself; when hot, it lies belly down in its burrow.

Mink, American
Range: N. America, introduced Britain
Habitat: Wetland, riverbanks
There are two species of mink: the North American mink and the slightly smaller European mink. Minks are usually seen near rivers or lakes, preying on waterfowl and fish, usually at night. Because of their soft, rich brown fur they have often been trapped and farmed to make fur coats. British minks have escaped from farms.

Mole, Eastern
Range: Eastern N. America
Habitat: Fields, lawns, gardens
The Eastern mole spends nearly all its life underground, digging through the soil with its powerful front paws. It is almost blind but finds the earthworms and insect grubs it feeds on with its sensitive nose.

Mole, European
Range: Europe, W. Asia
Habitat: Woodland, farmland
The mole spends most of its life burrowing tunnels underground, so is not often seen. The only signs of its activity are the soil heaps, called mole hills, that it makes while tunneling.

Mole, Giant golden
Range: South Africa
Habitat: Woodland
The rare giant golden mole is the biggest of all moles, up to 9½ inches (24 cm) long. Unlike other moles, this mole hunts aboveground for beetles, slugs and worms — even though it is blind, and so has to rely on smell, touch and sound. When frightened, it scurries for its burrow and seems to be able to find the entrance even though it cannot see.

Mole, Star-nosed
Range: Northeastern N. America
Habitat: Wetland, woodland
The star-nosed mole lives in wet places. Although it digs tunnels, it rarely feeds there. It has a ring of 22 fingerlike tentacles on the end of its nose, which it uses to feel for food such as small fish when it is underwater.

Mole-rat, Naked
Range: E. Africa
Habitat: Dry savanna
Naked mole-rats have pink, almost furless bodies and live underground in colonies of up to 100, controlled by a single female or queen. The queen and her fat helpers are fed by "workers."

Mongoose, Indian
Range: S. Asia,
introduced elsewhere
Habitat: Forest to desert
The mongoose is a swift, effective predator. It catches rats, mice and scorpions, but it is famed for the way it attacks snakes, such as cobras.

Monkey, Colobus
Range: Africa south of the Sahara
Habitat: Forests
The Angolan black and white is one of 15 species of colobus monkey. In the past it was killed for its long, silky hair and it is now quite rare.

Monkey, Golden
Range: C. Africa
Habitat: Savanna
The golden monkey has long, orange fur and blue patches over its eyes. It is mainly a leaf eater and lives in high mountain forests where conifers grow alongside broad-leaved trees. Although it is hunted for its fur, it is the destruction of its habitat that has put it in danger of extinction.

Monkey, Proboscis
Range: Borneo
Habitat: Rain forest, mangrove swamps
The male proboscis monkey gives the species its name, with its very long, pink nose. This normally dangles straight down but straightens out when he honks loudly.

Monkey, Red howler
Range: Tropical S. America
Habitat: Rain forest
The howler monkey gets its name from its incredible dawn and dusk shrieks, which can be heard echoing through the trees up to 2 miles (3 km) away. Red howlers are the biggest American monkeys.

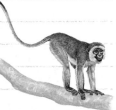

Monkey, Vervet
Range: S. and E. Africa
Habitat: Savanna, woods
Otherwise known as the green guenon, this monkey climbs, jumps, swims well and sleeps in trees; but it is quite happy running and foraging in open country.

Monkey, Woolly spider
Range: S.E. Brazil
Habitat: Coastal forest
The woolly spider monkey has long limbs and a prehensile tail, which it uses as an extra limb to help it move through the trees.

Moose
Range: Eurasia, N. America
Habitat: Taiga, tundra
The moose is the biggest of all deer and the antlers of bulls may be 6 feet (1.8 m) across. Moose shed the antlers in winter and grow bigger ones in spring. Bulls bellow to attract females and engage in fierce battles with rivals.

Mouflon
Range: S. Europe, C. and S. Asia
Habitat: Mountains
The mouflon is a tough mountain sheep that may be an ancestor of the domestic sheep. It seems able to eat virtually any vegetation, including plants other animals find poisonous.

Mouse, Deer
Range: N. America
Habitat: Woodland, grassland
The deer mouse makes nests underground, or in trees, where it starts to breed when only seven weeks old. It is a very nimble creature and feeds on insects, seeds and nuts.

Mouse, Wood
Range: Europe, N. Africa
Habitat: Woodland, farmland
Also known as the long-tailed field mouse, the wood mouse may be the most common European mammal, thriving everywhere from moorlands to suburban gardens. It often nests in burrows under trees and emerges at night to scurry around, foraging for seeds.

Muntjac, Chinese
Range: China, introduced Europe
Habitat: Forest
The muntjac is the size of a big dog and is now the smallest European deer. It is known as the "barking deer" in Asia because of its barklike cry.

Musk ox
Range: N. Canada, Greenland
Habitat: Tundra
The musk ox looks like a buffalo, but it is actually more closely related to the mountain goat. It lives in the Arctic tundra and has a long, shaggy coat to help it survive the bitter winter. Its big hooves stop it from sinking in soft snow.

Muskrat, Common
Range: N. America, introduced elsewhere
Habitat: Marshes, riverbanks
The muskrat lives in water and eats marsh vegetation. In winter it lives in a lodge like a beaver's, built with reeds and other plants.

Myotis, Little brown
Range: N. America
Habitat: Forest, suburbs
This common little bat often forms nursery colonies in attics and walls of buildings. Each bat can eat more than 1,200 insects an hour.

Narwhal
Range: High Arctic
Habitat: Cold oceans
The narwhal is a whale. The male has an extraordinary tusk, up to 10 feet (3 m) long, which is actually an extended tooth and is used to fight rival males.

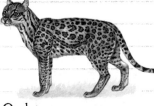

Numbat
Range: S.W. Australia
Habitat: Forest
The numbat is a small marsupial, but has no pouch. The young are dragged around clinging to the mother's nipples. It feeds on termites, and licks them up with its 4-inch-long (10 cm) tongue.

Ocelot
Range: C. and S. America
Habitat: Scrubland to forest
The ocelot sleeps by day in a tree or in dense vegetation, and emerges at night to hunt on the ground for small mammals, such as deer and peccaries. Its favorite food is agouti. Ocelots are among the most beautiful of cats, and they have been hunted intensively for their pelts. Hunting is now banned, and their numbers have increased to about 40,000.

Okapi
Range: C. Africa
Habitat: Forest
The okapi looks like a horse with a zebra's stripes on its back legs. In fact, it is a relative of the giraffe and browses on leaves, twisting them off with its long tongue.

Orangutan
Range: Sumatra, Borneo
Habitat: Rain forest
The orangutan is the second largest great ape after the gorilla. Unlike gorillas, it spends most of its life in trees and builds a platform of sticks for a nest. As its rain forest habitat has shrunk, so the orangutan's survival has been threatened.

Oryx, Arabian
Range: Arabian Peninsula
Habitat: Desert
The very rare Arabian oryx is well adapted to life in the desert and can endure long periods without water, getting most of its water from the plants on which it feeds.

Otter, Eurasian
Range: Europe, Asia, N. Africa
Habitat: Rivers, lakes, coasts
With its streamlined body, the otter is a strong, fast swimmer, using its tail to propel it through the water. It typically lives in a burrow in the riverbank and comes out at night to hunt for fish, frogs and voles.

Otter, Sea
Range: N. Pacific Ocean
Habitat: Rocky coasts
The sea otter spends most of its life at sea. It stays in shallow water close to beds of giant kelp seaweed. To eat shellfish, it floats on its back, rests a stone on its belly, and smashes the shellfish against the stone until the shell breaks.

Panda, Giant
Range: C. China
Habitat: Forest
The rare giant panda has the digestive system of a meat eater, but actually feeds only on the shoots of bamboo plants, which it eats sitting down, gripping the bamboo in its front paws.

Panda, Red
Range: S. Asia, China
Habitat: Mountain forest
The red panda looks a little like a raccoon. It sleeps during the day curled up on branches with its tail wrapped around to keep it warm. It comes down to the ground at night to feed on bamboo shoots, grass, roots, fruit, acorns and occasionally mice. When angry it rears up and hisses.

Pangolin, Giant
Range: W. and C. Africa
Habitat: Rain forest, savanna
Pangolins are the only mammals covered in scales. When threatened they roll themselves up into a ball and raise their scales so the sharp edges point outward. They feed on ants and termites, which they lick up with their long, sticky tongues. They have thick eyelids to protect their eyes from ant bites and can seal off their nostrils to keep the ants out.

Pangolin, Tree
Range: W. and C. Africa
Habitat: Forest
Like all pangolins, the tree pangolin is covered in scales, but it is also a good climber with a long, prehensile tail. It often sleeps on the ground during the day and climbs up trees to hunt ants by smell at night.

Peccary, Collared
Range: N., C. and S. America
Habitat: Forest, grassland, desert
Peccaries are piglike mammals that forage for a wide range of food, from insects to prickly pear cacti. The collared peccary is the most widespread of all peccaries.

Pika, Northern
Range: N. Asia
Habitat: Mountains, forest
The pika is like a rabbit without the big ears, but it usually lives high up in mountains. In summer it builds up little haystacks of grass among the rocks to eat during winter.

Platypus
Range: E. Australia, Tasmania
Habitat: Lakes and rivers
The platypus is one of the few mammals that lays eggs. It also has webbed feet and a bill like a duck, which it uses to probe riverbed mud for insect grubs.

Polecat, Western
Range: Europe
Habitat: Forest
The Western polecat is a small carnivore related to stoats and weasels. It hunts rodents, birds and lizards at night.

Porcupine, Crested
Range: Africa, Italy
Habitat: Forest, savanna
This is a big rodent, armed with fearsome spines, called quills, on its back, that measure up to 12 inches (30.5 cm) long. If threatened, it rattles its tail quills and charges backward, spines raised, at its foe.

Possum, Brush-tailed
Range: Australia, introduced New Zealand
Habitat: Woodland
This is a nimble, tree-climbing marsupial that feeds mainly on leaves, flowers and fruit. It is now quite at home in urban areas.

Potoroo
Range: Australia
Habitat: Damp scrub, grassland
Potoroos are small and ratlike with soft, silky fur. They bound along on their strong back legs. They eat a wide range of food, including plants, plant roots, grass, fungi and insects, which they forage for at dusk.

Prairie dog, Black-tailed
Range: C. U.S.
Habitat: Prairie
This squirrel lives in huge networks of burrows called townships. It gets its name from its doglike bark.

Pronghorn
Range: W. and C. U.S.
Habitat: Prairie
The world's fastest hoofed mammal, the pronghorn can reach 60 miles per hour (100 kmph). Its eyes are so good it can spot movements 4 miles (6.5 km) away.

Quokka
Range: S.W. Australia
Habitat: Dense vegetation
Once widespread, quokkas were shot for sport and now live in few places other than Rottnest Island. This island got its name, which means "Rat's Nest," because European explorers thought the quokkas were rats.

Quoll, Eastern
Range: Tasmania
Habitat: Forest
Quolls are a family of lithe, catlike marsupials that live in forests in Tasmania and New Guinea. They spend some time in trees where they hunt lizards and birds.

Rabbit, European
Range: Europe, introduced elsewhere
Habitat: Grassland, woodland, farmland
Rabbits live in burrows and breed very fast, with several litters a year. They eat grass and can also wreak havoc with farmers' crops of vegetables and grains.

Raccoon
Range: N. and C. America
Habitat: Woodland, suburbs
The raccoon is a woodland creature, but has learned to scavenge from humans and is renowned for its night raids on garbage cans. Its name is a Native American word meaning "scratches with hands."

Rat, Arizona cotton
Range: S.E. U.S.
Habitat: Dry grassland
Cotton rat populations sometimes expand so much that they are declared a plague. They normally feed on plants and small insects but may also feed on quail eggs.

Rat, Baja California rice
Range: Mexico
Habitat: Marshland
Rice rats generally live in marshland and feed on reeds and sedges, and sometimes on fish. They sometimes also eat rice crops and can become serious pests.

Rat, Brown
Range: Worldwide
Habitat: Cities, houses, farmland
Also known as the Norway rat, the brown rat originally came from Asia, but has spread with human habitation around the world. It eats almost anything.

Rat, Swamp
Range: C. and W. Africa
Habitat: Swamps
The swamp rat feeds on seeds, berries and fruits and lives in nests made of reeds and grasses.

Rhebok
Range: Southern Africa
Habitat: Grassland
The rhebok is a small antelope with soft hair. The ram (male) is aggressively territorial, marking out his range by clicking his tongue, whistling and urinating.

Rhinoceros, Black
Range: Africa south of the Sahara
Habitat: Savanna
Like the Sumatran rhino, Africa's black and white rhinos have two horns. The black is slightly smaller than the white and has a pointed upper lip to eat leaves — unlike the white, which has a wide lip for grazing.

Sable
Range: N. Asia
Habitat: Taiga
This small weasel-like predator eats small mammals, fish, nuts and berries. Its thick, soft fur insulates it against the icy Siberian winters, but has meant it is widely trapped for its fur.

Saiga
Range: C. Asia
Habitat: Steppe
The saiga is a goat-antelope with a trunklike nose that can filter out dust from the air in the summer, and warm frosty air in the bitter steppe winter.

Saki, Monk
Range: Amazon
Habitat: Rain forest
Saki monkeys are a family of long-tailed South American monkeys with long, coarse hair. The monk saki has long, shaggy hair around its face and neck that looks like a monk's cowl. It is a wary monkey that lives high in the forest canopy and rarely ventures down to the ground, clambering along branches on all fours. Occasionally it walks upright on large boughs and makes huge leaps from branch to branch.

Sea lion, California

Range: W. U.S.

Habitat: Coasts

The California sea lion is very fast, able to swim at speeds of 25 miles per hour (40 kmph), and can dive down 500 feet (150 m) for fish. Like all sea lions, it has front flippers strong enough to support its weight, and it can move quickly on land, almost galloping — unlike seals that only shuffle. It barks, wails and bleats.

Seal, Crabeater

Range: Antarctic

Habitat: Pack ice fringes

Surprisingly the crabeater seal does not eat crabs. Instead it feeds on shrimplike creatures called krill. Its main enemy is the killer whale.

Seal, Harbor

Range: Arctic and northern oceans

Habitat: Coastal areas

The harbor seal is also known as the common seal and is often seen basking on rocks or even swimming up river.

Seal, Harp

Range: N. Atlantic, Arctic Ocean

Habitat: Cold oceans

The harp seal is a superb swimmer and spends most of its life at sea. It swims large distances as it migrates between its northern summer feeding grounds and warmer oceans.

Seal, Leopard

Range: Southern Ocean

Habitat: Pack ice, cold oceans

The leopard seal is a fearsome predator with a wide mouth and sharp teeth. It mainly preys on penguins, which it snatches as they move off the ice.

Seal, Northern elephant

Range: N. America Pacific coast

Habitat: Offshore islands

The elephant seal lives up to its name. Males can grow up to 16 feet (5 m) long and weigh 2½ tons (2.2 tonnes). It feeds on fish and squid and dives very deep.

Seal, Ross

Range: Antarctic

Habitat: Pack ice

The little Ross seal is the smallest of the Antarctic seals and also the rarest. Altogether there may be fewer than 50,000 of them. The Ross seal feeds primarily on squid, fish and shrimplike krill, which it catches below the pack ice. It has enormous eyes adapted for hunting in the dim water under the ice. Its long flippers propel it through the water at surprising speed.

Seal, Weddell

Range: Antarctic

Habitat: Shore ice, inshore waters

This seal dives longer and deeper than any other seal, often staying down for an hour and reaching a depth of 2,000 feet (600 m) to feed on cod. Underwater they are lively and noisy; out of water they are quite sleepy.

Serval

Range: Africa south of the Sahara

Habitat: Savanna

The serval hunts birds, rats and other rodents in tall grass. Its long legs help it see over the grass but it pinpoints its prey, mainly with its astonishingly sensitive ears — then pounces on it and catches it with its front paws. Its hearing is so good that it can detect mole-rats tunneling underground. Typically it hunts at dusk and dawn.

Sheep, Bighorn

Range: W. U.S., Canada

Habitat: Mountains, deserts

Male bighorn sheep live up to their name, with massive horns curling right around and weighing up to 27 pounds (12 kg). Bighorns typically live in inaccessible mountain areas, but one subspecies lives in the desert and gets all its water from the plants it eats. Bighorns eat almost any plants and have a complex digestive process to get nutrients from poor-quality food.

Shrew, Armored

Range: C. Africa

Habitat: Forest

The armored shrew has an incredibly strong spine reinforced by bony flanges and rods. Mangbetu natives in the Congo call it the "hero shrew" because they can stand on its back without breaking it! In other respects it is much like other shrews, except that it moves slowly.

Shrew, Mole

Range: S. Asia

Habitat: Forest and woodland

Many shrews, including the Koslov's, and Gansu shrews, burrow tunnels through the thick leaf litter on the forest floor in search of insects to eat. Like moles, mole shrews (and shrew-moles) burrow right into the soil. They have tiny molelike eyes and hidden ears.

Shrew, Tree

Range: S.E. Asia

Habitat: Rain forests

Tree shrews are small creatures that live in the southeast Asian rain forests. They scamper up and down trees like squirrels, but spend much of their time on the ground, feeding on ants, spiders and seeds. Some scientists think that they should be in their own order.

Skunk, Striped

Range: N. America

Habitat: Grassland, woodland

When threatened, the striped skunk raises its tail and stamps its feet. If this fails, it turns around and emits a jet of foul smelling liquid from its anal glands.

Sloth, Three-toed

Range: Amazon

Habitat: Rain forest

The slowest of all mammals, the sloth moves barely 6½ feet (2 m) a minute flat out, hanging upside down from branches.

Solenodon, Cuban

Range: Cuba
Habitat: Woods
This strange shrewlike animal forages on the forest floor for insects and fungi, but it also has a venomous bite that it can use to kill lizards, frogs and small birds.

Squirrel, European red

Range: Eurasia
Habitat: Coniferous woodlands
The red squirrel is a rodent that lives in nests called dreys, which it builds in trees. It is an agile creature, using its sharp claws to grip as it scampers head first up and down trees. In fall, when food is plentiful, it buries stores of acorns for winter when its summer food of fungi and fruit is scarce, to supplement its main diet of pinecone seeds.

Stoat

Range: N. America, Eurasia, introduced New Zealand
Habitat: Forest, tundra
The stoat is a fierce little predator that kills rodents and rabbits with a swift bite to the back of the prey's neck. It often kills rabbits three times its own size. In winter many stoats turn creamy white, so that they are less visible against snow. In this winter coat they are called ermine.

Tamarin, Golden lion

Range: S.E. Brazil
Habitat: Coastal forest
The golden lion tamarin with its extraordinary orange-gold, silky fur has become severely threatened as the forests on the Atlantic coast of Brazil have been cut down. Sadly, many of these beautiful creatures have also been caught and sold as pets. International efforts are in progress to save them.

Springbok

Range: Southern Africa
Habitat: Savanna, desert
Springbok once formed herds 10 million strong and 100 miles (160 km) long as they trekked to find water in times of drought. Millions have been slaughtered, but quite large herds are still seen.

Squirrel, Gray

Range: Eastern N. America, introduced Europe
Habitat: Hardwood forests
A native of the oak, hickory, and walnut forests of eastern North America, this squirrel eats a lot of acorns, hickory nuts and walnuts. Here its numbers are controlled by predators such as owls, foxes and bobcats. It was introduced into Europe in the 1800s and has flourished away from its natural predators.

Takin

Range: Himalayas
Habitat: Forest
Takin live in dense bamboo and rhododendron thickets near the upper limits of the forest in some of the world's most rugged country, over 8,000 feet (2,400 m) up. They are clumsy looking, solid animals, but move easily around the steep hills, looking for grass, young bamboo and willow shoots to eat.

Tapir, Malayan

Range: S.E. Asia
Habitat: Rain forest
There are four species of tapir: three in South America and one, the Malayan tapir, in Southeast Asia. They are all shy creatures with piglike bodies and long snouts, which they use to feel for food in much the same way as an elephant does with its trunk.

Springhare

Range: Southern Africa
Habitat: Savanna
The springhare is a small rodent about the size of a hare with powerful back legs. When frightened or on the move, the springhare bounds along like a kangaroo, leaping over 10 feet (3 m) at a time using its big, bushy tail as balance. When feeding it stands on all fours.

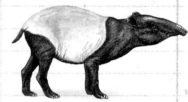

Squirrel, Red giant flying

Range: S. Asia
Habitat: Rain forest
The large flap of skin between the limbs of this squirrel allows it to glide up to 330 feet (100 m) between trees. This way it can move around the forest canopy without ever coming down to the ground. Typically this squirrel rests in hollow trees by day and emerges at dusk to forage for nuts, fruit, soft twigs, leaves and flower buds. Young squirrels are never seen on their mother's back, so it is assumed that they are placed in a safe refuge while the mother searches for food.

Tamarin, Emperor

Range: Amazon
Habitat: Rain forest
Tamarins are small monkeys that live in the rain forests of South and Central America. They can grip with their hands but they cannot swing like other monkeys. Instead, they scamper along branches like squirrels.

Tarsier, Western

Range: Sumatra, Borneo
Habitat: Forest scrub
Tarsiers are tiny primates with amazingly long tails, fingers and toes and gigantic eyes that help them find prey, such as insects, by staring through the gloom of dusk. They are great jumpers.

Tasmanian devil
Range: Tasmania
Habitat: Woodland
No bigger than a small dog, the Tasmanian devil is the most fearsome marsupial hunter, wrongly famed for killing sheep. In fact it feeds mainly on dead birds, dead wombats and dead sheep, as well as lizards, frogs and insects.

Tenrec, Streaked
Range: Madagascar
Habitat: Scrub, forest
Tenrecs are small, shrewlike mammals that live on Madagascar. The streaked tenrec eats woms and insects and it has spines that protect it like a hedgehog's.

Tiger, Caspian
Range: Around the Caspian Sea
Habitat: Grassland
In 1900, there were nine subspecies of tiger, of which three have already become extinct, including the Bali and Java tigers, due to the destruction of their forest habitats. The Caspian was the most recent to disappear, in the 1970s.

Tiger, Indo-Chinese
Range: Myanmar to Vietnam
Habitat: Mixed woodland
Tigers are the largest big cats, measuring 10 feet (3 m) from head to tail. They prey at night on large animals, such as deer, stalking their prey then pouncing. The Indo-Chinese tiger lives mostly in mixed forest. It is disappearing fast, as they are regularly trapped, shot or poisoned.

Tiger, Siberian or Amur
Range: Siberia
Habitat: Taiga
This is the biggest of the tigers and paler in color. It can survive bitter Siberian winters. There are just 400 or so left.

Tiger, Sumatran
Range: Sumatra
Habitat: Rain forest
The Sumatran tiger is the last of the three Indonesian subspecies to survive. It is darker colored and smaller than other tigers. Their numbers are estimated to be between about 450 and 700.

Vaquita
Range: Gulf of California
Habitat: Warm coastal waters
The vaquita is one of the smallest porpoises, less than 5 feet (1.5 m) long. It is also one of the rarest, with perhaps fewer than 500 still surviving.

Vicuña
Range: Central Andes
Habitat: Mountains
The vicuña is related to the camel. It lives over 13,000 feet (4,000 m) up in the Andes. The air is thin here but it still manages to run uphill at 30 miles per hour (50 kmph).

Vole, European water
Range: Europe, east to Siberia
Habitat: Freshwater banks, grassland
The water vole makes a burrow in the bank of a river or stream or burrows into the ground, if far from water. If feeds mainly on grasses and other plants and breeds in summer, producing several litters of four to six young.

Wallaby, Bridled nail-tailed
Range: Queensland, Australia
Habitat: Thick scrub
Wallabies are similar to kangaroos, but half the size, and tend to live in more vegetated areas. Some wallabies live in scrub; some in rocks. The nail-tailed wallabies are scrub wallabies that get their name because of the tiny nail at the tip of their tails.

Wallaby, Swamp
Range: E., S.E. Australia
Habitat: Rocky gullies, thickets
Swamp wallabies live in small herds, but are often difficult to spot because they lie down when danger approaches — then suddenly burst out in different directions if the threat comes too close. They usually bound about 7 feet (2 m) or more from a standing start.

Walrus
Range: Arctic Ocean
Habitat: Pack ice, rocky islands
The walrus is a huge creature that is like a sea lion, but up to 11½ feet (3.5 m) long. The males have huge tusks. It was once thought these were used to help them feed, but it is now believed that they are status symbols that help the male attract a mate.

Warthog
Range: Africa south of the Sahara
Habitat: Savanna
The warthog is a very tough creature. It feeds on short grass, fruit, bulbs and tubers in open savanna, and in this almost treeless environment it can be seen very easily by predators. If hunted it may run to take cover in a burrow, but may often stand and fight with its sharp tusks. Warthogs like to wallow in mud to keep cool.

Weasel, Least
Range: Eurasia, N. America, N. Africa, introduced New Zealand
Habitat: Farmland, woodland
The least weasel is the world's smallest carnivorous mammal, about 8 inches (20 cm) long and little thicker than a finger. It is so small that it can pursue the mice it preys on right into their burrows.

Whale, Blue

Range: Worldwide
Habitat: Cold oceans
The blue whale is the biggest animal alive today, 105 feet (32 m) long and weighing over 140 tons (127 tonnes). This mammal feeds on tiny shrimplike krill, which it strains out of the water through the baleen plates in its mouth. It consumes up to 4 tons (3.6 tonnes) of krill a day. In summer it feeds in polar waters, then migrates in winter toward the Equator to mate.

Whale, Humpback

Range: Worldwide
Habitat: Oceans
The humpback feeds on plankton through baleens like the blue whale, and migrates huge distances. The male is famous for its complex songs.

Whale, Northern right

Range: Northern hemisphere
Habitat: Cool seas
Right whales got their name because they swim slowly and float when dead, so whalers thought them the "right" whales to hunt — so right, that the Northern right whale has been hunted almost to extinction.

Whale, Killer

Range: Worldwide
Habitat: Cool oceans
The killer whale is the largest dolphin and one of the world's largest predators. It hunts mainly fish and squid but often hunts seals. It lives and hunts in family groups, communicating by sound.

Whale, Sperm

Range: Worldwide
Habitat: Warm oceans
The sperm whale is the largest of the toothed whales, with a fearsome jaw up to 16½ feet (5 m) long. The sperm whale is the world's largest predator. Its huge head is filled with a waxy substance called spermaceti that helps focus sound and control buoyancy.

Whale, Minke

Range: Worldwide
Habitat: Coastal waters
The minke whale is the smallest of the rorquals — whales, like the humpback and blue — that feed on plankton strained through the baleens in their mouths. The minke whale is typically 26–33 feet (8–10 m) long.

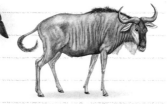

Wildebeest, Blue

Range: S. and E. Africa
Habitat: Savanna
This large cowlike antelope is Africa's most successful species. In the dry season huge herds migrate 940 miles (1,500 km) or more across the savanna in search of fresh grass and water — there are 1.5 million in Tanzania alone.

Wolf, Gray

Range: Eurasia, N. America
Habitat: Tundra, taiga, woodland, grassland
The gray wolf is the largest member of the dog family. Long persecuted, it now lives only in remote regions, especially dense forests. Gray wolves live in packs and work together when they hunt to bring down much bigger animals, such as caribou and moose.

Wolverine

Range: N. Eurasia, northern N. America
Habitat: Taiga, tundra
This heavily built creature, about the size of a small dog, is the largest of the weasel-like mustelids and is famed for its strength. It is so fierce that it can often drive even bears away from their kills. It is also famed for its appetite and is sometimes known as the "glutton." Wolverines often trek over 25 miles (40 km) in a day to find food.

Wombat, Common

Range: S.E. Australia, Tasmania
Habitat: Forest, scrub
Wombats are powerfully built marsupials that look and behave like badgers. They dig huge burrows where they rest during the day. At night they emerge to eat grass and other plants. Of the three species of wombat, the common wombat is the largest, weighing up to 77 pounds (35 kg).

Woodchuck

Range: Northern N. America
Habitat: Forest, farmland
The woodchuck, or groundhog, is a squirrel that can swim and climb trees, but lives in large underground dens where it hibernates all winter. Its emergence in spring is celebrated as Groundhog Day.

Yak, Wild

Range: Himalayas
Habitat: Mountains
With its thick, shaggy overcoat and warm, woolly undercoat, the yak is well suited to coping with icy conditions high in the Himalayas. It is also surprisingly sure-footed and grazes on slopes up to 20,000 feet (6,100 m), higher than any other large mammal.

Zebra, Grevy's

Range: N. Africa
Habitat: Savanna, semi-desert
Grevy's zebra is the largest of the zebras and able to live in drier places than the others. It grazes early in the morning and rests in the shade during the heat of the day.

Zorilla

Range: Africa south of the Sahara
Habitat: Savanna
The zorilla, or striped polecat, looks a little like a skunk and emits an equally foul smell from its anal glands when threatened. It hunts at night for rodents, reptiles, insects and birds' eggs.

REPTILES

UNLIKE mammals, reptiles are cold-blooded or "ectothermic" — that is, their temperature varies with their surroundings. Over 10,000 species of these scaly-skinned creatures are known, and live in all the world's warmer regions, on land, in the sea and in fresh water. The four main kinds are the crocodilians (crocodiles and alligators), squamata (lizards and snakes), turtles and the tuatara (a lizardlike New Zealand reptile).

Chameleon, Jackson's
Range: E. Africa
Habitat: Savanna trees
In common with all chameleons, Jackson's can change color to suit its background, and shoots out a sticky tongue as long as its body to catch insects. Unlike other chameleons, Jackson's chameleon has three horns on its head.

Adder, Saw-scaled
Range: N. Africa, S.W. Asia
Habitat: Desert, semiarid regions
The saw-scaled adder survives in some of the hottest places in the Sahara, using its potent venom to quickly kill its prey, which includes small rodents, skinks and geckos. Its bite is fatal to humans.

Anaconda
Range: Tropical S. America
Habitat: Swamps, rivers
The anaconda is one of the world's longest snakes, growing to more than 29 feet (9 m) long in the wild. It can climb trees, but spends most of its time lurking in murky water waiting for prey, such as capybaras and turtles. It is a constrictor, killing its victims by squeezing them in its coils.

Boa, Emerald tree
Range: S. America
Habitat: Rain forest
This boa lives in trees but catches much of its prey on the ground, dangling from a branch by its prehensile tail. It constricts its prey and swallows it while still dangling.

Chameleon, Meller's
Range: E. Africa
Habitat: Savanna trees
This is the largest chameleon in mainland Africa. Its body is covered in distinctive yellow stripes. Yet, despite its size and bold markings, it is very hard to spot, especially when it sways like a leaf in the breeze.

Agamid, Arabian toad-headed
Range: Middle East
Habitat: Desert
This is one of over 300 kinds of agamid lizard, which all have chisel-shaped heads and feed mainly on insects. The toad-headed agamid lives in burrows, but also buries itself in sand.

Anole, Green
Range: S.E. U.S.
Habitat: Woods, old buildings
The green anole changes color like a chameleon, depending on how warm it is, where it is and its mood. When a rival male approaches it turns from brown to green in seconds. It uses the pink flap under its chin to attract females.

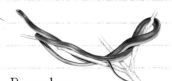

Boomslang
Range: Africa south of the Sahara
Habitat: Savanna
The boomslang snake is tree-dwelling and is easily mistaken by its prey — such as chameleons, frogs and birds — for a branch. It is one of Africa's most poisonous snakes.

Chuckwalla
Range: S.W. U.S.
Habitat: Rocky desert
The chuckwalla is a plant-eating desert lizard that hides in rocks during the night. When threatened it scurries into a rock crevice and gulps air so that it swells up and becomes wedged in place.

Alligator, American
Range: S.E. U.S.
Habitat: Rivers, swamps
The American alligator is one of the biggest reptiles in the Americas, growing up to 18 feet (5.5 m) long. It lives in rivers and swamps and eats anything from turtles to deer. In summer it often wallows in deep holes.

Boa constrictor
Range: C. and S. U.S.
Habitat: Rain forest, savanna
The boa constrictor is one of the world's biggest snakes, growing up to 18 feet (5.5 m) long. The boa catches its prey by lying in wait for victims to pass by, but it can go many weeks without eating. It swallows its victims whole.

Caiman, Spectacled
Range: C. America and Amazon basin
Habitat: Lakes, swamps
The spectacled caiman is the most common of the six species of caiman. It lives in Central America and the waters of the Amazon. Its name comes from the spectaclelike ridges between its eyes.

Cobra, Indian
Range: India, S.E. Asia
Habitat: Rain forest, farmland
The Indian or spectacled cobra is one of 12 species of Asian cobra. They are highly venomous snakes that eat rodents, lizards and frogs. They are also responsible for thousands of human deaths.

Cobra, King
Range: S. and S.E. Asia
Habitat: Forest
This is the world's largest venomous snake, growing 16 feet (4.9 m) or more long. It has very toxic venom that it uses to prey on other snakes. It lunges more than 6 feet (1.8 m) when it strikes.

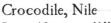

Crocodile, Nile
Range: Africa (except N.W.)
Habitat: Rivers, lakes, marshes
Like all crocodiles, the Nile preys on animals that come to the water's edge to drink, such as zebras. They seize their victim, drag it into the water, stun it with a blow from their powerful tail, then drown it.

Crocodile, Estuarine
Range: S.E. Asia, N. Australia
Habitat: Estuaries, mangrove swamps
The estuarine or saltwater crocodile is the world's biggest reptile, growing up to 19 feet (5.8 m) long. It is also the most dangerous. It is said to kill 1,000 people every year and can kill animals as big as buffaloes. The female lays 25–90 eggs in a mound of sand and leaves on land, and guards the eggs until they hatch.

Fer-de-lance
Range: C. and S. America
Habitat: Coastal lands
This is a large, poisonous snake of the pit viper family. Pit vipers have heat-sensitive pits between their eyes and nostrils that they use to track down warm-blooded creatures — mammals.

Crocodile, Mugger
Range: Indian subcontinent/Sri Lanka
Habitat: Marshes, lakes
The mugger crocodile is the most alligatorlike of all crocodiles, with a broad, heavy snout. One of the things that makes crocodiles different from alligators is that the fourth tooth of the lower jaw is visible when the mouth is shut.

Gavial
Range: N. India
Habitat: Rivers
The gavial or gharial is a crocodile with a long, thin snout, with 100 sharp teeth — perfect for catching fish and frogs underwater. When it catches a fish it flicks it in the air to turn it around so that it can swallow the fish head first.

Gecko, Giant leaf-tailed
Range: Madagascar
Habitat: Rain forest
This large gecko spends most of the day lying still, head down, on tree trunks where its mottled color and big, leaf-shaped tail make it very difficult to spot. If threatened it gapes its huge, flip-top mouth.

Gecko, Web-footed
Range: S. W. Africa
Habitat: Desert
This rare, desert-living gecko has webbed feet that act like snowshoes to stop it from sinking into soft sand. It digs a burrow in the sand, then sits waiting in the entrance to pounce on insects, such as termites.

Gila monster
Range: S.W. U.S., N. Mexico
Habitat: Desert
Named after the Gila river in Arizona, the Gila monster is one of only three venomous lizards in the world — the others are the beaded lizard of Mexico and Guatemala, and the Komodo dragon. Its tail acts as a food store for times when food is scarce.

Hawksbill
Range: Atlantic, Pacific and Indian oceans
Habitat: Coral reefs, tropical oceans
The hawksbill turtle has been hunted almost to extinction for its beautiful shell. Hunting is now widely banned, but the turtle is still in danger. It feeds on sponges.

Iguana, Common
Range: C. and S. America
Habitat: Forest trees near water
Iguanas are 35 or so species of lizards living mainly in the Americas. The common iguana is one of the biggest plant-eating reptiles, growing up to 6 feet (1.8 m) long. It spends most of its time basking in waterside trees, but can also swim.

Iguana, Marine
Range: Galapagos islands
Habitat: Lava rocks
The marine iguana is the only lizard that lives in the sea. It is a strong swimmer and dives for up to 20 minutes at a time as it searches for seaweed. It comes on land to incubate its eggs in the warm vents of volcanoes.

Iguana, Rhinoceros
Range: Haiti, Dominican Republic
Habitat: Scrub
Rhinoceros iguanas are large, heavily built lizards that get their name from the three or five hornlike scales on their noses. They live among thorn, manchineel and poisonwood trees.

Jungle runner
Range: C. and S. America, introduced Florida
Habitat: Forest clearings
This fast-moving, sun-loving lizard is often seen scooting across the ground as it forages for food, flicking out its long, forked tongue to take in insects.

Kingsnake, Scarlet
Range: S.E. U.S.
Habitat: Woodland

The scarlet kingsnake is the smallest of the very common American milk snake family. It is actually completely harmless, but looks similar to the deadly coral snake.

Komodo dragon

Range: Komodo and nearby islands
east of Java
Habitat: Grassland
The Komodo dragon is the world's biggest
lizard, up to 10 feet (3 m) long and strong
enough to bring down deer and wild boar.
Like all the monitor lizards, the Komodo
has strong legs and a long, forked tongue
which it uses to test the air for traces of
prey. There are about 5,000 left.

Lizard, Frilled

Range: Australia
Habitat: Rain forest, woodland
This lizard has a spectacular rufflike
collar of skin around its neck. The lizard
is actually harmless, but when threatened,
it opens up the ruff and gapes its bright
red mouth, then sways and hisses, making
it look far bigger and more dangerous
than it really is.

Matamata

Range: Amazon
Habitat: Creeks and lakes
The weird shape of the matamata helps
this turtle stay hidden among leaves on
the riverbed. When a fish comes close, it
opens its mouth wide so that water rushes
in, taking the fish along with it.

Racer, Northern black

Range: U.S.
Habitat: Woods, grassland, fields
Racers are long, fast-moving snakes. They
hunt with their heads held high for a better
view — then, when they spot prey, such as
frogs, lizards and mice, they make a quick
dash and bite their victim repeatedly.

Pond Slider

Range: S. U.S., C. America, Amazon
Habitat: Slow rivers, ponds
Pond sliders spend most of their lives
in water and are often seen basking
on floating logs. The young feed on
insects, snails and tadpoles, but adults
are omnivorous and will also eat plants.

Rattlesnake, Western diamondback

Range: S.W. U.S., Mexico
Habitat: Rocky canyons, hillsides
Rattlesnakes kill more people in the
United States than any other. Like all
rattlesnakes, this species has horny
tailpieces that it rattles when frightened.
It eats birds, small mammals and lizards.

Leatherback

Range: Worldwide
Habitat: Warm oceans
The leatherback is the world's largest
turtle, weighing 770 pounds (350 kg) and
growing up to 8 feet (2.4 m) long. It gets
its name from its shell, which is made from
a thick, leathery material as opposed to the
hard plates of other turtles. It is a strong
swimmer and can travel vast distances
across the ocean, often following jellyfish,
its main food.

Lizard, Mongolian agama

Range: China, Mongolia
Habitat: Desert
The Mongolian agama lizard is one of
over 300 plump-bodied lizards called
agamids. They nearly all have thin tails,
long legs and triangular heads with
chisel-shaped jaws. Like other desert
agamids, the Mongolian agama is a
burrowing creature, and spends the cold
winter asleep deep below ground.

Python, Carpet

Range: Australia, New Guinea
Habitat: Forest, savanna
Carpet pythons are the most widespread
of Australian pythons. The dark
carpetlike pattern on their bodies looks
like dead leaves, allowing them to lurk
almost invisibly among plant debris.

Sidewinder

Range: S.W. U.S., N.W. Mexico
Habitat: Desert
This poisonous snake has a unique way of
moving over sand. Instead of slithering, it
throws its body sideways, touching the
ground with only two small sections of its
body. This keeps the snake out of contact
with the hot sand and uses less energy.

Lizard, Desert night

Range: S.W. U.S.
Habitat: Desert
The desert night lizard lives in arid lands
in rock crevices or under plant debris. It
is often found near yucca plants and
agaves where it feeds on termites, ants,
beetles and flies. Despite its name, it hunts
from dawn to dusk.

Mamba, Eastern green

Range: Southern Africa
Habitat: Savanna, forest
Green mambas are extremely poisonous
snakes, but they are not usually aggressive
and tend to flee from danger. They spend
much of their lives in trees feeding on
birds and lizards. In the breeding season
males have ritual fights for females.

Python, Indian rock

Range: India
Habitat: Rain forest, mangroves
Rock pythons are huge snakes, up to 23
feet (7 m) long, that can easily kill a small
deer or a boar. They crush their prey in
their coils, then swallow it whole. They
are often used by Indian snake charmers.

Skink, Great Plains

Range: U.S., Mexico
Habitat: Prairie, woodland
Unusually for a lizard, the female Great
Plains skink is very maternal. She guards
her eggs carefully and turns them to warm
them evenly. She rubs her new hatchlings
into action and cares for them for 10 days.

Skink, Western blue-tongued
Range: S. Australia
Habitat: Desert
Blue-tongued skinks are large lizards with big heads, short tails and distinctive blue tongues. If threatened, they stick out their tongues and make a hissing noise. They eat insects, snails and berries.

Snake, Black rat
Range: N.E. U.S.
Habitat: Farmland, hardwood forest
These big snakes are powerful constrictors that prey on rats and squirrels. They are good climbers and are often found in barns and derelict buildings.

Snake, Egg-eating
Range: Africa south of the Sahara
Habitat: Savanna
This snake is one of the few snakes to feed entirely on birds' eggs. Its mouth can gape gigantically to swallow an egg whole. Inside its body, special backbones crush the shell, then the egg passes into the stomach and the shell pieces are regurgitated.

Snake, Northern water
Range: E. U.S.
Habitat: Ponds, lakes, rivers
Water snakes feed mainly on small fishes and frogs — though anglers often wrongly blame them for eating all the game fish. They can be seen basking on branches overhanging the water in spring or summer.

Slider, Red-eared
Range: S.E. U.S.
Habitat: Quiet waters
Red-eared sliders make popular pets and millions are raised each year on turtle farms. They do not actually have red ears, but a large red stripe behind each eye. Some red-eared sliders have lived to over 40 years of age in captivity.

Snake, Eastern coral
Range: S.E. U.S.
Habitat: Pine woods, lake edges
The eastern coral snake uses its powerful venom to paralyze the snakes it feeds on. Its stripes and coloration are much like the harmless scarlet snake's, but it has a black snout and red and yellow bands side by side.

Snake, Gopher
Range: W. U.S.
Habitat: Pine woods, prairie, scrub
Gopher snakes are large constrictor snakes that eat rats and mice. When the gopher is threatened it flattens its head, hisses loudly and shakes its tail like a rattlesnake — it then launches itself in a sudden attack on its enemy. In winter it often shares dens with rattlesnakes.

Snake, Paradise tree
Range: S.E. Asia
Habitat: Rain forest
The paradise tree snake is also known as the flying snake because of the way it glides through the air from tree to tree. It stretches out its body and glides down 66 feet (20 m) or more before landing gently.

Slow worm
Range: Europe, W. Asia, N. Africa
Habitat: Fields, scrub
The slow worm is a lizard with no legs that moves like a snake and can shed its tail if seized by an enemy. It feeds mainly on slugs and worms.

Snake, Smooth
Range: Eurasia
Habitat: Dry rocky areas, heathland
Often mistaken for vipers, smooth snakes are not actually venomous — they subdue their prey by surrounding it in their coils and then swallowing it alive. They like warm, shady areas under rocks.

Snake, Banded sea
Range: Indian Ocean, Pacific Ocean
Habitat: Tropical coastal waters
Sea snakes are related to cobras and one species has the most powerful poison of any snake, which it uses to kill fish. They have flat tails that work like paddles to help them swim.

Snake, Eastern hog-nosed
Range: E. U.S.
Habitat: Sandy areas, grassland, woodland
If in danger, the hog-nosed snake hisses, puffs itself up and flattens its head to scare its enemy. If this does not work, it rolls over, sticks out its tongue, convulses then plays dead.

Snake, Grass
Range: Europe, N. Asia, N. Africa
Habitat: Damp meadows, marshes
The grass snake is a good swimmer and feeds mainly on frogs, toads and fish, though it occasionally eats small mammals and birds. It typically swallows its prey alive. If caught in the open it remains completely still and pretends to be dead.

Snake, Spotted water
Range: N. Australia, S.E. Asia
Habitat: Fresh water
Like a number of snakes, spotted water snakes are well adapted to living in water. They have small, upward-pointing eyes and pads of skin to close off their nostrils when diving.

Tuatara

Range: New Zealand
Habitat: Woods

Tuatara are unique reptiles found only in New Zealand — the last survivors of an ancient group called rhynchocephalians (beak heads). Unusually, tuataras do not breed until they are at least 10 years old.

Tortoise, African pancake

Range: E. Africa
Habitat: Rocky outcrops

This tortoise gets its name from its shell, which is soft and flat. It does not retreat into its shell when threatened, but wedges itself into a rock crevice by inflating its lungs.

Turtle, Alligator snapping

Range: Mississippi Valley, U.S.
Habitat: Deep rivers, lakes

This is the largest freshwater turtle. It lurks on riverbeds with its mouth gaping to reveal a wiggling, pink appendage, which fish come to investigate. They are then snapped up by the turtle.

Turtle, Murray River

Range: S.E. Australia
Habitat: Rivers

Unusually, the shape of this turtle's carapace (shell) changes as it grows. When it hatches, the shell is round, then it grows at the back and finally becomes oval in adult turtles.

Turtle, Wood

Range: N.E. U.S., Great Lakes
Habitat: Woods, meadows, marshes

The wood turtle spends most of its life on land and is a good climber, feeding on fruit, worms, slugs and insects. It is a popular pet but has been hunted so much that it is now rare in the wild.

Snake, Western blind

Range: S.W. U.S.
Habitat: Desert

This snake looks a little like an earthworm. It has black spots where its eyes should be, but it is actually totally blind. It tracks ants and termites by following their scent trails.

Tortoise, Spur-thighed

Range: N. Africa, S. Europe, S.W. Asia
Habitat: Meadows

The spur-thighed tortoise has large spurs on its thighs, but otherwise is very similar to the highly domed Hermann's tortoise of southeastern Europe, for which it is often mistaken.

Soft-shell, Spiny

Range: N. America
Habitat: Rivers, creeks, ponds

Unlike other turtles, soft-shells have shells of skin rather than horny plates. Spiny soft-shells are great swimmers that can make a fast getaway if threatened when basking on a sand bar.

Turtle, Eastern box

Range: E. U.S.
Habitat: Forest

Box turtles get their name because their plastron (underside) is hinged, so they can fold up into a box shape to protect themselves from predators. The eastern box feeds on worms, slugs, mushrooms and fruit. In hot summers, it may bury itself in muddy pools to keep cool.

Viper, Common

Range: Eurasia
Habitat: Moors, heaths, scrub

Known in Britain as adders, vipers are venomous snakes, but they are very timid and rarely bite humans. They hibernate in winter but emerge only when it gets warmer than 46°F (8°C).

Terrapin, River

Range: S.E. Asia
Habitat: Tidal rivers

Also known as the batagur, this is a plant-eating turtle that nests on sand banks where it lays 50 eggs at a time. People have dug up so many of its eggs for food that it is now quite rare.

Tortoise, Galapagos giant

Range: Galapagos islands
Habitat: Varied

The Galapagos giant tortoise is the biggest of all tortoises, weighing up to 770 pounds (350 kg). It lives on land and feeds on almost any plant, especially cacti. It can live for over 100 years, but in the past many were killed by sailors for food. At least 13 subspecies of giant tortoise have evolved on the islands of the Galapagos group. The subspecies vary in size, length and shape of the carapace (shell).

Turtle, Loggerhead

Range: Pacific, Indian, Atlantic oceans
Habitat: Coastal waters and ocean

In the summer breeding season the female loggerhead comes ashore at night and digs her nest at the foot of sand dunes, laying up to five clutches, each of about 100 eggs. Sadly, numbers of loggerheads have been reduced by coastal development and fishing nets.

Viper, Gaboon

Range: W. C. and S.E. Africa
Habitat: Rain forest, woodland

The two species of gaboon viper are among the largest vipers, growing up to 6 feet (1.8 m) long. They are slow moving and often lie in wait for their prey, which include rats, squirrels and even small antelopes.

AMPHIBIANS

LIKE reptiles, amphibians are cold-blooded, but have no scales, and their skin is kept moist by secretions from mucus glands. Most amphibians begin life in water, or in a fluid-filled egg sac, and have gills to help them breathe in water. As they develop, they leave the water and spend their adult lives on land. Most of the 7,650 species live in the tropics, and there are three main kinds: frogs and toads (6,740 species), newts and salamanders (700) and caecilians (200).

Frog, Glass

Range: Northern S. America
Habitat: Rain forest
Glass frogs get their name because most have semitransparent skin on the underside, making their internal organs clearly visible. They spend their lives in trees and are great climbers. They lay their eggs on leaves above pools and streams, so that the tadpoles can drop into the water as they hatch and burrow into the mud on the stream bed.

Axolotl

Range: Lake Xochimilco, Mexico
Habitat: Mountain lakes
Axolotl is Aztec for "water monster." Uniquely, this salamander never fully grows. Although it grows four legs, it remains a tadpole all its life, even breeding in this state.

Eel, Congo two-toed

Range: S.E. U.S.
Habitat: Swamps, bayous
Congo eels look like eels but are salamanders and live in the southeast United States, not the Congo. The two-toed Congo eel has tiny, useless legs with two toes.

Frog, Corroboree

Range: New South Wales (Australia)
Habitat: Mountains, marshes
With its striking yellow and black markings, the corroboree frog is instantly recognizable, but there are now fewer than 300 of them left in their habitat in the Snowy Mountains.

Frog, Golden poison arrow

Range: C. and S. America
Habitat: Rain forest
There are about 100 species of poison arrow frogs, most of which are brilliantly colored like the golden poison arrow frog. Glands on their skin contain deadly poisons used by forest peoples to tip their arrows for hunting. The brilliant colors warn predators that they are poisonous, so that they can feed in broad daylight.

Bullfrog

Range: N. America, Mexico
Habitat: Lakes, ponds, slow streams
As big as a young rabbit, the bullfrog is an awesome predator, snapping up other frogs, small snakes, fish and even songbirds. Its call is a grumbling, throaty croak.

Ensatina

Range: Western N. America
Habitat: Forests, under logs and rocks
Ensatinas are a varied group of small salamanders. One feature they all share is a narrow base to their tails. If the tail snaps off when escaping a predator, it grows back after two years.

Frog, Darwin's

Range: Southern S. America
Habitat: Cold streams in forests
Unusually, the eggs of the Darwin's frog are cared for by the male. After the female lays the eggs, the male gulps in a dozen or so and keeps them safe in the croaking sac in his throat until they hatch.

Frog, Horned

Range: Northern S. America
Habitat: Rain forest
The Amazonian horned frog has a plump body that is as wide as it is long. It cannot move very fast, so hides in leaf litter on the forest floor until its prey passes by. Its mouth is so large that it can catch animals that are almost as big as itself, such as small frogs and rodents. The "horns" are projections on its eyelids.

Caecilian, South American

Range: S. America
Habitat: Usually forest
Caecilians look like earthworms, but they are actually amphibians. Most live in soft soil in rain forests and tunnel through the soil feeding on worms, insects, and centipedes.

Frog, Common

Range: N. Europe, W. Asia
Habitat: Moist areas near ponds
The common frog lives mostly on land, but in spring returns to ponds to mate. Each female lays 3–4,000 jelly-coated eggs that float in the ponds in large masses called frogspawn.

Frog, European green tree

Range: Europe, W. Asia
Habitat: Trees, bushes near lakes
The European green tree frog is one of the few tree frogs that live outside the tropics. It is a great climber with sticky pads on its toes for clinging onto trees. It feeds mainly on insects.

Frog, Marsh
Range: Europe, W. Asia
Habitat: Freshwater
The marsh frog is bright green and often quite conspicuous, sitting on lily pads and croaking very loudly. Males are particularly loud in the breeding season in spring. It feeds mainly on invertebrates, but also small birds.

Frog, Marsupial
Range: Central Andes
Habitat: Forest
The marsupial frog gets its name because the female has a pouch on her back into which the male packs her eggs after she has laid them. When the eggs hatch into tadpoles she uses her toe to release them into the water.

Frog, Northern leopard
Range: N. America
Habitat: Varied including wet meadows
Leopard frogs get their name from the bold black spots all over their backs. They are very adaptable creatures and will live in almost any kind of place near water.

Frog, South African rain
Range: Southern Africa
Habitat: Savanna
This very plump frog gets its name from its habit of hunting for insects during rainstorms. Otherwise the frog spends most of its time in underground burrows, digging with its back feet.

Frog, Termite
Range: Southern Africa
Habitat: Savanna
The striking colors of the termite frog indicate to potential predators that it has a foul-tasting skin. As its name implies, it feeds mainly on termites and ants. To get at its prey it may often clamber up tree stumps and rocks, or burrow into the ground. It breeds in shallow pools, attaching its jelly-coated eggs to plants.

Frog, Wallace's flying
Range: S.E. Asia
Habitat: Rain forest
Flying frogs do not really fly, but glide huge distances from tree to tree. The huge webs between their toes and fingers act like wings to keep them in the air and allow them to glide gently down to another branch. Flying frogs are thought to lay their eggs in nests of foam, high in the trees.

Hellbender
Range: Eastern U.S.
Habitat: Rocky-bottomed streams
Up to 30 inches (80 cm) long, the hellbender is one of the world's largest salamanders and often scares fishermen who see it lurking on stream beds. It is feared poisonous, but is actually completely harmless and feeds on crayfish and snails.

Mudpuppy
Range: Central N. America
Habitat: Lakes, rivers, streams
Mudpuppies are nocturnal hunters that crawl through muddy shallows in search of crayfish. They have huge, feathery gills to help them breathe underwater — the muddier the water, the bigger the gills.

Newt, Eastern
Range: Eastern N. America
Habitat: Ponds (adults), moist leaves (efts)
Eastern newts begin life in water before spending up to seven years on land as brightly colored red "efts" (adolescents). They then return to the water to become mature adults.

Newt, Warty
Range: Europe
Habitat: Still water
The male warty, or great crested, newt develops a long crest down its back during the breeding season, perhaps to impress the larger female. He usually performs a vigorous mating dance for the female then deposits his sperm for her to walk over.

Olm
Range: Southern Europe
Habitat: Water in caves
The olm is one of the few amphibians completely adapted to life in water and retains its feathery gills throughout its life. It lives in total darkness in its cave home and is virtually blind.

Salamander, Californian slender
Range: California, S.W. Oregon
Habitat: Redwood forest, grassland
With its long, slender body, the Californian slender salamander can hide easily in rotting logs and under leaf litter. It moves almost like a snake, curving its body from side to side.

Salamander, Fire
Range: W. Eurasia, N. Africa
Habitat: Woodland
The striking coloring of the fire salamander is a warning to predators that it is poisonous. It lives in forests and emerges at night, often after rain, to hunt for earthworms.

Salamander, Red
Range: E. U.S.
Habitat: Springs and streams
The red salamander reaches its most brilliant red when about two years old and then fades gradually. Like some other salamanders, it has no lungs but breathes through its skin.

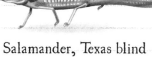

Salamander, Spotted
Range: S. Canada, E. U.S.
Habitat: Hardwood forest
Spotted salamanders spend most of their life underground, feeding on slugs and worms, but in early spring heavy rains encourage them to gather around breeding ponds where they mate and lay eggs in the water.

Salamander, Texas blind
Range: Texas, U.S.
Habitat: Cavewater
The Texas blind is a rare salamander that lives in water in caves. Its very pale pink body, tiny eyes and feathery gills are perfectly adapted for this dark underwater habitat.

Salamander, Tiger
Range: N. America, Mexico
Habitat: Dry plains, damp meadows
The tiger salamander is the world's biggest land salamander, up to 16 inches (41 cm) long, with a stout body, broad head and small eyes. It lives near water among plant debris.

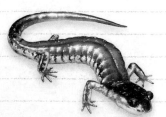

Salamander, Yonahlossee
Range: Blue Ridge Mountains, U.S.
Habitat: Wooded hillsides
The yonahlossee is a striking-looking salamander with a red back. It got its name from the place it was discovered — Yonahlossee Road on Grandfather Mountain, North Carolina.

Siren, Greater
Range: S.E. U.S.
Habitat: Shallow freshwater
The siren looks like an eel with its long, thin body and tiny front legs, but it is in fact a kind of salamander that retains its tadpole gills all its life.

Spring peeper
Range: Eastern N. America
Habitat: Ponds and swamps
Spring peepers get their name from their call, often heard early in spring in New England when they move to ponds where the ice has cleared. They are agile frogs that can jump 17 times their own height.

Toad, African clawed
Range: South Africa
Habitat: Ponds and lakes
The African clawed toad spends its entire life in water, with its eyes and nostrils above the surface. It is an extraordinary swimmer, able to dart through the water as fast as any fish and even swim backward. Its fingers are tipped with claws.

Toad, American
Range: Eastern N. America
Habitat: Woodland, gardens, parks
Easily recognized by the line running down its back, this toad is covered in warts. It rests during the day, but it can often be heard trilling when it is active at night, hunting for insects and other small invertebrates. These toads breed in ponds and streams in spring, with the females laying up to 8,000 eggs.

Toad, Common
Range: N. Eurasia, N. Africa
Habitat: Varied, usually dry
The common toad is one of the largest European toads. Like most toads, it has a warty skin and short back legs and hides away during the day. In cold places it hibernates in winter, then congregates to breed in spring.

Toad, Giant
Range: C. and S. America, introduced Australia
Habitat: Varied, near pools
Also called the cane toad, the giant toad is the world's largest, often weighing up to 3 pounds (1.4 kg). Introduced to Australia to control beetles, it has become a serious pest.

Toad, Midwife
Range: W. Europe
Habitat: Woodlands
The midwife toad gets its name because after the female has laid her eggs in long strings, the male wraps them around his back legs. He then carries the eggs for a month or more, helping to protect them from predators until they hatch.

Toad, Natterjack
Range: Europe
Habitat: Sandy places
The natterjack toad has an incredibly loud call that sounds like a machine and carries well over a mile (1.6 km). It usually lives near the sea and may even breed in saltwater.

Toad, Oriental fire-bellied
Range: Russia, China
Habitat: Mountain streams, rice fields
From above, the fire-bellied toad is a dull green, but when frightened it rears up, flashing a startling scarlet and black belly. It lives mostly in ditches and streams and can often be seen floating on the water surface.

Toad, Western spadefoot
Range: Great Plains, U.S.
Habitat: Dry grassland
The spadefoot toad gets its name from its broad back feet, which it uses like shovels to dig into sandy ground. It likes dry, sandy soil, but, if it rains, it crawls out on to the surface to mate and lay its eggs in rain pools where they hatch two days later.

BIRDS

FROM soaring condors to swooping swallows, most birds are masters of the air, flying as easily as fish swim in the sea. Yet it is not flight that makes birds unique, but their coat of feathers. Not all birds can fly, but all have feathers. There are some 9,000 species of bird, from tiny hummingbirds to huge ostriches, and they live in virtually every habitat open to the sky, from Antarctica to the Sahara.

Blackbird, Red-winged
Range: N. and C. America
Habitat: Marshes, fields
In recent years, the red-winged blackbird population has exploded and they are now perhaps the most numerous North American birds. After breeding, males gather into flocks a million or more strong.

Albatross, Wandering
Range: Southern oceans
Habitat: Oceans
The wandering albatross has the biggest wings of any bird, with a span of up to 11 feet (3.4 m). On these giant wings it can glide for weeks at a time over the ocean.

Anhinga
Range: S. U.S. to Argentina
Habitat: Lakes, rivers
The anhinga is a cormorantlike bird that dives deep after fish, paddling with its feet, ready to dart down and impale prey on its sharp beak.

Avocet, Pied
Range: Breeds Eurasia; winters Africa
Habitat: Mudflats
Unlike other shorebirds, avocets do not probe for food in the mud. Instead they stride through the shallows, sweeping their bills from side to side to find insects.

Barbet, Double-toothed
Range: E. Africa
Habitat: Savanna
Barbets are brightly colored birds with big beaks. They are related to woodpeckers and toucans and feed on fruit, especially figs and bananas.

Bee-eater, European
Range: Breeds W. Eurasia; winters Africa and Middle East
Habitat: Open woodland
Bee-eaters prey mostly on bees and wasps, which they seize nimbly in the air with their long, downward-curving bills. They then rub the insect on a branch to remove its sting.

Bird of paradise, Blue
Range: New Guinea
Habitat: Mountain forest
The beautiful male blue bird of paradise performs a spectacular display to court the much plainer female, hanging upside down from a branch and flashing open its blue plumes.

Bird of paradise, Raggiana
Range: New Guinea
Habitat: Rain forest
If anything, the male raggiana bird of paradise is even more spectacular than the blue, with its yellow head and crimson tail, which it shows off in the breeding season by posing in treetops to the much drabber female.

Bird of paradise, Ribbon-tailed
Range: New Guinea
Habitat: Mountain forest
The male ribbon-tailed bird of paradise has brilliantly colored green feathers around its head and incredibly long, ribbonlike tail feathers, nearly 3 feet (1 m) long, which it swishes to impress females.

Bird of paradise, Wilson's
Range: New Guinea
Habitat: Rain forest
Birds of paradise got their name because, when Europeans first saw their feathers 500 years ago, they thought they came from paradise. Like all birds of paradise, Wilson's feeds mainly on fruit, but also catches insects.

Bluebird, Asian fairy
Range: India to S.E. U.S.
Habitat: Hill forest
Fairy bluebirds are brilliantly colored birds that spend most of their time high up in the branches of evergreen coral trees. Their fluting calls and their bustling search for fruit are commonplace in East Asian woods.

Bobwhite, Northern
Range: S.E. U.S.
Habitat: Fields, farmland, scrub
The name bobwhite comes from the sound of the male's call during the mating season. For most of the year bobwhites move around in flocks of 30 or so birds, then in spring flocks break up and the birds pair for mating.

Bowerbird, Satin
Range: E. Australia
Habitat: Forest
Male bowerbirds make "bowers" to attract a mate. Some bowerbirds build rings or thatched huts. The satin makes an avenue of sticks that it paints with fruit and saliva.

Budgerigar
Range: Australia, introduced U.S.
Habitat: Scrub
Now very popular as a cage bird in various colors, the budgerigar is a small, green parrot in the wild. It is active early in the morning and late in the afternoon when flocks of the birds scour the ground for grass seeds.

Bulbul, Red-whiskered
Range: S. Asia, introduced U.S., Australia
Habitat: Scrub
Bulbuls are noisy tropical birds that feed on fruit, berries and nectar. Red-whiskered bulbuls are considered pests.

Bunting, Snow
Range: Arctic
Habitat: Tundra
The snow bunting is the most northerly breeding bird. In its white breeding plumage the male perfectly matches his snowy habitat. To escape the cold, these plump little birds sometimes burrow beneath the snow.

Bustard, Great
Range: N. Eurasia
Habitat: Steppe
This is the world's heaviest flying bird. Outside the breeding season, bustards move around in large flocks searching for seasonally available food.

Buzzard
Range: Europe, Asia, E. Africa
Habitat: Woodland, moorland
The buzzard sometimes hunts by watching from a treetop perch, but more often it soars over woodland edges scanning the ground for small mammals, dropping down swiftly on to its victim. In winter, the buzzard may feed on carrion.

Capercaillie, Western
Range: N. Europe
Habitat: Pine and oak forest
This turkeylike bird is the biggest of all grouse and is renowned for its leks (courtship displays), when the male's calls echo through the forest. It feeds on pine seeds in winter and leaves and fruit in summer.

Cardinal, Northern
Range: E. U.S.
Habitat: Woodland, gardens, shrubbery
Cardinals get their names from the red robes worn by Roman Catholic cardinals. Their range is extending farther north, perhaps due to global warming and they now winter as far north as Maine.

Cassowary
Range: New Guinea, N. Australia
Habitat: Rain forest
Cassowaries are large, flightless birds with a big, bony shield, or casque, on their heads — thought to help them break through the undergrowth as they search for fallen fruit.

Chickadee, Black-capped
Range: N. America
Habitat: Forest, gardens
The black-capped chickadee is a small bird with thick, fluffy feathers that help it cope with the winter cold as far north as Alaska. In winter it feeds mainly on seeds and berries.

Chicken, Greater prairie
Range: Great Plains, U.S.
Habitat: Grassland
As its habitat has shrunk, the once abundant prairie chicken — famous for the male's spring courtship — has become increasingly rare.

Cock-of-the-rock, Andean
Range: Andes
Habitat: Forest gorges
Cock-of-the-rocks are brilliantly colored birds that move in swift, weaving flights through rain forest gorges. Females build the nest alone on sheer cliff faces.

Cockatoo, Sulfur-crested
Range: New Guinea, Australia
Habitat: Rain forest
These noisy parrots gather in huge flocks for most of the year to feed on seeds, fruits and insects. Sulfur-crested cockatoos make popular pets because they mimic human speech remarkably well.

Courser
Range: Africa, India, Australia
Habitat: Desert, semidesert
Coursers are a group of nine species of desert bird found in Africa, India and Australia. They are strong fliers, but they are more often seen chasing the insects they catch by sprinting along the ground, or resting between bursts of running. The picture shows the cream-colored courser of Africa.

Crane, Common
Range: Breeds N. Eurasia; winters S. Eurasia and N. Africa
Habitat: Breeds forest swamps; winters wetlands
Cranes are long-legged birds, famous for their dancing displays, when they walk in circles, bowing, bobbing and tossing things over their heads.

Crane, Whooping
Range: Breeds Canada; winters Texas
Habitat: Breeds prairie pools; winters coastal marshes
One of the world's rarest birds, with fewer than 400 remaining in the wild, whooping cranes are opportunist feeders that feed on a wide range of plant and animal food in shallow water and on land.

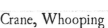

Crow, American
Range: N. America
Habitat: Varied
The adaptable American crow lives almost anywhere and feeds on almost anything. To confuse predators, males often build decoy nests.

Cuckoo, Common
Range: Breeds Eurasia; winters Africa
Habitat: Farmland, heath
The cuckoo returns to the north in late March and the loud breeding call of the male is traditionally taken as the first sign that summer is on its way. Cuckoos are renowned for laying their eggs in the nests of other birds, such as pipits and warblers. The cuckoo chick pushes the other eggs out of the nest and is then fed by its foster parents.

Curassow, Great
Range: C. America
Habitat: Forest, scrub
Curassows are the only game birds to nest in trees. Although they feed on the ground on leaves and fruit, they quickly fly up into the branches if disturbed.

Curlew, Eskimo
Range: Breeds Canada; winters S. America
Habitat: Breeds tundra, winters pampas
Huge flocks of these birds were once seen on their migrations, but so many millions have been shot that they are now very rare.

Dipper, North American
Range: N. America
Habitat: Upland streams
This little bird can often be seen dipping its head into mountain streams to snatch insects and other small creatures from the stream bed. A special membrane shields its eyes from the water.

Diver, Red-throated
Range: N. America, N. Eurasia
Habitat: Tundra, taiga, arctic waters
Divers are superb swimmers with streamlined bodies and strong webbed feet that can propel them down to 250 feet (75 m). Dense plumage keeps them warm in icy arctic waters.

Dove, Collared
Range: Eurasia
Habitat: Farmland
The collared dove is a very common bird that lives close to human habitation. It often feeds on scraps put out by humans as well as its natural diet of seeds and berries.

Dove, Mourning
Range: N. and C. America
Habitat: Dry grassland, desert
The mourning dove gets its name from its mournful call; and its wings make a distinctive whistling when the bird takes to the air. Adults feed their young by coughing up partially digested food, which is called pigeon milk.

Dovekie
Range: Arctic, N. Atlantic
Habitat: Cold oceans
Also known as the little auk, this seabird breeds in vast colonies among the rocks on Arctic shores, where the chicks are constantly preyed upon by glaucous gulls. The dovekie can fly and swim well and feeds on fish.

Duck, Mallard
Range: N. America, N. Eurasia
Habitat: Wide range of waters
Mallards are dabbling ducks that feed by upending in ponds, lakes and rivers to sift plant matter and invertebrates from the water. The colorful males are called drakes.

Duck, Mandarin
Range: E. Eurasia, introduced Europe
Habitat: Forest rivers, lakes
Long celebrated in Asian art, male mandarin ducks have orange wing feathers that they display like a pair of sails in the breeding season. Mandarins are most active at dawn and dusk, feeding on plant food and on insects, snails, and small fish.

Eagle, Bald
Range: N. America
Habitat: Lakes, rivers, coasts
The United States' national symbol, the bald eagle is one of the world's largest birds of prey, up to 3 feet (1 m) long. Hunting and poisoning from DDT pesticide reduced numbers to below 2,000, but the bird is now protected and there are approximately 300,000 remaining today.

Eagle, Crested serpent
Range: India, S.E. Asia
Habitat: Forest, savanna
This eagle can be hard to spot in the rain forest, except when it is soaring high above the trees. Like other serpent or snake eagles it preys mostly on snakes and watches for its quarry by perching in a tree, then dropping down suddenly and gripping the snake with its talons.

Eagle, Golden
Range: Eurasia, N. America, N. Africa
Habitat: Mountains, plains, coasts
One of the most magnificent birds of prey, the golden eagle is a superb flier. It preys on rabbits, marmots and other mammals, making a fast, low-level attack, then pouncing. Golden eagles nest on crags or in trees where they make a large platform, or aerie, from sticks. They are now rare in most places.

Egret, Great

Range: Worldwide

Habitat: Freshwater wetland

Also known as the American egret, the great egret belongs to the heron family and, like all herons, has a long neck and a powerful bill, which it uses for stabbing fish. It hunts by standing in wait in the water or by slowly stalking its prey. In the 19th century millions were killed for hat feathers, but they remain widespread.

Eider, Common

Range: N. America, N. Eurasia, Arctic

Habitat: Coastal waters

Eider ducks have very warm plumage to keep out the Arctic chill and people have long valued the down feathers for quilts. The female plucks these feathers from her breast to line the nest.

Emu

Range: Australia

Habitat: Bush

The emu is the world's second-largest bird after the ostrich. It is completely flightless and walks far through the bush searching for food, often up to 600 miles (1,000 km) a year.

Falcon, Peregrine

Range: Worldwide except for Sahara, C. Asia, S. America

Habitat: Mountains, sea cliffs

To catch birds in flight, falcons climb high then dive, or stoop, on their target at speeds of 125 miles per hour (200 kmph).

Finch, Blue-faced parrot

Range: Australasia

Habitat: Rain forest

Parrot finches are grass finches unrelated to the finches of the northern hemisphere. They feed on seeds in bushes, alone or in pairs.

Finch, Purple

Range: N. America

Habitat: Woodland

Outside the breeding season purple finches feed together on seeds in large flocks. In the breeding season the male dances around the female, beating his wings and singing a warbling song.

Finch, Zebra

Range: Australia and islands

Habitat: Woodland, scrub

The zebra finch is largely sedentary, moving only to find seeds on the ground. Like most grass finches, it builds a domed nest of grass and twigs.

Flamingo

Range: S. Eurasia, Africa, C. America, Caribbean

Habitat: Lagoons, lakes

The flamingo is a tall, startlingly pink bird that swims and flies well. Huge colonies are often seen as a pink mass on lagoons and lakes. It feeds on mollusks that, uniquely for a bird, it filters from the water in the same way as a baleen whale.

Flycatcher, Royal

Range: C. and S. America

Habitat: Rain forest, cloud forest

The royal flycatcher has a dull brown body, but the male has a brilliant crimson crest of feathers that it flashes up like a fan when courting. Like all flycatchers, it snaps up flies in the air.

Frigate bird, Great

Range: Indian and Pacific oceans

Habitat: Warm oceans

Frigate birds are wonderful fliers, with a wingspan of almost 6½ feet (2 m). But they are also the criminals of the seabird world, often attacking other birds and stealing their catch.

Gannet

Range: N. Atlantic

Habitat: Oceans

Gannets are superb divers. When they spot a fish in the water they dive from at least 100 feet (30 m), folding back their wings just as they plunge into the water. Their strong skulls protect them from the impact.

Goldeneye, Common

Range: N. America

Habitat: Lakes in summer; coastal bays in winter

The goldeneye duck is also known as the whistler because of the whistling sound made by its wings as it flies.

Goldfinch, American

Range: N. America

Habitat: Woodland, fields

These little finches can often be seen feeding in flocks on roadside thistles, taking off and swirling around every time a vehicle passes by. Their nests are lined with milkweed fluff and thistledown.

Goose, Canada

Range: Arctic, N. America, introduced Europe

Habitat: Wetland

Canada geese breed in the north and migrate south in fall, following the same route year after year. They graze on water and land plants.

Goshawk, Pale chanting

Range: S. Africa
Habitat: Desert, semidesert
This small goshawk is often seen in the Namib Desert perching on a tree — or even walking about on the ground, looking very much like a secretary bird. Indeed, it spends far more time on the ground than any other hawk — perhaps to save energy — and often runs after prey at great speed.

Grebe, Great crested

Range: Europe, S. Eurasia, S. Africa, Australia
Habitat: Still freshwater
Few birds have more elaborate courtships than this grebe. Both male and female have dark head plumes that they fan out during their "weed dance." In the dance, pairs shake, dive and rise from the water breast to breast to present each other with weeds.

Grebe, Pied-billed

Range: N. and S. America
Habitat: Marshes and ponds
The pied-billed grebe is a waterbird that can dive so fast it is nicknamed "hell diver." To escape predators it can sink into the water so that only its bill — and its nostrils — are above water.

Grosbeak, Pine

Range: N. America, N. Eurasia
Habitat: Coniferous forest
The pine grosbeak is a large finch that feeds mainly on berries and buds. The most northerly grosbeaks migrate south and west for winter, often in large numbers; more southerly birds stay put.

Grouse, Black

Range: N. Eurasia
Habitat: Moor, forest
Black grouse are famous for their courting displays during which the males jump around looking threatening, while the females strut nonchalantly between them.

Gull, Great black-backed

Range: N. Atlantic coasts
Habitat: Coasts, locally inland
The great black-backed gull is a strongly built aggressive bird with a hook-tipped bill. It feeds on anything from crabs and fish to small birds, such as puffins and mammals, such as mice and voles.

Gull, Herring

Range: N. hemisphere beyond tropics
Habitat: Coastal, inland
The herring gull's natural food is rarely herrings — more often shrimps, prawns and crabs. It has also learned to scavenge rubbish dumps and is now well established in many towns.

Harrier, Pallid

Range: Europe, C. Asia
Habitat: Plains, bogs, moorland
Slender, long-winged pallid and pied harriers are birds of prey that nest on the ground or in bushes. They catch birds, lizards and small mammals such as jerboas, by swooping low over the ground. The Gobi winter is too cold for the harriers, so they migrate to India by fall.

Hawk, Red-tailed

Range: N. and C. America, Caribbean
Habitat: Varied, typically near trees
The red-tailed hawk is able to live anywhere from deserts to alpine meadows. It is a versatile hunter, catching a wide range of prey, including rabbits, snakes and lizards. It sometimes swoops down from a high perch, but it can also chase prey at low levels, or hover in the air.

Heron, Great blue

Range: N. and S. America
Habitat: Rivers, marshes, swamps
The largest of the American herons, the great blue is a fearsome hunter. It stands still as a statue in shallow water, watching for fish or frogs. When it sees a target it makes a lightning strike with its sharp bill. Occasionally it hunts actively, running through the water and flicking its wings. It nests in colonies high up in trees.

Hoatzin

Range: Amazon and Orinoco
Habitat: Rain forest
With its long neck and spiky crest, the hoatzin is an odd-looking bird that clambers clumsily through the trees, occasionally flapping its wings. Nestlings have claws on their wings that they use to cling onto twigs as they explore. These claws are reminiscent of the earliest known bird, Archaeopteryx. If threatened, hoatzin chicks drop into water and climb out when danger has past. Adults loaf in trees and feed on leaves.

Honeycreeper, Purple

Range: Trinidad, tropical S. America
Habitat: Rain forest
Honeycreepers feed on fruit, especially bananas, but they also suck nectar from rain forest flowers through their long, curved bills. The male purple honeycreeper is a brilliant violet color, while the female is a deep green. The female builds a neat cup-shaped nest in a tree.

Hoopoe

Range: Eurasia, Africa
Habitat: Woodland, grassland
The hoopoe is notorious for the horrible smell of its nest in holes in trees and walls. The smell is thought to deter predators, but it remains a favorite prey of falcons.

Hornbill, Great Indian

Range: S. Asia
Habitat: Tropical Rain forest
The great Indian is a large hornbill and the casque, or ridge, on its bill amplifies its loud, honking calls. In flight, its wing beats swish so loudly they can be heard more than half a mile (800 m) away. It lives in the rain forest canopy, feeding mainly on fruit.

Hornbill, Southern ground

Range: Southern Africa
Habitat: Savanna
Unlike other hornbills, the large southern ground hornbill lives mostly on the ground and feeds on small animals rather than fruit. It typically catches small animals while walking around its territory.

Hornero, Rufous

Range: S. America
Habitat: Trees
The rufous hornero gets its name from its extraordinary nests, built out of wet mud and straw. Hornero is Spanish for baker and the nest looks like an old-fashioned baker's oven.

Hummingbird, Bee

Range: Cuba
Habitat: Forest
Hummingbirds are tiny, jewellike birds that feed on nectar, hovering in front of flowers as they feed. The bee hummingbird is the tiniest bird in the world, no bigger than a human thumb.

Hummingbird, Ruby-throated

Range: Breeds N. America; winters C. America
Habitat: Woodland
This tiny, dazzlingly colored hummingbird can fly more than 500 miles (800 km) over the Gulf of Mexico when it migrates.

Hummingbird, Sword-billed

Range: Andes mountain range
Habitat: Shrubby slopes
This hummingbird has the longest bill of any bird relative to its body, enabling it to probe into the deepest flowers. When it perches it holds its bill vertically.

Ibis, Glossy

Range: S. Eurasia, Africa, Australia, Caribbean
Habitat: Marshes, lakes
The beautiful glossy ibis is the most widespread of the ibises, living on lakes right around the world, often in large colonies. It eats insects and water creatures that it picks from the mud with its long bill.

Ibis, Hermit

Range: Morocco, Turkey
Habitat: Mountains, deserts
The hermit ibis, also known as the northern bald ibis or waldrapp, was once widespread through southern Europe and the Middle East. Now, perhaps because of changes in the climate, it has become very rare and breeds only in Morocco and Turkey.

Jacamar, Rufous-tailed

Range: C. and S. America
Habitat: Rain forest
Jacamars are 17 species of brilliantly colored birds that perch on twigs waiting for insects. The rufous-tailed jacamar typically lives in pairs or family groups and its mournful call can often be heard echoing through the rain forest. The female jacamar digs a breeding tunnel where it lays and hatches its eggs.

Jacana

Range: S. U.S., C. America
Habitat: Vegetated freshwater
The eight species of jacana have toes so long that they spread their weight as they walk, so they can seemingly walk on water, treading on the leaves of water lilies. This is why they are also called "lily trotters."

Jay, Blue

Range: Eastern N. America
Habitat: Woods, parks
The blue jay is often seen in gardens gathering seeds and nuts. It sometimes buries hoards to tide it over the winter. Even so, many blue jays from the north fly south for the winter. The blue jay also feeds on insects. When there are population explosions of moth caterpillars, it eats very well.

Jungle fowl

Range: S.E. Asia
Habitat: Forest
The ancestor of the domestic chicken, the jungle fowl lives on the edge of forests where it finds seeds and insects by scratching with its feet. Like cockerels, male jungle fowl make a noisy, crowing sound. They usually breed in the dry season from March to May.

Kestrel, Common

Range: Eurasia, Africa
Habitat: Open country, fields
Kestrels are small falcons that hunt rodents and insects. They have very acute eyesight and hover over open ground, watching with their wings beating. When prey is targeted they drop down gently on it. They need a head wind to hover, but they are among the biggest of all hovering birds. Typically, they lay their eggs on a ledge or in a hole abandoned by other birds.

King of Saxony's bird of paradise

Range: New Guinea
Habitat: Rain forest
The king of Saxony's bird of paradise was named by European naturalists exploring the forest of New Guinea in honor of their monarch. It looks fairly ordinary except for two amazing plumes that extend from its head. When displaying, the male sits on a high branch with its plumes up, bouncing up and down, swelling its back feathers and hissing. When a female approaches he sweeps his plumes down in front of her then follows her to mate.

Kingbird, Eastern

Range: breeds
N. America; winters
S. America

Habitat: Open country with trees
The eastern kingbird will defend
its territory dauntlessly, attacking
much larger birds like hawks and raining
them with blows. It even attacks aircrafeet.

Kingfisher, Belted

Range: Breeds N. America;
winters Caribbean

Habitat: Streams, rivers, ponds
This kingfisher likes to perch on branches
overhanging the water where it can see
fish and dive after them. often, though, it
hovers over the water. It also eats frogs
and crabs.

Kite, Brahminy

Range: India, S. China,
S.E. Asia, Australasia
Habitat: Near water, coasts
This kite feeds on frogs, crabs, snakes,
fish, insects and some carrion. It also
scavenges off human waste for scraps
and refuse.

Kookaburra

Range: Australia
Habitat: Open
country with trees
Famous for their
raucous cry, laughing
kookaburras live in the
bushlands of eastern Australia.
They are the largest member of
the kingfisher family, but they
prey on lizards, snakes, small mammals
and frogs rather than fish, often beating
their victims against a rock to kill them.

Lapwing, Northern

Range: Europe, Africa, Asia
Habitat: Grassland, farmland, marshes
Lapwings are also known as peewits, after
the cry they make when on the wing.
Unlike other lapwings, the northern
lapwing lives in damp, grassy fields rather
than close to water. In the breeding season
the males often soar up into the sky in a
spectacular aerial display, then
tumble down.

Lark, Desert

Range: Africa, Middle East to
N.W. India
Habitat: Desert
The desert lark lives in the warm
deserts of southwestern Asia and India
across to the Sahara, and builds its nest
against a rock or tuft of grass. Its
plumage is perfect camouflage against
the sandy soil. A dark species lives on
black sandy areas; a pale species lives
on areas of white sand.

Limpkin

Range: S. U.S.,
C. and S. America, Caribbean
Habitat: Swamps
The limpkin is a marsh
wading bird, similar to
cranes, that probes the
mud for water snails
with its beak. It
was hunted
almost to
extinction in
the last
century but is
now protected
by law.

Longclaw,
Yellow-throated

Range: Africa south of the Sahara
Habitat: Damp grassland
Longclaws are related to pipits and
wagtails and, like them, forage on
the ground for insects. Longclaws get their
name from their 2 inch-long (5 cm) hind
claw. They live in pairs. When flying, they
occasionally dive into the grass for insects.

Loon, Common

Range: Far north America and Eurasia
Habitat: Lakes, coasts
Loons, also known as divers, are the
grebes of the polar regions — perfectly
adapted for underwater swimming. They
are very clumsy when it comes to walking
on land because their feet are set so far
back that they constantly tip forward.

Lorikeet, Rainbow

Range: E. Australia west to Bali
Habitat: Forest, gardens
Unlike other parrots, the lorikeet does not
feed on fruit and seeds. Instead, it licks up
nectar and flower pollen with its tongue.
Typically, the rainbow lorikeet will fly off
to search for food in the trees shortly after
dawn, screeching loudly.

Lyrebird, Superb

Range: S.E. Australia
Habitat: Mountain forest
Lyrebirds get their name from their
lyrelike tails. They are ground-living
birds, but hop up into trees to roost. Just
before mating the male builds several
mounds of earth, then dances on them,
spreading out his tail before the female.

Macaw,
Scarlet

Range: C. and S.
America

Habitat: Forest, savanna
Macaws are the largest of all
parrots. The scarlet macaw is a
brilliantly colored parrot that
feeds high up in the trees on
seeds and fruits. Although the
most common of the macaws, it is
declining in numbers because of the
destruction of the rain forest and the
trapping of young birds for
sale as pets.

Magpie,
Black-billed

Range: Eurasia,
N. America, N. Africa
Habitat: Open country with trees
Magpies are lively birds that feed on
insects, snails, slugs and spiders,
although they will sometimes steal eggs
and nestlings. In recent years they have
moved into suburban areas.

Manakin, Wire-tailed
Range: Tropical S. America
Habitat: Rain forest, plantations
Manakins are small, colorful birds that typically forage alone for insects and fruit. They prefer humid areas in the forest canopy or just below, but are often seen in clearings and cocoa plantations.

Martin, Sand
Range: Breeds Eurasia, N. America; winters S. America, Africa, S.E. Asia
Habitat: Steep sand or gravel banks
Like swallows, sand martins feed on insects on the wing, gaping their beaks wide to take the insect in. But their flight is slightly less graceful than the swallow's.

Meadowlark, Eastern

Range: Breeds N. America; winters S. America
Habitat: Prairies, farmland
The eastern meadowlark's whistlelike song is one of the first heard on the prairies in spring. It nests on the ground and probes the grass for grasshoppers, ants and worms with its sharp beak.

Merganser, Red-breasted
Range: Breeds Northern N. America, Eurasia; winters Southern N. America, Eurasia
Habitat: Coastal, inland waters
Mergansers are saw-billed ducks, which means their beaks have serrated edges to help them grasp slippery fish. They nest in shallow depressions in the ground, lined with grass, leaves and down.

Mockingbird, Northern
Range: N. America
Habitat: Open woodland, gardens
Mockingbirds are tireless singers, singing day and night — mimicking anything from a ringing telephone to a croaking frog. The record for one bird is 39 bird cries and 50 other calls.

Moorhen
Range: Worldwide except Australia
Habitat: Swamps, marshes
Despite its name, the moorhen is not a moorland bird; the "moor" comes from an Anglo-Saxon word meaning "bog." It is a small, timid bird that swims well and also forages on land.

Motmot, Blue-crowned

Range: C. and S. America, Caribbean
Habitat: Rain forest, plantations
Motmots live in dense vegetation on the forest floor where they ambush insects, spiders and lizards. They often perch on low branches, swinging their tail from side to side like a pendulum as they wait for prey. They nest in burrows.

Nighthawk, Common
Range: Breeds N. America; winters S. America
Habitat: Grassland, desert, open woods
Nighthawks are not hawks but are related to nightjars. They are on the wing at dawn and dusk "hawking" for insects with their large mouths.

Nightingale
Range: Breeds Eurasia; winters Africa
Habitat: Woodland, thickets
The nightingale is famed for its beautiful song, which is often heard in woods from dawn to dusk and even at night. It is a secretive, dull brown bird that is hard to see, foraging for food, such as worms and berries, among dense vegetation on the woodland floor. It hops around, rather than flying.

Nightjar, Eurasian
Range: Breeds Eurasia; winters Africa
Habitat: Open country, woods, sand dunes
During the day nightjars lie motionless on the ground, often almost invisible in dead leaves. They take to the air at dusk and catch moths in their wide, gaping beaks.

Oriole, Golden
Range: Breeds Eurasia; winters Africa, India
Habitat: Forest, orchards
The brilliant yellow golden oriole is surprisingly hard to see as it hides among the leaves in woodland trees. It rarely comes to the ground and its flight is swift and winding. A courting male chases a female at top speed through the branches.

Osprey
Range: Almost worldwide
Habitat: Lakes, rivers, coasts
The osprey, or fish hawk, feeds almost exclusively on fish. It flies high over the water, flapping and gliding, then, when it spots a fish, it plummets to the water, entering feet first with a large splash to grab the fish in its talons. After surfacing, it shakes its feathers and carries the fish back to its nest of sticks.

Ostrich
Range: Africa
Habitat: Savanna
The ostrich is the world's largest bird. It cannot fly, but it can run at up to 45 miles per hour (70 kmph) for over 22 miles (35 km). Several females lay in a single nest on the ground, producing a combined clutch of up to 30 eggs.

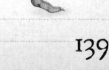

Owl, Barn
Range: Almost worldwide except N. Asia
Habitat: Open country, farmland
The barn owl is easily recognized by its heart-shaped face. It roosts by day in places like barns, and hunts for rodents at night, flying low and silently, then swooping.

Owl, Snowy
Range: Canada, Greenland, N. Eurasia
Habitat: Tundra, coasts
The snowy owl lives in the Arctic, where its white plumage makes it almost invisible against snow. It hunts during the day, preying on lemmings, hares and small birds. It usually nests in mid-May in a shallow pit scraped into the ground, lined with moss and feathers.

Parula, Northern
Range: Breeds Eastern N. America; winters Caribbean, C. America
Habitat: Pine forest (summer), mixed woodland (winter)
This blue warbler forages in trees for insects, especially caterpillars, creeping over branches and hopping from perch to perch. Its nest is built in hanging lichen.

Pelican, Brown
Range: N., C. and S. America
Habitat: Coasts
Unlike its cousin the great white, the brown pelican hunts in the sea, but it has the same big pouch under its beak for scooping up fish. It typically catches fish by diving down sharply with its wings back from about 50 feet (15 m) up. Cushioning air sacs in its chest soften the impact as it plunges into the water.

Owl, Eastern screech
Range: Eastern N. America
Habitat: Woodlands, wetlands
With their phenomenally acute directional hearing and their keen eyesight, owls can weave through the wood in almost pitch darkness and pinpoint prey, such as small nocturnal mammals, with deadly accuracy. Woodland owls include barn owls, great horned owls and the fiercely territorial eastern screech owl, known for its eerie, rising and falling, whistling wail.

Oystercatcher, Common
Range: Breeds Eurasia; winters Africa, S. Asia
Habitat: Coasts, estuaries
These handsome shorebirds sometimes use their long beaks to draw worms out of the sand and sometimes to hammer a hole in the shells of cockles, mussels and limpets. Their courtship display is among the noisiest of all shorebirds, as they walk around "piping" agitatedly.

Peafowl, Congo
Range: Congo, Africa
Habitat: Rain forest
The Congo peafowl is Africa's largest and most spectacular game bird, only discovered in 1936. It is the only one of 49 pheasant species not native to Asia. Although it looks quite similar to the Asian peafowl and eats the same variety of fruits and insects, it breeds quite differently. Both male and female are equally splendid and form lifelong pairs.

Penguin, Adelie
Range: Antarctica
Habitat: Oceans, rocky coasts
Apart from the Emperor penguin, the Adelie penguin lives nearer to the South Pole than any bird, nesting in large colonies along shores that are free of ice only in summer. The Antarctic summer is so short that all the females in each colony lay their eggs within two days in November.

Owl, Long-eared
Range: N. America, N. Eurasia, N. Africa
Habitat: Coniferous forest
The long-eared owl hunts exclusively at night, using its sharp ears to detect voles and mice — in contrast to the short-eared owl, which often hunts in broad daylight.

Parrot, Gray
Range: C. Africa
Habitat: Lowland forest, savanna
Gray parrots roost together on forest edges or on small islands in rivers, and fly off in pairs at sunrise to find seeds, nuts, berries and oil palm fruit. They are great mimics and one has been taught 750 human words.

Peafowl, Indian
Range: Originally India, Sri Lanka
Habitat: Forest, farmland
Now kept in parks and gardens all over the world, the male peafowl, or peacock, is one of the most spectacular of all birds, with its huge tail of 150 or more long iridescent feathers that it raises in a huge fan.

Penguin, King
Range: Subantarctic, Falkland Islands
Habitat: Ocean, breeds coasts
The king penguin is one of the biggest penguins, almost 40 inches (1 m) tall — exceeded only by the huge emperor penguin. It is also one of the deepest diving of the penguins, plunging 150 feet (45 m) or more in pursuit of fish and squid.

Penguin, Little

Range: New
Zealand, Australia
Habitat: Coasts
Also known as the fairy
penguin, the little
penguin is the smallest of the penguins
— less than 16 inches (41 cm) tall. It is also
one of the few to remain active after sunset.

Petrel, European storm

Range: Atlantic, Mediterranean
Habitat: Oceans
The smallest of European seabirds,
the storm petrel was believed to warn of
a storm when it followed a ship. In fact,
it probably follows to feed on fish brought
to the surface by the disturbance.

Pheasant

Range: Originally C. and S.E. Asia;
introduced worldwide
Habitat: Woodland, forest edge, heath
Called the pheasant in Europe and North
America, the common pheasant is one of
49 species of pheasant, many of which,
like the common pheasant, came originally
from Southeast Asia.

Pigeon, Victoria crowned

Range: New Guinea and islands
Habitat: Rain forest
This is the biggest of the pigeons — about
the size of a chicken. It has an amazing
fan of feathers on its head. It lives in
rain forests and feeds on fallen fruit on
the forest floor.

Pipit, Water

Range: Breeds Eurasia;
winters S.E. Asia and Japan
Habitat: Breeds mountains;
winters lowlands
Pipits are small birds that nest on the
ground. The water pipit breeds well above
the tree line on mountains, usually close to
rushing streams and occasionally next to
glaciers in the snow.

Pitta, Garnet

Range: Burma, Sumatra, Borneo
Habitat: Swampy forest
Pittas are stout, thrushlike birds of the
tropics. The garnet pitta is a colorful bird
of swamp forests that runs about the forest
floor foraging for ants, beetles and other
insects as well as snails and fruit.

Plover, American golden

Range: Breeds far north America and
Asia; winters S. America and Asia
Habitat: Tundra, grassland
Every year this plover, also known as the
lesser plover, flies one of the longest
migrations of any land bird, almost
8,000 miles (13,000 km) each way.

Poorwill, Common

Range: Breeds northern N. America;
winters in the south
Habitat: Breeds open woods; winters
desert
The common poorwill, almost uniquely
among birds, spends the winter in a state
like hibernation, when its heart rate slows
and its body temperature drops from
106°F (41°C) to 64°F (18°C).

Potoo

Range: Caribbean, C. and S. America
Habitat: Forest edge, farmland
Potoos are related to nightjars and look a
little like them, but they catch their insects
more like flycatchers — that is, by darting
out from a perch. But, like nightjars, they
hunt mainly at night and by day sit stiffly
upright on a broken branch.

Ptarmigan, Rock

Range: Arctic, far north America
and Eurasia
Habitat: Tundra
The ptarmigans are part of the grouse
family but live in the very far north.
In winter their plumage turns almost
completely white, matching the snow.

Puffin, Atlantic

Range: N. Atlantic
Habitat: Rocky
coasts
With its big, colorful bill,
the puffin looks a little
like a parrot and is
sometimes called the sea
parrot. With this bill it can catch as
many as 10 small fish in succession without
having to swallow. Puffins breed in
colonies in shallow burrows that they dig
in the soft turf on cliff tops.

Quail, California

Range: W. U.S.
Habitat: Scrub, farmland
The California quail is an elegant bird
with a characteristic head plume that
feeds on leaves, seeds and berries. In the
breeding season it feeds in small groups,
but in winter California quails gather into
larger flocks for security from predators.

Quelea, Red-billed

Range: Africa south
of the Sahara
Habitat: Savanna
The red-billed quelea is probably the
world's most abundant bird and often
forms huge, cloudlike flocks containing
over 100,000 birds. Because of the damage
they do to crops, they have been hunted
on a huge scale.

Quetzal, Resplendent

Range: C. America
Habitat: High-altitude
rain forest
The resplendent quetzal is
an extraordinary bird that inhabits
the lower layers of the tropical
forest. Besides its brilliant emerald
green and crimson plumage, it also has
extraordinary tail feathers, over 2 feet
(60 cm) long, which were much prized
by the ancient Mayans and Aztecs. Yet
surprisingly, the quetzal is hard to
spot because it sits motionless for
long periods. It feeds on oily fruit
and insects.

Redshank, Common

Range: Breeds Europe, C. and E. Asia;
Winters S. Europe, N. Africa, S. Asia
Habitat: Breeds marshes, moorland;
winters muddy and sandy shores
This "sentinel of the marshes" sends
off a harsh, piping alarm to warn of
intruders. It adapts to many coasts,
feeding mostly on small shrimps, snails
and worms on the surface.

Robin, European
Range: Eurasia
Habitat: Woodland, gardens
With its striking red breast, the little robin is easily identified. It is very bold, often following gardeners to eat worms turned up during digging. It is also very possessive of its territory, guarding it fiercely from other robins.

Rhea, Greater
Range: S. America
Habitat: Grassland
Rheas are the biggest birds in the Americas. Like their African cousin the ostrich, they are completely flightless and, as with ostriches, females often share nests to lay their eggs.

Shrike, Northern
Range: Breeds N. America, Eurasia
Habitat: Varied
Shrikes are songbirds that feed mainly on insects. They are often called "butcher birds" because they sometimes impale their prey on a thorn to save it to eat later.

Rosella, Crimson
Range: S. and E. Australia, introduced New Zealand
Habitat: Mountain forests
Crimson rosellas are one of the region's many parrot species. They live mainly in the gum tree forests in southeast Australia, but escaped pets have colonized parks around Wellington, New Zealand. Green rosellas live in Tasmania. Swift parrots breed in Tasmania and migrate to mainland Australia for the winter.

Secretary bird
Range: Africa south of the Sahara
Habitat: Savanna
The secretary bird is actually a bird of prey like the hawk, but it has the most extraordinary long legs and strides along the ground, perhaps walking 20 miles (30 km) a day. It catches prey by running after it.

Sicklebill, White-tipped
Range: C. and S. America
Habitat: Tropical forest
The sicklebill is a tiny hummingbird with a very long, downward-curving bill that allows it to sip nectar from heliconia flowers and also coryanthes orchids. It often clings to the blooms with its feet as it sips.

Roadrunner, Greater
Range: S.W. U.S.
Habitat: Desert, semidesert
Roadrunners are actually a kind of cuckoo, but spend most of their time on the ground. Although they can fly, they usually run, often at speeds of up to 15 miles per hour (25 kmph). They use their tail and wings for balance to help them to swerve around obstructions. They feed mostly on insects, such as crickets and grasshoppers, killing them with a sudden pounce. They nest in cacti or thornbushes.

Seriema, Red-legged
Range: S. America
Habitat: Grassland
This bird rarely flies. Instead, it escapes danger by running along at terrific speed with its head down. It is a predator that preys on snakes. Farmers sometimes use them as watchdogs.

Skua, Great
Range: N. Atlantic
Habitat: Oceanic
Skuas are big, strong birds that live over the cold waters of the North Atlantic. They not only attack other birds to steal their prey, but also kill and eat birds such as puffins, kittiwakes and gulls, and take their eggs.

Sandgrouse, Pallas's
Range: C. Asia
Habitat: Desert steppe
Pallas's sandgrouse is a plump ground bird about the size of a pigeon. It is a strong flier, but finds the seeds that it eats on the ground and is able to cope with the grit of the desert.

Sheathbill, Snowy
Range: Subantarctic, S. Georgia, Falkland islands
Habitat: Coasts
The snowy sheathbill is a scavenger that makes the most of almost anything edible in its South Atlantic home. It haunts penguin colonies, feeding on carcasses, feces and offal, or snatching penguin eggs and chicks. It even eats seaweed for the invertebrates that live on it.

Sandgrouse, Black-bellied
Range: Eurasia, N.W. Africa
Habitat: Grasslands
The need for water plays a key role in the life of the black-bellied sandgrouse. It roosts in small flocks on open ground, then at dawn it flies to a water hole, where several flocks may jostle for water. When it has young, it soaks its breast feathers to take water back for the chicks to drink.

Robin, American
Range: N. and C. America
Habitat: Woodland, gardens
Originally a woodland species, the American robin has thrived in suburban gardens. It can often be seen on lawns and in flower beds, drawing earthworms from the ground.

Sparrow, House
Range: Eurasia, introduced worldwide
Habitat: Farmland, urban areas
The house sparrow is an amazingly adaptable little bird. A few birds were taken to New York in 1850 and they have now spread all over the Americas.

Sparrow, Song
Range: N. America
Habitat: Thickets
This is the most widespread of all American native sparrows. There are various races and each can be identified by its own particular song dialect. The biggest race is the northern song sparrow from the Aleutian Islands.

Starling
Range: Eurasia, introduced worldwide
Habitat: Farmland, suburbs
Starlings are one of the most familiar birds in cities, often massing in huge, swooping flocks before settling. In winter, flocks may feed out in the countryside, then pour into the city to roost as the sun goes down.

Sunbird, Malachite
Range: C. Africa
Habitat: Mountains
Sunbirds are the hummingbirds of Africa and Asia. They feed in the same way on nectar from flowers and have the same brilliant coloring. But they cannot hover like hummingbirds and have to perch on flowers to sip. The malachite sunbird feeds on giant lobelias and protea bushes and also insects.

Sunbird, Yellow-backed
Range: India, S.E. Asia
Habitat: Forest, farmland
The yellow-backed, or crimson, sunbird eats insects but usually clings to stems and twigs to suck nectar from flowers. Its pear-shaped nest hangs from a branch.

Swallow, Barn
Range: Breeds N. hemisphere; winters s. hemisphere
Habitat: Breeds farmland with buildings
The barn swallow makes its nest from mud and grass in buildings and under bridges, but it spends much of its time in the air, catching insects on the wing.

Swan, Tundra
Range: Breeds Arctic; winters N. America, Eurasia
Habitat: Breeds marshy tundra; winters marshes
The tundra swan is the most northerly breeding of all the swans. Most breeding pairs return each winter to the same spot on the tundra.

Swift, Crested tree
Range: Malaysia, Indonesia
Habitat: Forest edge, woodland
Unlike true swifts, crested swifts can perch and typically they sit on branches and telephone wires from where they can swoop down on insects.

Swift, White-throated
Range: N. America
Habitat: Mountains, cliffs
Swifts spend almost all their life on the wing, even mating in flight. The white-throated swift is the fastest flying bird in North America, flying up to 186 miles per hour (300 kmph).

Tanager, Scarlet
Range: Breeds eastern N. America; winters S. America
Habitat: Forest
Tanagers are tropical birds that feed on bees, other insects and their larvae. The scarlet tanager is one of the few that migrates north to breed. The male is brilliant scarlet before breeding, then molts to the same olive green as the female.

Tern, Common
Range: Breeds eastern N. America, N. Eurasia; winters to the south
Habitat: Coasts, estuaries
Terns nest in huge colonies on isolated beaches, islands and cliffs, where pairs scrape a hollow in the ground. Noisy terneries sometimes fall silent when all the birds rise and sweep out over the sea for a minute or two.

Tinamou, Great
Range: C. and S. America
Habitat: Tropical forest
Tinamous are large birds a little like pheasants, but can barely fly at all. When in danger they lie still and rely on their plumage to hide them. This is why the great tinamou prefers areas of rain forest where there is dense undergrowth. If frightened it may burst from the floor with a roar of wings and fly, but for only a short way. Usually, though, it pecks on the ground for insects and berries.

Toucan, Plate-billed mountain
Range: Andes in Columbia, Ecuador
Habitat: Mountain forest
Also known as the laminated toucan, the plate-billed mountain toucan is the highest living of the toucans, living up to 10,000 feet (3,000 m) in the Andes. Like other toucans it feeds on fruits and berries.

Toucan, Toco
Range: S. America
Habitat: Tropical forest
Toucans are tropical birds related to woodpeckers. They have huge, colorful beaks that are full of air spaces to keep them light. Toucans use them to nip fruit and berries from the trees.

Tragopan, Temminck's
Range: China, Myanmar, Tibet
Habitat: Mountain forest
Tragopans are colorful birds related to pheasants that feed on the ground on seeds, buds and leaves in the damp forests of Southeastern Asia and China.

Tropic bird, Red-tailed
Range: Indian and Pacific oceans
Habitat: Oceans
With its long, dark red tail feathers, the red-tailed tropic bird is an unusual looking seabird. In the breeding season it goes slightly pink.

Turaco, Red-crested
Range: Africa
Habitat: Forest, savanna
Turacos are colorful African relatives of cuckoos. They live in tropical forests and feed on fruit. The red-crested turaco is a poor flier, but runs, hops and climbs very nimbly and swiftly through the branches of rain forest trees.

Turkey, Wild
Range: U.S., Mexico
Habitat: Wooded country, scrub
Wild turkeys are big fowl that strut around woodlands in groups of 20 or so for most of the year, foraging for seeds, nuts and berries. They are strong fliers over short distances and roost in trees.

Vireo, Red-eyed
Range: Breeds N. America; winters S. America
Habitat: Forest
The red-eyed vireo is a tireless songster, singing right through the day. It builds a neat cup-shaped nest in a tree fork. Nestlings leave the nest after 12 days.

Vulture, King
Range: C. and S. America
Habitat: Rain forest, savanna
Like the giant condors of California and the Andes, the king vulture is one of seven American vulture species. Like African vultures it feeds on carrion and has a bald head for plunging into messy carcasses. But unlike African vultures, king and other American vultures are related to storks, not birds of prey. The king vulture relies on smell to track prey.

Vulture, Lappet-faced
Range: Africa, Middle East
Habitat: Savanna, desert
This is the biggest of the African vultures and, though often last to arrive at a carcass, it pushes the other vultures out of the way. With its big, powerful beak it can cut easily through flesh and its bald head saves its plumage from getting soiled with blood.

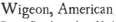

Warbler, Willow
Range: Breeds Eurasia; winters Africa, S. Asia
Habitat: Woodland, farmland
The willow warbler is one of more than 300 warblers spread widely across Eurasia and Australia. All mainly eat insects and each has a distinctive song.

Warbler, Yellow
Range: Breeds N. America; winters C. and S. America
Habitat: Thickets by streams, swamps
The yellow warbler is one of the most widespread of American wood warblers. Like all warblers it forages in trees for insects.

Wigeon, American
Range: Breeds northern N. America; winters in the south
Habitat: Marshes
Wigeons are called dabbling ducks, but they find very little food by dabbling. Usually they graze on grass in marshes in huge, tightly packed flocks. They may even snatch the food of other diving birds.

Woodcock, American
Range: Breeds N. America; winters to the south
Habitat: Woodland
Woodcocks are actually waders but they have left the shore to live in woods where they probe soft soil for worms with their long bills.

Woodpecker, Gila
Range: S.W. U.S., Mexico
Habitat: Desert scrub
These woodpeckers build their nests in holes inside saguaro cactuses or mesquite trees. The male has a red cap on top of its head, which is missing from females and young.

Woodpecker, Great spotted
Range: Europe, N. Africa, Asia
Habitat: Forest
Like all woodpeckers, the great spotted clings to tree trunks with its strong feet and uses its long bill to drill for insects. Insects are its main food, but it also eats fruit, berries and even nestlings of other birds. In spring, it can be heard drumming rapidly on trees to mark out its territory.

Wren
Range: Eurasia, N. Africa
Habitat: Woodland, farmland
Wrens are tiny songbirds with short, upright tails that hop about the ground searching for insects and spiders. They nest in hollow tree stumps or among tree roots.

Zitting cisticola
Range: S. Eurasia, N. Africa, Australia
Habitat: Damp grassland, rice fields
This little warbler is well known for the male's song flight, during which it spirals up to 100 feet (30 m) above the ground while singing.

INVERTEBRATES

CREATURES without backbones, such as insects, snails and worms are called invertebrates. Most invertebrates are small, but there are more of them than all other animals put together. Of the world's million and a half known animal species, at least a million are insects, and there are many other invertebrates living on land — including centipedes, arachnids such as spiders, and crustaceans such as woodlice.

Bedbug
Range: Worldwide
Habitat: Human and animal hosts, crevices
Bedbugs stay hidden during the day, but come out at night to feed on the blood of birds and animals, including humans.

Ant, Army
Range: C. and S. America
Habitat: Rain forest
Unlike other ants, army ants do not make a permanent nest. Instead they crawl across the forest floor, devouring any small creature in their path, and then spend the night in a temporary nest called a bivouac, with walls made by ants clinging to each other.

Ant, Harvester
Range: Worldwide
Habitat: Fields
These ants get their name from their habit of gathering seeds and storing them in special granary areas in the nest, ready to eat in times of need.

Ant, Velvet
Range: Worldwide, especially tropics
Habitat: Varied
These are not ants but wasps, covered with velvety hair. They get their name because the females are wingless and antlike.

Bee, Carpenter
Range: Worldwide
Habitat: Near flowers
Female carpenter bees chew into wood, making a tunnel-like nest for their brood cell. They line the nest with sticky pollen, lay a single egg, then seal the cell.

Ant, Carpenter
Range: Worldwide
Habitat: Wood
Colonies of carpenter ants make their nests in wooden buildings or in rotting tree trunks. The nests can destroy the timber in roofs or walls.

Ant, Leafcutter
Range: C. and S. America
Habitat: Rain forest
Leafcutter ants spend the night in nests under the rain forest floor, then at dawn workers crawl out and climb trees to cut pieces of leaves to bring back to the nest. Instead of eating the leaves, they use them to make a compost on which a fungus grows. They eat the fungus.

Ant lion
Range: Worldwide, especially tropics
Habitat: Scrub and dry, sandy areas
Ant lions get their name from their larvae, which dig a pit in sandy soil to trap ants. When an ant comes near, the larvae tosses soil at it so that it falls into the trap.

Bee, Cuckoo
Range: Worldwide
Habitat: Near flowers
Cuckoo bees cannot carry pollen so, like cuckoo birds, they lay their eggs in the nests of others — in this case, bees. The cuckoo bees' eggs hatch first and the larvae eat up their host's food store.

Ant, Fire
Range: S. America, introduced N. America
Habitat: Woods, fields
Fire ants get their name because they inflict a very painful bite, which they use to attack other insects. They were introduced into Alabama from South America and are now major pests because they build huge nests, damage grain and attack poultry.

Ant, Red wood
Range: Eurasia
Habitat: Woodland
By preying on plant-eating insects, wood ants play a key role in reducing the damage done to forest trees. Wood ants also feed on the sticky honeydew secreted by aphids.

Aphid
Range: Worldwide
Habitat: Green plants
Aphids are tiny insects that feed on the sap of leaves and plants and can do great damage. They multiply rapidly, but may be eaten by ladybugs and wasps.

Bee, Leafcutter
Range: Worldwide
Habitat: Varied
Leafcutter bees live alone rather than in swarms. They cut out pieces of leaf with their jaws and use them to line their nests — usually a tunnel in rotting wood.

Bee, Mining
Range: Worldwide except Australia
Habitat: Near spring flowers
The mines of mining bees are long, branching tunnels they dig into the ground. They stock them with nectar and pollen for their larvae to eat when they hatch.

Bee, Orchid
Range: Tropics worldwide
Habitat: Near orchids
Orchid bees feed on the nectar from orchids, such as the gongora. They play a crucial role in spreading the pollen of these flowers. Some orchids mimic the bees' shape to attract them.

Bee, Plasterer
Range: Worldwide, especially
s. hemisphere
Habitat: Soil
Plasterer bees nest in tunnels in the ground, which they line with a secretion from glands in their abdomen. The secretion dries to form a clear, waterproof "plaster."

Bee, Stingless
Range: Tropics worldwide
Habitat: Woodland
Stingless bees cannot sting, but they can protect their nests by biting the skin of intruders, coating them with resin and getting up their nose. often the bees simply retreat into their underground nests.

Beetle, Actaeon
Range: S. America
Habitat: Rain forest
Of all the South American rain forest's many beetle species, none is more spectacular than the actaeon beetle. This is one of the world's biggest beetles, growing up to 3½ inches (9 cm) long and 2 inches (5 cm) wide.

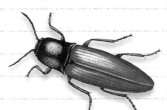

Beetle, Click
Range: Worldwide, especially tropics
Habitat: Leaf litter, rotten wood
If a click beetle finds itself upside down, it arches its body and snaps itself straight with a loud click, launching its body into the air. If threatened, it can feign death.

Beetle, Darkling
Range: Worldwide, especially deserts
Habitat: On the ground
Darkling beetles are especially common in deserts. They come out in the cool of the night to forage for food such as rotting wood and insect larvae.

Beetle, Diving
Range: Worldwide
Habitat: Bogs and lakes
Diving beetles live in ponds and lakes. Their hind legs are covered with hairs that flatten out like paddles to drive them through the water. When they dive they can stay under the water for some time, breathing air trapped under their wing cases.

Beetle, Goliath
Range: C. Africa
Habitat: Rain forest
The goliath beetle is among the largest of all beetles — 5 inches (13 cm) long. The larvae help to break down rotting wood and so enrich the soil.

Beetle, Jewel
Range: Worldwide, especially tropics
Habitat: Forest
Jewel beetles come in brilliant metallic colors, often with stripes, bands and spots. They like to lay their eggs in wood in freshly burned forests, and the larvae chew oval tunnels in the wood. Adults feed on flower nectar.

Beetle, Longhorn
Range: Worldwide, mainly tropical
Habitat: Forest
Longhorn beetles have antennae up to four times as long as their bodies. Their larvae are serious pests as they eat into timber and trees.

Beetle, Rove
Range: Worldwide
Habitat: Soil, fungi, leaf litter
Rove beetles are long beetles with short wings and, like the Devil's coach horse beetle, have an abdomen that they curve up like a scorpion if threatened.

Beetle, Stag
Range: Worldwide, especially tropics
Habitat: Broad-leaved forest
With large heads and massive jaws, stag beetles are fearsome-looking beetles, but they are actually quite harmless, feeding mostly on tree sap. However, males often lock antlers to fight over females.

Beetle, Whirligig
Range: Worldwide
Habitat: Pond and stream surfaces
These shiny, black beetles are the only beetles that can swim on a film of water. They gather together and swim rapidly in whirling circles.

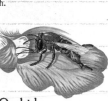

Biddy
Range: Worldwide
Habitat: Woodland streams
Biddies, or spiketails, are large black-and-yellow dragonflies, often seen hovering above woodland streams. Unlike some other dragonflies, the adults have eyes that meet at the top of their head.

Bug, Assassin
Range: Worldwide, especially tropics
Habitat: Varied
Assassin bugs are killers that attack other insects such as caterpillars. They stab their prey with their proboscis and inject a toxin that dissolves tissue. The bugs then suck out their victim's body juices.

Bug, June
Range: Americas and Europe
Habitat: Farmland
June bugs are one of more than 30,000 kinds of scarab beetle, once held sacred by the ancient Egyptians. June bugs mostly feed on leaves, but their white grubs or larvae feed on the roots of plants and can cause tremendous damage to crops such as corn and sugar cane.

Bumblebee
Range: Worldwide, except southern Africa and Australia
Habitat: Near flowers
Bumblebees are large, hairy bees, typically black and yellow. Like all bees, they sip nectar from flowers to turn into a honeylike substance, and also play a crucial role in pollinating flowers.

Butterfly, Cabbage white
Range: Originally Eurasia, now also N. America, Australia
Habitat: Farmland
Known also as the large white, the caterpillar of this butterfly feeds on cabbage, stripping the leaves. It is regarded as a pest in some places.

Butterfly, Cairns birdwing
Range: S.E. Asia, N. Australia
Habitat: Rain forest
The largest Australian butterflies, Cairns birdwings can measure over 6 inches (15 cm) across. They typically live on pipevines in forest clearings.

Butterfly, Copper
Range: Eurasia, N. America
Habitat: Hedges, scrub, gardens
Coppers are a large family of butterflies that includes small coppers, one of the most common butterflies in the northern hemisphere. The caterpillars feed on dock and sorrel.

Butterfly, Fluminense swallowtail
Range: Amazon
Habitat: Swamps, scrub
The fluminense is one of the world's most endangered butterflies because its habitat has been cleared and drained to make way for factories, houses and banana plantations.

Butterfly, Monarch
Range: Americas, spreading elsewhere
Habitat: Milkweed (caterpillar)
Every fall millions of monarchs fly thousands of miles from Canada to Mexico. They lay their eggs the following spring, on their way back north. Young adults continue the journey north for the summer.

Butterfly, Morpho
Range: S. and C. America
Habitat: Tropical rain forest
With their shimmering blue coloring, morphos are among the most beautiful of all butterflies. They are fast flying and flit through the forest, with males often chasing each other through patches of sunlight. They feed on the juices of fallen fruit.

Butterfly, Queen Alexandra's birdwing
Range: Papua New Guinea
Habitat: Rain forest
The female Queen Alexandra's birdwing is the world's biggest butterfly, 11 inches (28 cm) across. The male has a bright yellow abdomen indicating to predators that it is poisonous. This butterfly is so highly prized by collectors that it has been hunted almost to extinction.

Butterfly, Swallowtail
Range: N. America
Habitat: Forest, orchards
The giant swallowtail is one of the largest butterflies in North America, growing up to 5½ inches (14 cm) across. The caterpillar feeds on orange trees in southern North America. Adults eat plants such as lantana and azalea.

Centipede
Range: Worldwide
Habitat: Varied, especially leaf litter
Centipedes are tiny predators, typically with 15 pairs of legs. They are not insects but belong to their own class. They use poison claws to kill prey such as insects and spiders.

Cicada
Range: Worldwide, mostly warmer places
Habitat: Shrubs and trees
Cicadas are famous for the loud mating song of the males. The song is made by a pair of structures called tymbals on the abdomen that are vibrated by special muscles.

Cockroach, American
Range: Originally Africa, now worldwide
Habitat: Moist, dark crevices
Cockroaches have flat bodies, which allow them to squeeze into crevices in order to find food or escape from predators. Certain pest species thrive in warm, dirty places, especially where there is food.

Cockroach, German
Range: Worldwide
Habitat: Leaf litter, garbage, buildings
The German cockroach is a common pest in kitchens and food stores. It multiplies rapidly. Unlike common cockroaches, such as the American, it has proper wings.

Cockroach, Madagascan hissing
Range: Madagascar
Habitat: Rain forest
Males of this species fight each other. When they win they often hiss by squeezing air out of the breathing holes on their bodies called spiracles. Males also hiss to court females.

Crane fly
Range: Worldwide
Habitat: Typically near water
Crane flies look like large, long-legged mosquitoes, but they do not bite. In fact, they do not eat anything at all because they do all their eating when they are larvae.

Cricket, Mole
Range: Worldwide
Habitat: Damp sand or soil near streams
Looking remarkably like tiny moles, mole crickets are covered in velvety hairs and burrow through the ground with their large, spadelike legs.

Cricket, True
Range: Worldwide
Habitat: Woodland, on the ground in meadows
True crickets "sing" to attract mates by rubbing together special ridges at the base of their forewings. The sound is a high-pitched chirrup.

Damselfly
Range: Worldwide
Habitat: Swamps, bogs, pools
Damselflies, such as stalk- or spread-winged damselflies, are related to dragonflies but are smaller and thinner. When they rest, they cling vertically to stalks with their wings out.

Damselfly, Narrow-winged
Range: Worldwide
Habitat: Ponds, bogs, streams
Damselflies feed on small insects on plants. The narrow-winged damselfly folds its wings together when at rest on stalks.

Darter
Range: Worldwide
Habitat: Varied, including mountain forest near streams
Darter, or skimmer, dragonflies get their name from their fast, darting flight, often skimming just over the surface of the water as they pursue their prey.

Dragonfly, Club-tailed
Range: Worldwide
Habitat: Ponds, lakes, rivers
Unlike other dragonflies, the club-tailed dragonfly spots its prey by watching from a perch. Once it sights its prey, it darts out to seize it, then returns to the perch.

Dragonfly, Darner
Range: Worldwide
Habitat: Sluggish water
Darners, also known as hawkers, include some of the largest, most powerful and fastest flying of all dragonflies. When hunting, they zoom back and forth prepared to seize their prey.

Dysedera crocata
Range: Worldwide
Habitat: Crevices in wood
Most spiders have eight eyes; dysderid spiders like crocata have only six, set in a circle. The crocata spends the day hiding under stones, then comes out at night to hunt woodlice. This spider can pierce a woodlouse's tough body armor with its huge fangs.

Earthworm
Range: Worldwide
Habitat: Mostly damp soil
Earthworms are the most common of the segmented worm group. As they tunnel into the ground, they swallow soil and digest dead leaves and rotting plant matter, then excrete the rest. This mixes up the soil and helps to keep it fertile.

Earwig, Common
Range: Originally Europe, now worldwide
Habitat: Varied
Earwigs eat plants and other insects. They have pincers at the end of their body to catch prey. They often live in flowers and are considered garden pests.

Earwig, Long-horned
Range: Worldwide, mainly tropics
Habitat: Shores, leaf litter, debris
Also known as striped earwigs, long-horned earwigs are nocturnal, coming out at night to prey on other insects. If attacked, they squirt out a foul-smelling liquid.

Firebrat
Range: Worldwide
Habitat: Hot, damp places
Firebrats are a kind of silverfish. They live in hot places in buildings, such as near ovens and hot pipes. They run quickly and scurry around finding crumbs of food to eat.

Firefly
Range: Worldwide
Habitat: Woodland, moist grassland
Fireflies, or lightning bugs, emit flashes
of cold, green light when mating. The
males fly, flashing, just above the ground
and females flash back from the ground or
trees to guide the males toward them.

Flea, Cat
Range: Worldwide
Habitat: On cats
Fleas are tiny insects that live on mammals
and feed on their blood. They have no
wings, but they are amazing jumpers, able
to jump 200 times their own length to get
from host to host. Cat fleas are the most
common in homes, biting people and dogs
as well as cats.

Flea, Chigoe
Range: Americas, tropical
Habitat: Mammal and
bird hosts
Chigoe fleas — also called jiggers — are
parasites that attack various animals,
including humans. Typically, pregnant
females burrow into people's feet where
the flea causes a reaction that makes the
skin of the foot grow to engulf the insect.
When the fleas hatch, they drop off
their host and spend the rest of their
life on the ground.

Fly, Fruit
Range: Worldwide
Habitat: Typically fruit
Fruit flies feed on nectar from flowers and
the juice of overripe fruit. Some species
lay their eggs on the skin of fruit such as
oranges, and the larvae eat away the fruit.

Fly, House
Range: Worldwide
Habitat: Flowers, dung, garbage
House flies are among the most numerous
animals on Earth. They suck liquid from
anything sweet or rotting. Typically their
larvae grow up in dung or garbage.

Fly, Hover
Range: Worldwide
Habitat: Typically flat-topped flowers
Hover flies are amazing fliers, able to dart
this way and that, backward and forward
as they search for flowers to sip for nectar.
Some hover flies deter predators by
mimicking wasps.

Fly, Large caddis
Range: Mainly N. hemisphere
Habitat: Near ponds, lakes, rivers
Caddis flies look a little like moths, but
moths have scaly wings, while caddis fly
wings are made from a membrane. Females
typically lay strings of eggs encased in
jelly on plants just below the water
surface. The larvae transform to adults and
then emerge from the water.

Fly, Robber
Range: Worldwide
Habitat: Varied, especially
dry grassland
These are fast-flying, powerful insects
that catch and kill other insects in midair,
or pounce on them on the ground. They
stab their victims through the neck and
suck them dry.

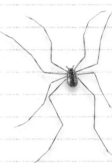

Froghopper
Range: Worldwide, especially tropics
Habitat: Shrubs, trees
These little insects can jump like tiny
frogs. They lay their eggs on plant stems.
When the nymphs hatch they cover
themselves in a foam a little like saliva.

Grasshopper,
Long-horned
Range: Warm areas worldwide
Habitat: Typically in grass
Grasshoppers are part of a large order
called Orthoptera, along with crickets,
katydids and locusts. Grasshoppers and
locusts are vegetarians, feeding mainly
on plants.

Grasshopper,
Short-horned
Range: Warm areas worldwide
Habitat: Typically in grass
Short-horned grasshoppers have short
antennae. Like all grasshoppers, they
have powerful back legs that they use
to jump huge distances, aided by their
small wings.

Harvestman
Range: Worldwide, mainly temperate
Habitat: Under stones, in leaf litter
Harvestmen look like spiders, but their
bodies are more oval and have no waist.
They feed on small insects such as
springtails, but do not spin a web.

Head louse
Range: Worldwide
Habitat: On humans, apes, monkeys
The head louse is a small, flat insect.
It clings on to its host's hairs with its
strongly clawed legs and then sucks on
their blood.

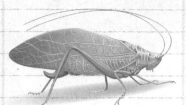

Katydid
Range: Worldwide, mainly tropics
Habitat: On vegetation, in forests
Also called bush crickets, katydids are narrow grasshoppers that look a little like green leaves and are hard to spot on the bushes where they live. They get their name from the song of the northern katydid male; it sounds like "Katy did."

Honeybee, Western
Range: Worldwide
Habitat: Near flowers
Honeybees are very similar to bumblebees, but smaller and more slender. The western honeybee is the best-known honeybee. Originally from Asia, it has now spread around the world — partly because it makes honey, partly because it helps to pollinate flowers.

Leafhopper, Scarlet-and-green
Range: Americas
Habitat: Anywhere with vegetation
The scarlet-and-green leafhopper is a brilliantly colored insect. It feeds on plant juices and has powerful back legs to help it hop from plant to plant.

Louse, Bark
Range: Worldwide
Habitat: On bark
Bark lice are not part of the same insect order as body lice. In fact, most of them have wings. Most live on the bark of trees and feed on lichen and algae. Similar insects called book lice feed on paper and stored food.

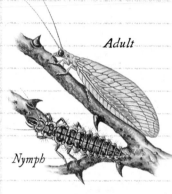

Adult

Nymph

Louse, Feather
Range: Worldwide
Habitat: On birds
Feather lice are the bird equivalent of head lice. They have two claws on each leg, which they use to cling onto their host's feathers. They feed by biting off pieces of feather with their strong jaws.

Hornet, Giant
Range: Eurasia, N. America
Habitat: Woodland
Hornets belong to a group of insects called social wasps and live in huge paper nests made from chewed wood. In the nest, the colony is controlled by a queen. Hornets have a dangerous sting and prey on other insects; they also sip nectar.

Lacewing, Green
Range: Worldwide, especially dry areas
Habitat: Vegetation, ants' nests
Lacewings prey on aphids, thrips and mites when they fly at night. They are attracted to lights and may come into houses to hibernate in fall.

Leaf insect
Range: Tropical Asia, Australia
Habitat: Leaves
These strange-looking insects are shaped just like the leaves they live on, right down to the veins. Even their eggs look like plant seeds, so they are hard for predators to spot.

Ladybug
Range: Worldwide
Habitat: On leaves
Ladybugs are small beetles. Because they feed on aphids that destroy plants they are greatly valued as pest controllers. The ladybug's bright colors warn enemies that it tastes unpleasant.

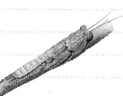

Horsefly
Range: Worldwide
Habitat: Near mammals
Horseflies have huge iridescent eyes. Males feed on nectar and pollen, but the females feed on the blood of mammals — not only horses but deer, humans and other large mammals. These flies may spread disease from animal to animal.

Locust
Range: Africa, Asia
Habitat: Warm places
Locusts are plant-eating grasshoppers. The most well known is the desert locust. In certain weather conditions, billions of insects gather together in a swarm, which can devastate crops when the locusts land and begin to feed.

Mantis, Angola
Range: Angola
Habitat: Tropical rain forest
The Angola mantis is almost impossible to see on a lichen-covered branch. It waits motionless for prey, then strikes in an instant.

Mantis, Flower
Range: Tropics worldwide
except Australia
Habitat: Vegetation
Flower mantises prey on the insects
that live on flowers. They are often
colored to help them hide on the flower.

Mantis, Praying
Range: Worldwide, mainly
warmer places
Habitat: Vegetation
Praying mantises are deadly hunters that
catch their prey by remaining perfectly
still, then striking suddenly. While they
wait they hold their powerful front legs
together as if they are praying.

Mantisfly
Range: Worldwide, mainly
warm regions
Habitat: Lush vegetation
Mantisflies are relatives of lacewings,
but they look exactly like small praying
mantises and use their front legs to seize
prey in just the same way.

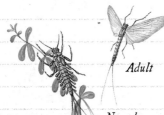

Adult

Nymph

Mayfly
Range: Worldwide
Habitat: Streams, rivers, ponds
Mayflies live for several years as nymphs
underwater, feeding on algae, but once
they leave the water as adults they cannot
eat, and they die in a few hours — just
enough time to mate and lay eggs.

Midge
Range: Worldwide
Habitat: Near ponds, streams
Midges are tiny flies that are either biting
or nonbiting. Both are seen in swarms at
dusk. Biting midges suck blood and have
a very irritating bite.

Millipede, Armored
Range: N. hemisphere
Habitat: Leaf litter
Armored, or flat-backed, millipedes have
an unusually flat shape for a millipede. If
attacked when crawling through the leaf
litter, they can spray poisonous chemicals.

Millipede, Cylinder
Range: Mainly N. hemisphere
Habitat: Leaf litter, rotting wood
Millipedes are not insects, but long
creatures in a class of their own. They
move through leaf litter and eat plants.

Adult

Mite, House dust
Range: Worldwide
Habitat: Houses
Mites are a huge group of tiny arachnids
(like spiders). House dust mites feed
on scales of skin found in house dust
and their droppings can often cause
allergic reactions.

Mite, Velvet
Range: Worldwide, especially tropics
Habitat: Mostly in or on soil
Velvet mites have red or orange velvety
bodies. They live in the soil and feed
mostly on insect eggs. At certain times
of year, usually after rain, adults emerge
to mate.

Moth, Atlas
Range: S. Asia
Habitat: Tropical forest
With wings measuring 10 inches (25 cm)
across, this is one of the world's largest
moths. Its wings are richly colored and
each has two triangular windows that
are almost transparent.

Moth, Sphinx
Range: Worldwide
Habitat: Grassland
The sphinx, or hawk, moth flies by day
and looks remarkably like a bee as
it hovers, sipping nectar from flowers.
Bee sphinx caterpillars feed on the leaves
of canthium.

Moth, Bombycidae (silkworm)
Range: Originally China
Habitat: Woodland
Many Bombycidae moth caterpillars make
silk, but the best known is Bombyx mori.
The Bombyx mori caterpillar, or silkworm,
feeds on mulberry trees and has been
farmed for 4,000 years for the silk it
spins to create its cocoon. Originally from
China, silkworms are farmed all over the
world, but are now extinct in the wild.

Moth, Cotton boll
Range: Warm regions in the Americas
Habitat: Cotton
Cotton boll moths are night-flying moths
with two eye flashes on their wings. Their
yellow-green caterpillars feed on cotton
plants and can do tremendous damage
to cotton crops.

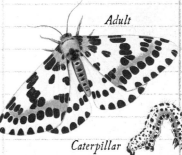

Adult

Caterpillar

Moth, Geometrid
Range: Worldwide
Habitat: Broad-leaved woods
Geometrid moths are unusual among moths
in that they spread their wings flat when
at rest. Their caterpillars, known as
inchworms, form geometrical loops on
leaves that can be damaging to the tree.

Moth, Gypsy
Range: Originally Eurasia, now also N. America
Habitat: Temperate forests
Gypsy moths were brought to North America in 1869 to provide silk. The project failed, the moths escaped and in the wild their caterpillars do a great deal of damage, eating their way through both evergreen and broad-leaved forests. They can sometimes strip a whole forest in a single season.

Moth, Hummingbird
Range: Eurasia except south, N. America
Habitat: Scrub
Hummingbird moths can look remarkably like hummingbirds when they hover in front of flowers, sipping on nectar through their long feeding tube.

Moth, Oleander sphinx
Range: Africa, S. Asia; summer Europe
Habitat: Subtropical forests
The oleander sphinx or hawk moth is strikingly colored in green and purplish pink, but the patterns camouflage it very well against leaves. Its caterpillar feeds on oleander, periwinkle and grapevine.

Moth, Poplar sphinx
Range: Europe, W. Asia
Habitat: Caterpillar on poplar trees
Like other sphinx or hawk moths, the poplar feeds at night. During the day it rests on tree trunks, where its patterning keeps it remarkably well camouflaged against the bark.

Caterpillar

Adult

Moth, Puss
Range: Europe, Asia, N. Africa
Habitat: Forest
Woodland moths feed mostly at night. By day, they sleep camouflaged in leaf litter like lappet moths, or against tree bark like oak tree moths. Each kind of wood attracts its own moths. Oak woods draw tortrix and puss moths. When threatened, puss moth caterpillars squirt out formic acid from their tails.

Moth, Tiger
Range: Eurasia, sometimes N. America
Habitat: Woodland, gardens
Tiger moths are so brightly colored that they look almost like butterflies. The colors warn predators that they taste nasty or mimic other nasty-tasting species.

Moth, White-lined sphinx
Range: C. and N. America
Habitat: Warm open places, including deserts and gardens
Like all sphinx or hawk moths, the white-lined is one of the fastest-flying insects and can reach speeds of over 30 miles per hour (50 kmph). It also flies long distances to breed.

Plant bug
Range: Worldwide
Habitat: Vegetated areas
Bugs are tiny insects that have needlelike mouth parts for piercing food and sucking out juices. Most plant bugs feed on leaves, including crops, but others feed on aphids.

Pseudoscorpion
Range: Worldwide, especially warmer regions
Habitat: Leaf litter, tree bark
Pseudoscorpions are tiny relatives of the scorpion that live in leaf litter, but instead of stings in their tails they have venom glands in their pincers.

Sawfly, Common
Range: Worldwide, especially cool N. hemisphere
Habitat: Gardens, pastures, woods
Sawflies look a little like wasps, but do not have a sting. The female lays eggs on leaves, forming scars or galls.

Scorpion
Range: Worldwide, mostly warm places
Habitat: Typically deserts
Many scorpions have a dangerous sting in their tails that can be fatal to humans. However, they usually catch their prey with their pincers.

Scorpion, Whip
Range: Tropical N. America, S. America, S. Asia
Habitat: Soil, caves, deserts
Whip scorpions have a long, thin tail and no sting. They are sometimes called vinegaroons because they can spray a vinegary liquid from the base of their tail when threatened.

Scorpion, Wind
Range: C. America and southern N. America
Habitat: Warm, dry areas such as deserts
Wind scorpions, also known as sun spiders, are fast-running hunters that prey at night on insects and even small lizards.

Scorpionfly, Common
Range: Worldwide, mostly N. hemisphere
Habitat: Shady areas in vegetation
Scorpionflies get their name because the male has swollen, upturned genitals in its tail that look just like a scorpion's sting.

Silverfish
Range: Worldwide, especially warmer places
Habitat: Dark, warm places
Silverfish are tiny wingless insects. Some species live in dark, warm places indoors, eating flour, damp cloth, paper and wallpaper paste.

Skimmer
Range: Worldwide
Habitat: Typically near slow-flowing streams, ponds
Skimmers are dragonflies with stout, flat bodies but often quite long wings, with a span up to 4 inches (10 cm). They are usually seen flying near still or slow-moving water.

Slug, Great black
Range: Europe, N. America
Habitat: Woodland, farmland, gardens
Slugs are mollusks, like snails, but have no shell and, as they move, lay down a trail of shiny mucus or slime to ease their passage. Slugs find the plants they eat by smell.

Snail, Garden
Range: Originally Europe, introduced elsewhere
Habitat: Woodland, farmland, gardens
Snails are a kind of mollusk called gastropods, which feed on plants and animals using a special mouth part called a radula, filled with rows of teeth.

Snakefly
Range: N. hemisphere
Habitat: Woods, vegetation
Snakeflies get their name from their long necks, which they raise like a cobra to catch their prey, seizing it with a sudden lunge. They prey on beetle larvae and aphids.

Spider, Black widow
Range: S. U.S.
Habitat: Wood piles or garbage
Female American black widows have a bite with venom more deadly than a rattlesnake. Although the amount of venom is small, it can kill a person unless antivenin is given quickly.

Spider, Common house
Range: Eurasia, N. America, Australia
Habitat: Buildings
The house spider has long, hairy legs and builds large, flat webs in dark corners. It lurks in a silken tube under the web waiting for prey, then rushes out to catch any victim tangled in the sticky strands.

Spider, Crab
Range: Worldwide
Habitat: Meadows, gardens
Crab spiders get their name because they scuttle sideways like a crab. They do not make webs, although the smaller males use silk to tie the female down for mating. They usually lurk in wait for prey on flowers.

Spider, Funnel-web
Range: Worldwide
Habitat: Varied
These spiders live in burrows and make funnel-shaped webs to trap their prey. The Sydney funnel-web is very venomous.

Spider, Garden
Range: Worldwide
Habitat: Grassland, forest, gardens
This spider weaves a web at night and waits during the day for prey to get caught in it. If the web is damaged, the spider eats it and makes a new one rather than repairing it.

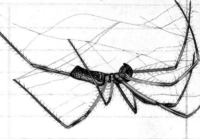

Spider, Golden-silk
Range: Subtropical, tropical Americas
Habitat: Damp open forests
These are spiders that build a strong web to protect them from predators and to capture prey. The drag line of their web is actually stronger than Kevlar, the fiber used in bullet-proof vests. Females weigh 100 times as much as males.

Spider, Green lynx
Range: Worldwide in warmer places
Habitat: Shrubs, tall grass
Lynx spiders are fast-moving hunters that rarely spin webs. Instead they chase their prey over plants, jumping from leaf to leaf. They have good eyesight and pounce on plant bugs, fire ants and other insects, using their green color to hide them.

Spider, Jumping
Range: Worldwide, especially warm regions
Habitat: Woods, grass, garden walls
Jumping spiders have unusually good eyesight for spiders and rely on jumping on victims to catch them rather than building a web. Before jumping, they attach a silk safety line to help them get back to their hideout.

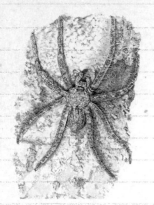

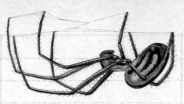

Spider, Orchard
Range: Worldwide
Habitat: Woodland, gardens
The orchard spider is an orb-web spider, but does not spin a web. Instead, it sits on tree branches and waits to grab passing moths with its strong front legs, perhaps relying on its scent to attract them.

Spider, Trapdoor
Range: Worldwide
Habitat: In the ground
Trapdoor spiders live in burrows with hinged lids at the top. The spider waits in its burrow until it senses prey moving overhead, then jumps out of the door and grabs the prey.

Stinkbug
Range: Worldwide
Habitat: Shrubs and trees
Stinkbugs get their name from the foul-smelling liquid that they squirt at any attacker. Like all bugs they suck nourishment from plants or insects.

Spider, Lichen
Range: Warm regions worldwide
Habitat: On the ground, tree trunks
Spiders such as the lichen rely on their drab colors and soft outline to keep them hidden as they hunt at night. They can move sideways with enormous speed to catch prey.

Spider, Purse-web
Range: Worldwide
Habitat: In the ground
This spider weaves a long silk tube inside a sloping burrow. The top of the tube projects above the ground but is camouflaged with leaves. When an insect lands on the tube, the spider grabs it and drags it inside.

Spider, Water
Range: Eurasia
Habitat: Slow flowing or still water
This is the only spider to spend its life underwater. It can swim and dive and is able to live in the water by spinning itself a bell-shaped air bubble from which it can launch its attacks on prey.

Stonefly, Common
Range: Worldwide except Australia
Habitat: Plants near streams
Stoneflies look a little like dragonflies, but they are not strong fliers and spend much of the day resting on stones with their wings folded. They also feed mostly on plants, though some hunt insects.

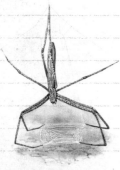

Spider, Nursery-web
Range: Worldwide
Habitat: On the ground, water plants
Nursery-web spiders weave webs not to catch prey but to protect their young. The female carries her egg sac with her until the eggs are almost ready to hatch, then spins a web around them. She then stands guard until they hatch.

Spider, Sheet web
Range: Worldwide
Habitat: Grassland, forests, gardens
This family of over 3,500 tiny spiders weaves sheetlike webs that hang from threads. Insects flying into these threads fall onto the web and are caught. Among many species are the money spiders and bowl-and-doilies.

Spider, Wolf
Range: Worldwide
Habitat: Varied
Wolf spiders are roving hunters with sharp eyesight that creep up on prey and seize it after a final dash. Females weave silk cocoons for their eggs.

Sweetheart underwing
Range: N. America
Habitat: Forest, gardens
This moth is usually very hard to see because its mottled colors blend so well into the bark of the tree where it rests during the day, but if alarmed it flashes the bright pink underwings that give it its name to startle the attacker.

Spider, Ogre-faced
Range: Worldwide
Habitat: Woodland, gardens
The ogre-faced spider gets its name from its large-eyed face. It is a net-casting spider, which means it carries its web with it, and throws it like a net over its prey.

Spider, Spitting
Range: Worldwide
Habitat: Under rocks, in buildings
This spider traps its prey by spitting out two zigzag lines of a sticky substance to literally stick the victim down.

Stick insect
Range: Worldwide, especially Australasia
Habitat: On shrubs and trees
Stick insects look so much like twigs that, when they are motionless during the day, predatory birds can hardly see them. They move to feed on leaves at night.

Tarantula, Red-kneed
Range: C. America
Habitat: Desert, forest
Tarantulas are big spiders. The largest are called bird-eating spiders because they sometimes prey on small birds. These can measure up to 11 inches (28 cm) across.

Termite, Subterranean
Range: Tropics
Habitat: In soil and wood
These termites live in underground nests in warm, wooded areas. They feed on the wood of rotting trees and their roots, but some species are also serious timber pests.

Tick, Hard
Range: Worldwide
Habitat: On bird, mammal, reptile hosts
Ticks are parasites that feed on the blood of birds, mammals and reptiles. Young ticks stick on their host for several days while feeding, then drop off to turn into an adult.

Termite, Drywood
Range: Tropics
Habitat: Dry wood, including timber
These termites attack dry wood, including furniture, beams and planks in houses. Microorganisms in their gut help them to digest the wood. Special soldier termites with large heads and horns defend the colony.

Treehopper
Range: Warmer regions worldwide
Habitat: On trees
These little bugs are sometimes known as thorn bugs because they have an extraordinary thorn-shaped extension on their thorax called a pronotum. This acts as a disguise and also makes them difficult to eat.

Termite, Snouted
Range: Tropics
Habitat: On the ground
Most termite colonies have special soldiers to defend them against enemies such as ants. The snouted termite soldiers have especially long snouts that they use to spray a sticky, foul-smelling fluid at any unfortunate intruder.

Wasp, Blue-black spider
Range: Worldwide, especially warmer regions
Habitat: Varied, near spiders
Adult spider wasps feed on nectar, but when they are about to lay their eggs, the female will catch spiders by paralyzing them with her sting. She then drags the spider to her nest, lays an egg and seals it. The spider will provide food for the hatchling.

Wasp, Common
Range: Eurasia
Habitat: Attics or burrows
These wasps build paper nests in attics or in the ground. They feed on nectar and ripe fruit, but also catch insects to feed their young. Such wasps are well known for the sting at the end of their tail.

Wasp, Gall
Range: Worldwide, mostly N. hemisphere
Habitat: Host trees, plants
Gall wasps are tiny wasps that lay their eggs on plants. The plant then produces a scar called a gall, which protects and nourishes the larvae as they hatch.

Wasp, Ichneumon
Range: Worldwide, especially temperate regions
Habitat: Host insects such as beetles
These wasps lay their eggs on or inside other insects or their larvae. When the eggs hatch the larvae feed on the host.

Wasp, Paper
Range: Worldwide
Habitat: Varied
Paper wasps belong to the family of social wasps that live in colonies organized around a queen. They build nests of papery material made from chewed wood and saliva.

Weta
Range: New Zealand
Habitat: Grasslands, woodland
The word "weta" comes from wetapunga, a Maori name for the giant weta that means "god of ugly things." There are more than 70 species of weta in New Zealand, besides the giant. Tree wetas spend the day in tree holes, with their spiked back legs sticking out. Ground wetas live in tunnels dug in the soil.

Woodlouse
Range: Eurasia
Habitat: Leaf litter, wood debris
Also known as roly-polies or pill bugs, woodlice are crustaceans like crabs, but live on land. They hide in moist, dark places in the day and come out at night to feed on decaying plant matter and insect corpses.

Yellow jacket
Range: N. America
Habitat: Forest, fields, towns
Yellow jackets are the American equivalents of European wasps. Like them, they feed on nectar and other sweet things, but prey on insects to feed their young. The female stings aggressively if her nest is threatened.

GLOSSARY

ALGAE: Plantlike organisms that usually live in water.

AMPHIBIAN: A four-legged vertebrate animal that can live on land and in water.

ARTHROPODS: The largest group of invertebrate animals, including insects and spiders.

BIOME: A large grouping of plants and animals adapted to survive in a particular area.

CAMOUFLAGE: Colors or patterns on an animal that make it hard to see against its background.

CARNIVORE: A meat-eating animal.

CARRION: The remains of recently dead animals.

CELLS: Microscopically small packages from which all living things are made up.

CLASS: Level in the system of animal classification below a phylum.

COLONY: Large group of animals of the same species living together.

DECIDUOUS: Tree that loses its leaves in fall.

DIURNAL: Active during the day, or occurring daily.

DORMANCY: A sleeplike state in which a plant or animal ceases to be active.

ECHOLOCATION: A way in which animals navigate, or find prey by sending out sounds and detecting the reflections.

ECTOTHERMIC: Animals like reptiles, with a body temperature that depends mainly on its surroundings. Also known as cold-blooded.

ENDEMIC: Species native to an area.

ENDOTHERMIC: Animals like mammals, that are able to maintain their own constant body temperature. Also known as warm-blooded.

EPIPHYTE: Plant that grows in trees, high off the ground.

ESTIVATION: A time of dormancy in hot or dry weather. Many animals in the subtropics estivate during the long dry season.

EVOLUTION: Gradual changing of animal species through time.

EXOSKELETON: A skeleton forming a hard shell around the outside of its body, like an insect's.

EXTINCTION: The final disappearance of a species.

FAMILY: A level in the system of animal classification below an order.

FOOD CHAIN: A series of organisms, each of which depends on the next as a source of food.

FOOD WEB: An interlinking network of food chains from a particular environment.

GENUS (PLURAL GENERA): A level in the system of animal classification below a family. Genera are divided into species.

GRUB: Young insect larva with a thick, soft body

HABITAT: The natural surroundings an animal needs to survive.

HERBIVORE: Animal that feeds mainly on plants.

HIBERNATION: Deep, sleeplike dormancy in winter during which an animal's body cools and its body processes slow down.

HOST: Animal used by a parasite for its food and home.

INCUBATION: The process whereby an embryo develops inside an egg before hatching.

INSECTIVORE: Animal that eats mainly insects.

INVERTEBRATE: An animal without a backbone.

KINGDOM: One of the five basic divisions of the living world, such as animals or plants.

LARVA (PL. LARVAE): A young animal that looks completely different from its adult form.

LIFE CYCLE: All the stages in the life of an animal, from its beginning through to its death.

MARSUPIAL: A mammal whose young are born before they are fully developed and are carried in a pouch on the mother's belly.

METAMORPHOSIS: The dramatic change in body shape as a young animal becomes an adult, such as when a caterpillar becomes a butterfly.

MIGRATION: Long journey made, often yearly, by animals to breed or find food.

MIMICRY: A kind of camouflage in which an animal looks like another animal, plant, or object.

NICHE: The place or role in a habitat that an animal can fill.

NOCTURNAL: Active at night.

NYMPH: Young insect resembling its parents, but without fully formed reproductive organs.

ORDER: Level in the system of animal classification below class.

PARASITE: An animal that lives or feeds on or inside another living animal.

PHOTOSYNTHESIS: The processes that allow plants to capture energy from the sun and store it as sugars.

PHYLUM (PL. PHYLA): Level in the system of animal classification below kingdom.

PLANKTON: Tiny organisms that float in lakes and oceans.

PREDATOR: Animal that kills other animals and eats them.

PREHENSILE: Able to curl around things and grip them.

PROBOSCIS: A nose or long noselike set of mouthparts. An elephant's trunk is a proboscis; so is a butterfly's tongue.

PUPA (PL. PUPAE): Stage in the life cycle of an insect in which the larva's body breaks down and is rebuilt as an adult. Pupae usually have a hard outer case, often inside a cocoon.

SCAVENGER: Animal that lives on leftovers, including human refuse and remains of predator's kills.

SPECIES: A single kind of living thing. Members of a species can breed with each other, producing offspring like themselves.

TEMPERATE: Zone with moderate temperatures — basically the areas of the world between the tropics and the polar regions.

TERRESTRIAL: Living mainly on the ground.

TERRITORY: Area claimed by an animal, either for feeding or breeding.

UNDERSTORY: Layer of vegetation on the forest floor.

VERTEBRATE: Animal with a backbone — basically fish, mammals reptiles, amphibians and birds.

INDEX

ACKNOWLEDGMENTS

Picture credits
(t=top, b=bottom, l=left, r=right, c=center)

6 Mattiaath/Dreamstime.com, 7br Cecil Dzwowa/Dreamstime.com, 11br Richard Kittenberger/Dreamstime.com, 19br butupa/CC Attribution, 20 Peter Wollinga/Dreamstime.com, 21br Bidouze Stephane/Dreamstime.com, 25br Davemhuntphotography/Dreamstime.com, 29br Ondrej Prosický/Dreamstime.com, 32l Tracy Hornbrook/Dreamstime.com, 34 David Steele/Dreamstime.com, 35br Patrick Poendl/Dreamstime.com, 39br Maxim Petrichuk/Dreamstime.com, 42bl Sergei Razvodovskij/Dreamstime.com, 48 Volodymyr Byrdyak/Dreamstime.com, 49br Honourableandbold/Dreamstime.com, 52br Paul Martin/Dreamstime.com, 60br Alexander Gaydenko/Dreamstime.com, 65br Hotshotsworldwide/Dreamstime.com, 66 Jim Parkin/Dreamstime.com, 67br Christopher White/Dreamstime.com, 74br Musat Christian/Dreamstime.com, 76 Nadezhda Bolotina/Dreamstime.com, 77br Yurataranik/Dreamstime.com, 80tr Lucaar/Dreamstime.com, 86 Nathaniel Luckhurst/Dreamstime.com, 87r David Watson/Dreamstime.com, 100 Photodynamic/Dreamstime.com, 101r Humandreams/Dreamstime.com